Awaken the Genius Within
A Guide to Lifelong Learning Skills

Samuel A Malone

GLASNEVIN
PUBLISHING

Glasnevin Publishing, 2nd Floor,
13 Upper Baggot Street, Dublin 4, Ireland
www.glasnevinpublishing.com

This edition published in 2014 by Glasnevin Publishing

ISBN: 978-1-908689-24-5

A CIP catalogue record for this book is available from the British Library

Layout and design: Glasnevin Publishing
Cover design: Bryan Mac Donald

Papers used by Glasnevin Publishing are from well managed forests and other responsible sources.

Glasnevin Publishing books are available at special quantity discounts for use in educational courses or for use in corporate training programs. For more information, please email info@glasnevinpublishing.com

Contents

Preface

This book is aimed at lifelong learners such as college students who want to improve their grades, adults who have returned to college seeking higher education, employees and professionals who want to progress in their careers, seniors who want to stave off or reverse the decline in their mental powers, and all those who want to develop and maintain a sharper mind. Mentors, coaches and trainers will find this book useful as a teaching guide to lifelong learning skills.

In this book you will learn how to use your brain more effectively at home, in study, in recreation and at work. You will learn how to concentrate better and develop the skills of effective reading. Discover how learning maps can help you in study, writing, research and at work. Memory is a vital skill for learning and you will be introduced to a wide range of memory skills to help you remember better and learn more. Anybody can develop the skills of creativity and this book will show you how.

You are born with the most amazing computer in your head but it doesn't come with an instruction manual. Just like an understanding of how a lathe works may help carpenters build better furniture, an understanding of how the brain works may help you use it more effectively. The brain needs learning, oxygen, nutrition and love to survive and thrive. Provided you look after it during your life the brain will serve you well into ripe old age.

Concentration is the discipline of being able to become totally absorbed in a topic. In any area of life you can't achieve anything worthwhile without developing and exercising your powers of concentration. A lack of concentration has resulted in students failing examinations, employees not getting the job they want, companies going bankrupt and sports people losing tournaments and games, with dire personal, professional and financial consequences. It is vital to learn the skills of concentration and how to use them to best effect. This book will show you how.

Good reading skills are critical for success in all areas of our personal and working lives. Reading feeds the brain with ideas and information, nourishes the imagination, expands our mental horizons, enhances creativity and builds our thinking skills. There are reading skills you can master which will improve your ability to read faster, smarter, and with greater comprehension and retention. Reading strategies give you choice as regards what you should read carefully, what you should skim and scan, and what you should skip and ignore. They can easily be adapted for different kinds of reading such as challenging non-fiction books, light novels, newspapers, magazines, letters and reports.

Learning maps are tree-like, radiant, nonlinear ways of organising information by showing graphically the connection between central ideas and supporting information. They are a way of capturing information, and provide a simplified pictorial overview of complex information, allowing learners to better understand relationships and find new connections. Over the past 50 years they have been adopted for note-taking, research and other purposes by millions of people throughout the world, including students, writers, lecturers, and trainers and leading companies.

If we fail to learn from our mistakes we will go on making them resulting in lost business, lost customers, lost time, lost opportunities and lost productivity. People should see their mistakes as learning opportunities and as feedback for continuous improvement. Most successful people will tell you that they learned more from their mistakes than from their successes. We can prevent mistakes recurring by asking questions and reflecting on what worked and what didn't work so that we constantly improve our performance.

Lifelong learning is continuous education and training from cradle to grave involving formal and informal methods of learning. It aims to provide the best possible development and opportunity in personal, social, recreational, working and professional life. To become a lifelong learner you must be totally committed, passionate and purposeful about the pursuit of learning, and believe that learning is a continuous journey and not an end in itself. You must identify your learning needs, set your learning goals, monitor your progress, and modify your learning strategies as necessary. Lifelong learning takes place in the workplace, in colleges, libraries, clubs and professional bodies, in the community and at home. In this book you will learn about the learning to learn skills you will need to become a more effective lifelong learner.

Memory is the power to remember and recall events, and is a central part of our identity and life story. It is impossible to function successfully without a good memory. Memory skills can be used in the home, study, personal development or at work. The effort and time involved in learning memory skills will be more than compensated by your improved memory, and overall ability to learn more effectively. There are simple strategies you can adopt to overcome everyday memory problems. Improving memory is a lifelong process and you should aim to make it an on-going integrated and enjoyable part of your life. Discover how your memory works and about the techniques that will help you remember better and learn more.

Creativity is often about seeing something unusual in the usual. Apart from making something new, creativity can also be about improving, refining, changing or combining things in new or novel ways. It is also about building on existing ideas and finding inspiration in unlikely places. Creativity turns problems and challenges into opportunities and solutions. Creativity has enriched our lives and provided us with the comforts and conveniences of modern living. Learn the techniques to generate creative ideas and learn about the creative problem solving approach. Use these techniques to enhance your creative ability in your personal, domestic and work life so that you become a more interesting, creative and successful person.

Samuel A Malone
January 2014

Acknowledgements

I would like to thank my publisher, Glasnevin Publishing for the great job done on layout, typesetting and editorial work. I would like to thank my grandson, Shane Malone Bsc. (Hons) who proofread an earlier script from a students perspective, and made several important suggestions that improved the readability and structure of the material.

About the Author

Samuel A Malone is a self-employed training consultant, lecturer and author. He is the author of 20 books published in Ireland, the UK and worldwide on learning, personal development, study skills and business management. Many of his books have been translated into foreign languages and gone into second editions. His most recent book (2011) is titled *Why Some People Succeed and Others Fail* (Glasnevin Publishing, Dublin). He has an M.Ed with distinction (in training and development) from the University of Sheffield and is a qualified Chartered Management Accountant (ACMA), Chartered Global Management Accountant (CGMA) and a Chartered Secretary (ACIS). He is a fellow of the Irish Institute of Training and Development (FIITD). Previous books published by the author include *Learning about Learning* (CIPD, London), *A Practical Guide to Learning in the Workplace* (The Liffey Press, Dublin), *Better Exam Results* (Elsevier/CIMA, London) and *How To Set Up and Manage A Corporate Learning Centre* (Gower, Aldershot, UK).

Chapter 1
Brain Skills

Humans have been ignorant about how their brains work for most of history. Aristotle thought that the purpose of the brain was to cool the blood. In relatively recent times brain scanning techniques have opened up the brain to scientific scrutiny, and added considerably to our knowledge about the brain. You are born with the most amazing computer in your head but it doesn't come with an instruction manual. Just like an understanding of how a lathe works may help a carpenter to build better furniture, an understanding of how the brain works may help you to use it more effectively.

A nodding acquaintance with the basics will help you use it more consciously, purposefully and successfully in your life. Knowing how the hemispheres of our brain function together will help you exploit your analytical and creative abilities to maximum effect, and optimise the use of your whole brain. To be successful in life you need to use both sides of your brain. The brain needs learning, oxygen, nutrition and appreciation to thrive and survive. There are differences between male and female brains. Provided you look after it during your life the brain can thrive into ripe old age.

Brain Capacity

The brain's capacity is enormous. It has more capacity than the world's telephone system, the internet or the national grid. There are as many neurons in an average human brain as there are stars in a galaxy. The brain is probably the most complex system in the universe. It is said to have between 50 and 100 billion nerve cells or neurons, and these in turn have thousands of connections. Neurons are brain cells that transmit signals at a speed of up to 200mph. Neurons in different parts of the brain have different shapes and structures, and operate as clusters that are functionally specialised to do particular jobs.

The neuron consists of a cell body with branching dendrites and a projection called an axon which conducts messages away from the cell body.

At the other end of the axon, the axon terminals transmit the electro-chemical signal across a synapse. The synapse is the gap between the axon terminal and the receiving cell. The neurons are stimulated by new experiences which grow branches called dendrites. Dendrites are root like projections receiving and transmitting information from one neuron to another. A typical neuron receives input signals from tens of thousands of other neurons. Information to and from neurons is transferred electrically via chemical neurotransmitters. The acronym SAND will help you recall the parts of the brain that can change as a result of learning and experience. This stands for

- Synapses,
- Axons,
- Neurons and
- Dendrites.

The brain is therefore a vast web of connections and networks that circulates information and determines how you think and act. Every time you speak, move or think, electrical and chemical communication takes place between tens of thousands of neurons. As your knowledge and experience grows your brain grows in tandem making new neurons and connections. It uses natural electricity and numerous chemicals to function effectively.

Figure 1
Structure of a Typical Nueron

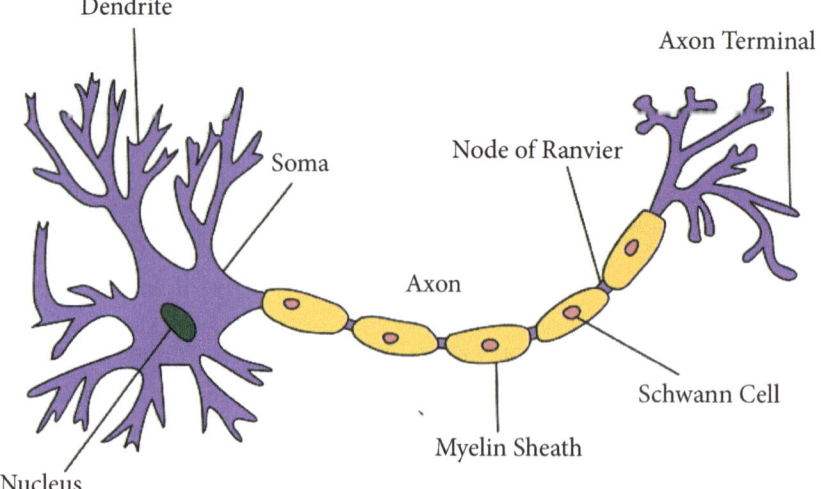

The Maturing Brain
When you are born you have almost all of the brain's neurons even though the brain is not fully developed. The baby brain looks quite smooth in contrast to the wrinkled appearance of a more mature brain. It becomes wrinkled as your neurons are stimulated through your senses by learning and experience. Our brain develops rapidly and by the age of two it has doubled in volume. By the age of four, the brain is 95 per cent of adult size, and by adolescence, the brain is fully grown but not yet fully mature. From the first days of life, infants actively perceive and learn about their environment, with the brain responding to experience by making con-

nections between neurons. You have no recollection of the first few years of life because your brain and particularly your hippocampus, a region critical for memory, learning and emotional processing, have not matured enough. Psychologists call this "childhood amnesia" i.e. the fact that you are unable to recall the first few years of your life.

The brain will continue to mature into your late teens and early twenties. The brain of a baby is far more flexible and malleable than an adult brain. It has more connections between neurons, but over time the unused connections are pruned and the ones in constant use are strengthened. Similarly, the brain of the teenager is fine-tuned and pruned during puberty. This means that the brains of young children and teenagers are uniquely designed to learn and explore. It is well known that languages are easier to learn at a younger age when the brain is most malleable, and more difficult to learn after puberty.

Size Doesn't Matter

Contrary to popular believe neuroscience has shown that we have no big untapped reservoir of unused brain power. You use more or less all of your brain, and not the 10 per cent often quoted by motivational speakers and personal development gurus. Physically the brain is unremarkable in appearance, looks like a creased spongy mass and is only about three pounds in weight. Women's brains are about 15 per cent smaller than men's, but the neurons in women's brains are more densely packed. In any event, size doesn't determine intelligence as Einstein had only an average sized brain, while Anatole France, who won the Nobel Prize for literature, had a brain that weighed only 2.2 pounds. Scientists believe it was the richness of connections in Einstein's brain and the use he made of it that accounts for much of his genius. Concentrated focused attention shapes the brain while strengthening existing connections and laying down new ones. Thinking is good for your brain.

Our ability to absorb information is vast. In 1986, Thomas Landauer, of Bell Communications Research in New Jersey, studied how much visual and verbal information subjects stored while examining images and text, and how quickly they forgot it. He estimated that the average adult stores around 125 megabytes of this type of information in their lifetime. This is equivalent to storing the contents of 100 books the length of Moby Dick. Indeed, it is language that has shaped our brain and distinguishes us from our first cousins the apes and monkeys.

Unlike apes and monkeys we use sophisticated language and the spoken word to communicate with others. In addition we cook food, travel around the globe and build houses, roads and bridges. Over thousands of years we have expressed our emotions in music, art, sculpture and architecture. Through recorded language, in the form of books, we compensate for the limitations of our memory, and learn from the experience of others by building on their ideas while taking them further. Thus humankind

Inspiration

"There are billions of neurons in our brains, but what are neurons? Just cells. The brain has no knowledge until connections are made between neurons. All that we know, all that we are, comes from the way our neurons are connected"
Tim Benners-Lee

3

has made amazing advances in modern technology and communication systems. We could not have done this without the contribution of our unique hands. Without hands there would have been no great works of art, no invention and manipulation of tools, no evolution of writing and consequently no recorded information. We use tools and machines as extensions of our hands, and in the case of computers as extensions of our brains.

Structure of the Brain

In this part we will deal with parts of the brain critical to learning and memory. The cortex is the most recent part of the brain and is the part most central to human intelligence. It is used for conscious perception, thought, language, interpersonal communication, social relationships and movement. The cortex is the grey matter which is wrapped around the other parts of the brain. It resembles a smooth cauliflower with ridges and valleys. It is now known that the cortex is not fully developed until we are in our mid- twenties. This is thought to be the reason why teenagers make irrational decisions and do foolish things because their brain is not fully mature.

Figure 2
The Cereberal Cortex of the Human Brain

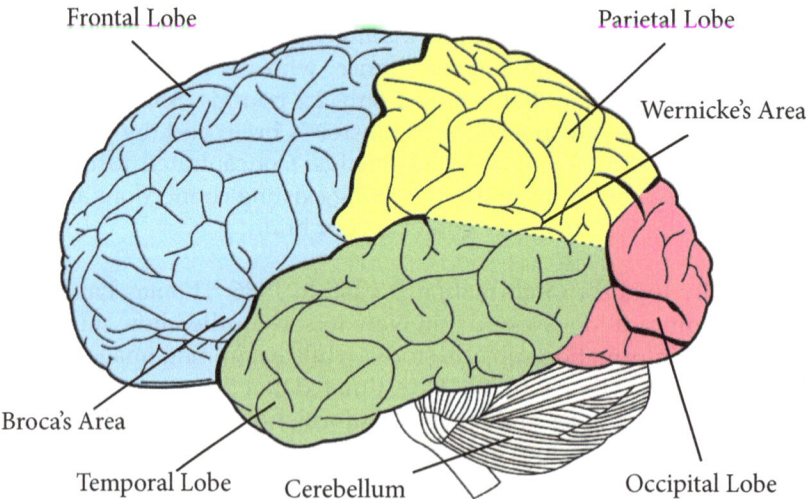

Damage in the cortex area of the brain gives rise to antisocial behaviour and an inability to relate to other people. The case study of a man called Phineas Gage dramatically illustrates this point. He survived a traumatic work based brain injury when a dynamite explosion propelled an iron bar deep into his skull. After the accident he seemed to be okay with his motor control, sensory perception and general intellectual ability intact. However, his behaviour changed radically afterwards. He became unreliable at work, a homeless drifter, and an alcoholic. Over time he exhibited a lack of moral sensitivity, with outburst of profanity, disrespect for others, and a general lack of prudence and self-control.

The part of the cortex concerned with language is a very complex area and still largely unexplored. What we do know is that thoughts before they become spoken words pass through two areas associated with the perception and expression of speech. The first is called Wernicke's area which interprets the meaning of words. Damage to this area means people will have no sense of the meaning of words. If you suffer a stroke in this region, for example, you will have difficulty understanding what others are telling you, and also what you yourself are thinking. Trying to speak results in garbled, nonsensical sounds that neuroscientists call 'word salad'.

The second area is called Broca's area which is the brain's speech production and processing centre. Here meaning is translated into sound and ultimately into a word. Words go to the motor cortex which activates the muscles to produce speech. Injure Broca's area, and though you may know what you want to say, you will be unable to do so, effectively rendering you mute.

The Cerebellum
The oldest part of the brain is called the cerebellum which is located just above the brain stem. The cerebellum is only one tenth of the brain's size but has about half of all its neurons. This is where movements are coordinated and habits are formed, and therefore it can function efficiently with the minimum amount of energy. In fact, many daily routines are conducted without much conscious thought, since these patterns have been learned and are stored in the cerebellum. The cerebellum manages all automatic motor activity that is 'over-learned,' or has become part of our subconscious.

Automatic processes like walking, talking, speaking, eating and reciting familiar information are handled by the cerebellum, leaving the cerebral cortex free to manage and concentrate on more complex activities. The cerebellum learns to handle coordinated motor activities by mimicking the electrical patterns occurring in the cerebral cortex, as you learn to drive a car, ride a bicycle, make a presentation, serve a tennis ball, play a guitar, or sing a song. Once you've learned the procedure thoroughly, the cerebral cortex delegates the task to the cerebellum, which usually handles it automatically afterwards. In fact, the brain is constantly trying to automate processes, and thus exclude them from our consciousness. In this way actions can be completed quicker and more efficiently, and with less energy. On the other hand, consciousness is slow, cumbersome, and subject to error.

A problem may arise if you try to consciously think about the process which comes naturally and instinctively to you, such as the detailed movements involved in driving a car. This used to happen to me when I was giving my son some driving lessons. I found it very difficult to put into words the detailed process that I had done automatically, subconsciously and successfully over many years. Apparently, it can cause anxiety and awkwardness when you try to let the cerebral cortex explain what the cerebellum does expertly and automatically without consciously thinking. In sport like golf, accomplished athletes learn to trust their well-trained bodies and cerebellum to do the subconscious movements that they are best at doing. This prevents their conscious minds from trying to take over at critical moments which may cause the person to make awkward swings and generally perform below par.

The Limbic System

Another important factor is the relationship between the cortex and the limbic system. The limbic system is an area in the centre of the brain associated with control of emotion and behaviour, especially perception, motivation, memory and thought. Emotion has a profound effect on learning. Positive feelings speed learning, while negative feelings slow down or stop learning. Our memory is better if we consciously link emotion with what we want to remember. Similarly, if we link something to music it has a better chance of going in to our long-term memory because music arouses deep emotions. You know this from everyday experience. A tune or song may evoke memories of long forgotten events. You remember people who made you laugh or the person who made you feel embarrassed about something.

Figure 3
The Limbic System

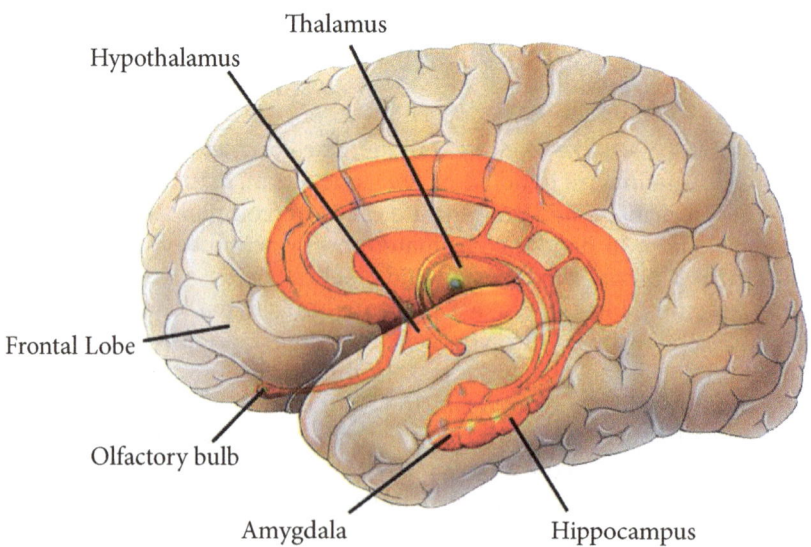

Thalamus
Hypothalamus
Frontal Lobe
Olfactory bulb
Amygdala
Hippocampus

A perceived threat, such as changes in work practices or some misfortunate accident that happened to you on the way to work, will arouse the limbic system. This in turn alerts the cortex which becomes preoccupied with the event, so that your ability to think effectively and rationally diminishes. Your judgement will be impaired so that any decisions you take will be dominated by emotion rather than rational thought. Major structures within the limbic system include the amygdala and hippocampus which I will now discuss briefly.

The Amygdala

The amygdala, an almond-shaped centre of the limbic system, plays a central role in social and emotional behaviour. The amygdala generates and processes unconscious emotional states and experiences relating to our fears. These fears are stimulated by events in the environment which are perceived as potentially dangerous or life threatening. For example, if you got sick after eating sushi in the past, you will have developed an unconscious aversion to it. This is known as taste aversion conditioning. The amygdala seems to play a critical role in this kind of long-term learning. Damage to the amygdala of rats and other animals may disrupt or even eliminate the animals' fear response. Humans with severe injuries to the amygdala suffer the same fate.

The Hippocampus

The limbic system is also involved in transferring information into the hippocampus. The hippocampus is named after its curving shape, which reminded neuroscientists of a seahorse. It is located under the temporal lobe (just inside the temples of the head), one on each side of the brain. The hippocampus is a brain structure concerned with memory and is critical for the formation of new autobiographical and fact based memories. It is thought to function as a memory 'gateway' through which new memories must pass before being permanently stored in the brain. It seems to be particularly important in learning and remembering spatial information, such as the ability to follow road routes.

Damage to the hippocampus may result in anterograde amnesia. This is the loss of ability to form new memories, although older memories may remain accessible. A person who is injured in the hippocampus may have a good memory of his childhood and the years before his injury, but relatively little memory of what has happened since.

When we are stressed our adrenal glands tend to produce more of a hormone called cortisol. This facilitates the fight-or-flight response in the short-term. This is the human response to a threatening situation to stay and fight or run away. However, stress occurring over the long-term may damage the hippocampus and impair memory.

The brain stem is the neurological network that connects the brain to the body. Damage to this part of the body may result in paralysis. The brain stem is linked to the spine via the central nervous system, which in turn is linked to all the parts of our body through neurological connections. This means that the brain and the body are totally integrated. Damage to the neurological pathways means our muscles are unable to function effectively resulting in motor neuron disease (MND).

Learning About the Brain

In the past we have learned about the brain when it has been damaged in some way. Chronic mental illnesses such as schizophrenia, developmental disorders such as autism, degenerative diseases of the nervous system, war injuries, and accidents and strokes that damage specific areas of the brain all help us understand how the brain works. Patients who have undergone procedures such as lobotomy and radical bisections provided valuable information about the brain.

Lobotomy was used in the past to treat severe depression, while a radical bisection of the brain was used to treat epilepsy. Soldiers who get brain injuries in war situations give the medical profession a rare opportunity to study the brain, discover how it works, and how it can be helped to recover from often massive traumatic brain injuries. New tools also lead to new scientific breakthroughs.

Functional Magnetic Resonance Imaging

The telescope revolutionised the science of astronomy moving it away from hearsay to scientific rigour. The microscope made similar advances in biology possible. Functional magnetic resonance imaging (fMRI) is likely to do the same for neurobiology and our understanding of the brain. Descartes said 'I think, therefore I am." Using fMRI the brain may be observed while a person thinks or performs various actions. The active part of the brain during any particular function will require more blood and so shows up on the scan.

It is important to remember that fMRI only shows changes in blood-oxygen levels in different areas of the brain. These changes are just a representation of actual brain activity, and not the real thing as we are so far unable to ascertain the thoughts going on in the brain. They are in fact pooled data, aggregated from multiple scans, and colour coded to represent average levels of blood flow and neurological activity. Nevertheless, they provide a good indication of brain activity at the time when people perform certain tasks, and are now considered to be the best method of studying the brain in action without invasive surgery.

Brain scanning technologies show that different parts of the cortex have different functions. For example, while talking, the Broca's area (speech) on the left frontal lobe shows activity. While reading aloud, the Broca's area and the occipital lobe in both hemispheres will light up. People with damage to this area are diagnosed with 'Broca's aphasia' which is the cause of speech impairments. Neuroscientists are trying to map these connections, and determine the function of different parts of the brain. This is not going to be an easy task because of the magnitude of the neurons and connections in the brain. It will need the cooperation of anatomists, brain imagers and computer scientists to solve the problem.

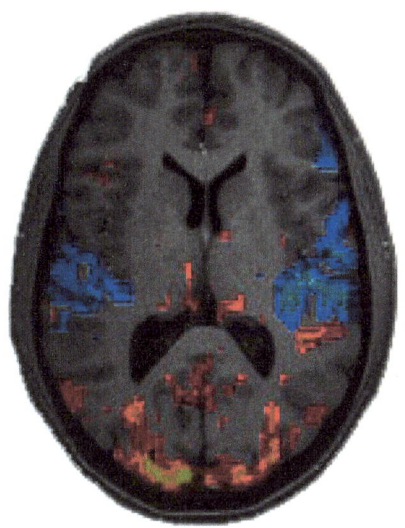

Figure 4
An Example of a fMRI
Scan

Hemispheres – Right and Left

The general functions of the right and left hemispheres were discovered after epilepsy patients had their corpus callosum cut to cure severe convulsions. After the operation both sides of the brain could no longer directly communicate, and consequently, both hemispheres seemed to be acting independently. Each side of the brain seemed to have its own awareness, as if there were two independent personalities occupying the same head. The most conspicuous part of the cortex is the right and left brain hemispheres joined by the corpus callosum. In an intact brain this acts as a constant two-way communication channel between the two halves.

There is much dubious pop psychology written by personal development specialists about left brained people and right brained people, as if they were separate beings. Many unsupported self-help therapies and claims stem from this oversimplification of how the brain works. What we do know is that we have two brains joined together, and interconnected by a thick bundle of fibres called the corpus callosum. This means that the two sides of the brain are continually interacting and talking to each other, and we need both sides to function properly.

Even though we have two thinking mechanisms, the brain functions as a totality as both hemispheres work in harmony with each other. In fact, brain specialisation is not a function of anatomy or dictated by genes but rather a result of experience. Women have a thicker corpus callosum which may account for their superior verbal skills. One research study showed that women say about 20,000 words a day compared with a mere 7,000 words for men.

The left brain tends to be logical, analytical, sequential and intellectual, while the right brain tends to be emotional, artistic, conceptual and creative. The left brain specialises in speech, writing, language and calculations, while the right brain specialises in facial recognition, spatial abilities, and some aspects of music perception and production. This means that to recognise a person we need to engage both sides of the brain: the right for facial recognition, and the left for name identification.

In fact, the specialisation between the sides is not clear cut, with each side having the ability to compensate for the other, while working simultaneously and in concert. Managers with dominant left hemispheres make good planners, because their brain is generally focused on logical and rational thinking. In contrast, managers with dominant right hemispheres make good leaders, because their brain is largely focused on imagination, creativity, visual imagery and emotional response. The ideal manager will show a judicious and balanced mix of left and right brain qualities.

Music

It was previously thought that the right hemisphere was the seat of music. Today we know that both sides of the brain are in harmony when listening to music as music engages the whole brain. Brain scanning studies show that rhythm activates the speech or Broca's area as well as the cerebellum. Melody activates both hemispheres, while harmony activates the left hemisphere more than the right. Pitch activates the left of the brain, while tone activates the right hemisphere.

Training in music enhances your memory, and improves your capacity for learning. There are hundreds of studies that confirm that creating and playing music, especially at a young age, is better for your brain than mere listening to music. In a study involving 90 boys between the ages of six and fifteen, it was found that musically trained students had better verbal memory, but showed no differences in visual memory. Musical training appeared to improve the ability of the brain's language areas to handle verbal learning. Further, the memory benefits appeared to be long-term.

When students who dropped out of music training were tested a year later, it was discovered that they had retained the verbal memory advantage gained while in music training. Brain scans show that musicians have a bigger corpus callosum than non-musicians, which means that they have better communication links between the left and right hemispheres of the brain. Music may therefore be a valuable tool for improving the integration and harmonisation of the brain.

The great men and women of history do not merely have superior brains;

they also have high levels of emotional commitment, interest, motivation, resilience and great powers of concentration. All of these reflect the highly integrated brain in action. Albert Einstein, as well as being the most famous scientist of all time, was also an accomplished violinist and painter. He thus had both scientific and artistic talents and knew the benefits of actively integrating the creative and rational sides of his brain. Similarly, Winston Churchill, the famous World War Two prime minister of England, in addition to his oratorical and political skills, wrote and painted as a way of relaxation.

Some people wonder what the position of brain specialisation with left-handed people is. You have probably guessed correctly. In left handed people the functions of the two hemispheres tends to be reversed, which means that the right deals with logic and language, and the left deals with concepts and creativity.

Brain Lobes and the Senses

The two hemispheres of the cortex are divided into four lobes or parts which are all inter-connected (see figure 2). These in turn are divided into left and right parts. Communication is two-way: back and forth through the senses and also from the brain.

These can be recalled by the acronym *F-POT*:
* **F**rontal lobes. This is located at the front of the brain behind the forehead, and is concerned with judgement, reasoning, planning, parts of speech, movement, emotions, impulse control, problem solving, and time management. It is considered to be our emotional control centre, and is home to our personality. It is often called the executive function of the brain, as it manages and organises what the rest of the brain does. One of the most common effects of damage to this part of the brain is a dramatic change in social behaviour. A person's personality can be significantly changed after an injury to this area. Because of its location it is the most vulnerable part of the brain.
* **P**arietal lobes. This is located at the top of the brain under the crown of the scull, and is involved in cognition, information processing, pain and touch sensation, spatial orientation, speech and visual perception. Damage to this part of the brain can cause difficulty with writing, problems with mathematics, disorder of language, and problems with spatial orientation and awareness.
* **O**ccipital lobes. This is located at the back of the brain, and is involved with converting information we receive through the eyes into images we understand. Information travels from the eyes through the thalamus first, and then to the occipital lobes. From here it goes to the various visual associative regions in the parietal and temporal lobes. Damage to this part of the brain may affect our ability to see properly.
* **T**emporal lobes. Structures of the limbic system, including the olfactory cortex (sense of smell), amygdala, and the hippocampus are located in the temporal lobes. The temporal lobes are situated behind

the ears and are involved with sound, language and speech production, as well as memory association and formation. Damage to this part of the brain may affect language and cause impaired memory for verbal material.

Techniques for whole brain learning

Inspiration

———————————

"Comparing the capacity of computers to the capacity of the human brain, I've often wondered, where does our success come from? The answer is synthesis, the ability to combine creativity and calculation, art and science, into a whole that is much greater than the sum of its parts."
Garry Kasparov

We know that the brain operates as a whole system, coordinating and integrating all its specialised functions. Whole brain learning means that you consciously try to involve all the parts of your brain when learning. One of the most prominent advocates of whole brain learning was Ned Herrmann, who developed the "whole brain model", which is widely used in industry. The areas where whole brain thinking is frequently applied are decision-making, problem solving, and improving team performance.

Herrmann was an American physicist and scientist who studied the brain and the connection between the brain and behaviour. He concluded that the brain has four distinct quadrants or preferred ways of learning. These are based on the cerebral hemispheres (quadrants A and D) representing higher level modes of thinking, and the limbic system (quadrants B and C) representing lower level modes of thinking. He reached his conclusion after integrating his own scientific and intuitive observations with the left brain-right brain theory and evolutionary models of the brain.

He classified the left quadrant of the brain into two halves: - A and B. The A upper left quadrant was logical, analytical, fact-based and quantitative. People with this learning style favour rational problem solving using facts and logic. They are technical minded with a direct communication style. People need to think through their ideas in a systematic and logical way. The B bottom left quadrant was organised, sequential, planned and detailed. A person with this style takes a linear, organised approach to their work and frequently create "to do" lists. They value routine, and want to be sure that things are done correctly and on time. People need form and structure to think through a plan of action to facilitate a problem's solution.

Hermann proved that everyone has at least a primary preference for one of the quadrants, although 90 per cent of us are multi-dominant. Each quadrant is associated with particular thinking styles and behaviours. Hermann's questionnaires, which are available on-line, are used to determine the thinking preferences of individuals. His research showed that better problem solving involved all four quadrants of the whole brain model. People with a dominant way of thinking are blinkered and unable to see all the ramifications of a situation.

Other approaches to whole brain learning
There are other approaches to whole brain learning which I will now address. You should adopt a growth mentality about your ability to learn

and develop. With this positive attitude you believe that your brain is capable of learning anything, and that it has the capacity and flexibility to go on learning for as long as you live. This will prevent you from being constrained by a belief in the limitations of your innate abilities, and provide you with the attitude and motivation that with hard work, persistence and resilience you can achieve what you desire in life. Excellence in any area of life is achieved more by hard work and constant practise than by innate ability.

If you feel you are more logical than creative or artistic then you should intentionally engage the right hand side of your brain. You can become more creative by thinking up alternative ways of solving everyday problems while considering feelings and intuitions about situations. You can also become more creative by reframing problems so that you see them from a different perspective. The topic of creativity is dealt with comprehensively in chapter 8.

There are different solutions to any problem, and the best one is the one suitable to the particular context and your preferences. On the other hand, if you are very creative you might consider adopting a more logical approach to everyday problems. In the modern world the ability to think outside the box, to see complex relationships, to synthesise new ideas, and look at the big picture are now more important than ever. These are the sort of skills that high tech companies like Google and Microsoft pay a premium for.

The brain learns in patterns just like the way it is organised. The brain under a microscope with its connected neurons, dendrites, synapses and axons has a map-like patterned shape. We learn by making meaningful memorable links and associations between information and experiences. Seeing how things are organised and connected helps us learn smarter and quicker, and give us a deeper understanding. The brain can't make sense of unrelated and disconnected information. By filling in the gaps and organising the material it constructs its own meaning. This is why learning maps which mimic the way the brain is organised make such good vehicles for learning. Learning maps are covered in chapter 4 of this book.

Do not believe gender based stereotypes attributed to brain research. The gender based differences are in fact very small and each gender is capable of doing anything that the other gender does. In fact, equality laws have demonstrated the truth of this statement, and shown that women are just as capable as men if given the same opportunities. Men are becoming nurses and women doctors are now commonplace. In science women are now reaching the same heights in this profession as men, and in accountancy women accountants outnumber men.

The brain performs best in a loving, caring and supportive environment.

Inspiration

"When you approach the learning situation from the standpoint of the whole brain, then you have greatly expanded the strategies available to you and the options for design and delivery."
Ned Herrmann

Companies like Facebook and Google are aware of this, and encourage their employees to be happy and enjoy themselves while they work. They know that a happy workforce is a productive and satisfied one.

Adopt an attitude of lifelong learning and do so into ripe old age. Neuroscientists now know that the brain grows new brain cells at any age if it continues to be challenged. Follow your passions. If you engage in activities that interest you and create a sense of wonder in you, your brain will stay flexible, and create more interconnections. They will also give you a sense of accomplishment and purpose, making you feel validated, and good to be alive.

Brain waves

Knowledge of how brain waves function may help you to use your brain more effectively. Brain waves can be recorded and studied on an electro-encephalogram (EEG). Death occurs when the brain can no longer be read off an EEG. Brain waves range from low arousal (sleeping) to high arousal (extreme alertness). From lowest to highest arousal levels these waves are known as beta, alpha, theta and delta.

They can be recalled by the acronym **BAT-D**:
1. **B**eta waves are the most common, and they happen when we are alert, during our normal waking hours. Beta provides us with the best problem solving state. In this state you experience focused attention, critical reasoning and improved analytical capabilities. They occur at the highest frequency of between 13 and 30 cycles per second. If you feel yourself perplexed by a problem, and struggling to solve it, you are almost certainly in a beta mode. Although essential for effective functioning in everyday life, higher beta waves can mean that you are anxious, restless and feeling stressed.
2. **A**lpha waves occur when we are relaxed and experiencing pleasant feelings. This often happens when we have our eyes closed, and when daydreaming. These are at a low frequency of between 8-13 cycles per second. A lack of alpha waves suggests anxiety and stress. People learn faster and remember more when physically relaxed, in a non-threatening, relaxed and friendly environment. Ornstein, the renowned brain researcher, found that when a person was doing maths, the EEG showed that the left hemisphere was active and in beta mode. However, the EEG simultaneously showed an increase in alpha mode in the right hemisphere. Thus, alpha mode allows for better integration of the two hemispheres of the brain. In general, the brain waves of clever people are more coordinated and coherent. This facilitates higher levels of brain functioning.
3. **T**heta waves occur during moments of reverie and deep relaxation, often just moments before we are about to fall asleep, or moments before we actually wake up. Theta waves occur naturally during meditation and the rapid eye movement (REM) dream state. These are at

a low frequency of 4-7 cycles per second. They may also occur during daydreaming. Theta provides the best learning state. In addition, people often get their most creative and inspiring ideas during theta waves. In fact, many of our famous inventors were inspired to create remarkable inventions during this dreamlike state.

4. Delta waves occur during sleep and during transcendental meditation where awareness is completely detached. Delta is the realm of the subconscious mind. These are at very low frequency of 0.5-4 cycles per second. Despite popular belief it is not possible to learn during sleep. However, there is some evidence to suggest that learning up to the time we go asleep can be very effective. It seems that sleep consolidates learning, and the less activity and interference we have in the interlude between the learning tasks and sleep the better.

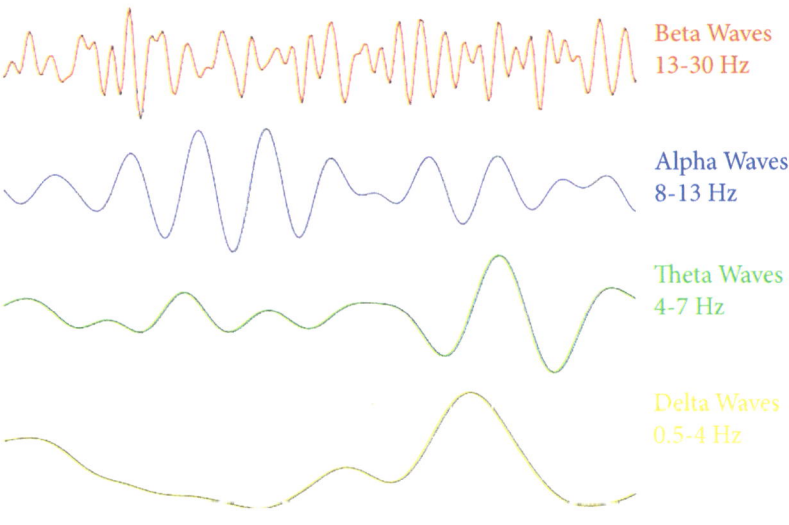

Beta Waves
13-30 Hz

Alpha Waves
8-13 Hz

Theta Waves
4-7 Hz

Delta Waves
0.5-4 Hz

Figure 5
Comparison of Brain Waves

What the Brain Thrives On

The brain needs learning, oxygen, nutrition and emotion to survive and thrive. It is, in fact, a huge consumer of these vital elements. The acronym LONE will prompt your memory when recalling the key points. This stands for learning, oxygen, nutrition and emotion.

Learning

Neuroscientists have known about the plasticity or malleability of the brain for years. Even the ancient Greeks, like Socrates, accepted the idea believing that people could train their brains the way gymnasts trained their bodies. Today neuroscientists have found that the brain thrives on learning. Eric Kandel, psychiatrist-neuroscientist, won the Nobel Prize for showing that when people learn something the wiring in their brain changes which is now called plasticity.

A 2005 study found that the effects of neuroplasticity occur more rapidly than previously thought. Medical students' brains were scanned during the time they were studying for their exams. In the space of a few months, the students grey brain matter increased significantly. It seems everything you do has an impact on the brain. Heretofore, it was thought that the brain was fixed when we were born and you couldn't change it. Now we know the brain remains plastic and changes until the day we die, which is excellent news for those of us who want to go on learning throughout our lives.

Neurons that Fire To-gether Wire Together

The brain grows and expands with use through experience and reflection. Learning affects our brain so that it develops and changes throughout our lifetime. The more experience and learning you acquire the larger, more complex, and more sophisticated the brain becomes. Your brain rewires in response to environmental stimuli and learning. In particular, the brain learns from successful outcomes. It only learns from mistakes if we intentionally reflect on where we went wrong, and take corrective action to make sure we don't repeat the same mistakes in the future. Similarly, we must get feedback on our substandard performance and the actions we must take to improve for the future if we are to learn.

In neuroscience they say that neurons that fire together wire together. That's the basis of how we learn. Studies of the brain have shown that the length of dendrites may vary by as much as 40 per cent between different individuals. Those who pursue intellectually demanding jobs have longer dendrites that those who do not.

Mirror Neuron

In the late 1990's researchers discovered that the structure of the brain can change as a result of thoughts we have. Neurons that are scattered throughout key parts of the brain not only fire when we perform a certain action, but also fires when we watch somebody else perform the same action. These are called mirror neurons, and account for our natural ability to learn from observing, mimicking, and modelling the behaviour of others. This means that when we intentionally and consciously see something being done by somebody else, our brain records similar patterns so that we can do the action ourselves. Thus if we want to become a good golfer we will imitate and practise the stance and swing of a professional, enabling us to learn from his experience by following the mental image of the elite actions.

The concept of mirror neurons explains empathy, and why laughter, smiling and yawns are contagious, and why an observer can experience the same emotions as the person they are observing. For example, a manager who laughs and is easy going will trigger a similar response in those that he manages. Similarly, a person watching the facial expressions of disgust, or pleasure in others, will often experience the same emotions themselves. The same phenomenon occurs when we listen to music. We visualise the music and words of the song in our heads, so that they are stored in our long-term memory. Long after you first heard it, when you retrieve the song from your memory, it activates the same mirror neurons as if you were hearing it live for the first time. For example, sometimes when lying in bed at night you can recreate music in your head as if it were playing live.

We now know that the human brain can change structurally depending on how it is used. A famous study of London taxi drivers showed that parts of their hippocampus, the part used when navigating streets, had greater volume than the normal person. The increase in size was proportional to the number of years of on-the-job experience they had. It typically takes two years of hard study for London taxi drivers to acquire the 'knowledge' in preparation for their licensing examination. They are expected to know the vast configurations and one-way systems of the streets of the metropolis, and consequently take you anywhere you want to go in London without reference to a map. Similarly, research shows that playing a string instrument increases the area of the brain that receives input from the fingers.

How Knowldge Shapes the Brain

Plasticity is also demonstrated by the fact that the brains of stroke victims can be re-educated to compensate for the damaged areas. Research has found that when the brain loses sensory input from part of the body, there is a tendency for neurons from neighbouring parts of the brain to compensate. Studies show that some stroke patients make unexpected progress when their functioning arms are tied down, and they are forced to use their non-functioning arms for everyday tasks. The forced activity literally rewires the damaged areas of their brain.

In addition, people with problems such as attention deficit disorder (ADD), depression, sleep disorders, anger management issues, and various phobias, now routinely do neurofeedback therapy to correct such problems. Neurofeedback has been used to help people achieve peak performance, and make the best of their capabilities. Specifically, it has been used to help managers and top athletes to coach their minds. It works by helping the brain to focus and be present in the moment with employees, customers and teammates. Training the brain, like training the body with physical exercise, allows it to learn to control and regulate certain body reactions such as stress.

In the laboratory, experiments were carried out on the brains of rats and mice to determine the effects of various types of environment on the structure of the brain. It was found that enriched environments facilitated the growth of dendrites or the connections between brain cells. The more connections neurons can make the more advantageous it is for the brain. The efficiency and effectiveness of our brain really depends on the number of connections we have between brain cells. The more connections we have the better we are at problem solving and decision making.

Enriched Environments Facilitate The Growth Of Brain Cells

Starve your brain of information and the dendrites wither and die off.

Inspiration

_____

"To exist is to change,
to change is to mature,
to mature is to go
on creating oneself
endlessly."
Henri Bergson

In sensory deprivation experiments, where people are kept in complete isolation, skills built up over a lifetime can quickly deteriorate. Your brain depends on stimulation from experience, learning, new challenges and the environment. Continually asking questions, and seeking out answers, stimulates your brain, and changes the dendritic map of the brain.

Education is food for the brain. The cerebral cortex grows rapidly in the first ten years of a child's life. By providing a stimulating and interesting environment during this period, the growth of dendritic connections between brain cells is facilitated. Intelligence is determined more by the density of dendritic connections than by anything else. This merely supports what educationalists have long known: that providing a wide variety of experiences and challenges to the growing child nurtures and enhances intellectual development. Some people feel that the crime of education is that it is sometimes perceived as boring rather than challenging. The opposite is also true. Old people put in to retirement homes without adequate mental stimulation become demoralised, senile and dependent. However, if they are challenged by learning experiences, and given responsibility and control over their own lives, they retain their mental powers.

Oxygen

Our brain is only about 2 per cent of our body weight, but consumes up to 20 per cent of the oxygen we need. This is why we feel lethargic and sleepy after a heavy meal, as the oxygen within the blood is diverted to the stomach to digest the food. An uninterrupted supply of oxygen and nutrients is essential for the proper functioning of your brain. In fact, the body treats the brain as a priority. Even if other organs need blood, the body attempts to supply the brain with a constant flow of blood. If the blood supply to your brain is cut off, a stroke happens. If this lasts for long enough, neurons will start to die because they haven't enough oxygen to survive. Paralysis, loss of mobility, loss of speech, and loss of memory, is a possible consequence of a stroke.

Generally your brain can go without oxygen for only three to five minutes before serious damage results. Starved of oxygen, your brain cells will die. Reduced oxygen to your brain will impair mental processing and the ability of your memory to store and retrieve information. In addition, it may cause sleeplessness, poor concentration, forgetfulness, mood swings, restlessness, depression and low drive.

An increase in oxygen is always accompanied by an improvement in mental sharpness, memory and judgement. The hippocampus which is concerned with memory is especially sensitive to lack of oxygen and this may result in serious damage to the hippocampus. This could happen during a heart attack, respiratory failure, sleep apnoea, carbon monoxide poisoning, or near drowning. The hippocampus is one of the first areas of the brain to show damage in Alzheimer's disease.

Aerobic exercise such as gardening, or going for walks in the fresh air, increases blood-flow to your brain, and burns off harmful stress hormones. Dancing is particularly good as it increases the number of connections between neurons as well as keeping you physically fit. So exercise is good for your brain as well as your body. By taking a thirty minute walk each day you can reduce the risk of heart attack, hip fracture, diabetes, colon cancer, and lower your weight and blood pressure, while increasing the flow of oxygen to your brain. A good brisk walk will also help to clear your head, and re-energise you to accomplish the things you need to do.

Aerobic Exercise

While you're walking remember to take in deep breaths. Breathe in through your nose as this will help you breathe in deeper. This will also relax you, and increase the supply of oxygen to your brain. It's good to do this before a test, or before any anxiety inducing activity, such as a job interview, or making a presentation that requires good use of your brain. On the other hand, smoking reduces the oxygen flow to your brain, which is bad for your brain as well as for your lungs and general health.

Inspiration

"An enchanted loom where millions of flashing shuttles weave a dissolving pattern, always a meaningful pattern though never an abiding one."
Sir Charles Sherrington

Nutrition And Exercise

The brain needs a nutritious diet to survive and thrive. A balanced diet of vitamins and nutrients is needed to keep your body and brain in peak condition. A healthy diet stabilises blood sugar levels, which is the only source of fuel for your brain. Brains consume about 25 per cent of all the glucose we absorb. We need a steady supply of glucose throughout the day, which means eating complex carbohydrates, fats and proteins. For example, complex carbohydrates, such as whole grains and fruit, are an essential part of any healthy diet. Plato said in 400 BC that a healthy body promotes a healthy brain, and a healthy brain promotes a healthy body.

It seems that the old wives tale that fish is good for your brain is true. There is now scientific evidence to support this statement. Studies show that fish like tuna and salmon rich in omega-3 fatty acids are good for your brain. Sixty per cent of the human brain is fat, and so fats eaten influence the composition of the brain. Omega-3 promotes the growth of neurons, and so allows the brain to repair damage.

Fish is Good for Your Brain

In 1998, Joseph Hibbein, a psychiatrist and lipid biochemist, at the National Institute on Alcohol Abuse and Alcoholism (NIAAA) in the USA, found that depression was up to 60 times rarer in countries such as Taiwan and Japan, where the diet consisted of a lot of oily fish, compared with the US and Germany where they don't consume as much fish. In particular, he found that in countries that consume a lot of fish, rates of bipolar disorder, post-natal depression, and seasonal affective disorder were low. In addition, it appears that healthy people with relatively low levels of omega-3 are more likely to become mildly depressed, pessimistic and impulsive.

Omega-3 also seems to have other positive effects on the brain as they act as anti-inflammatories. This means they dampen inflammation in heart disease, and may also suppress inflammatory processes in the brain. People, who take omega-3 supplements, show improved brain performance, with better short-term memory, arithmetic ability and concentration levels.

A study by Dr Lanka, as reported in the American Journal of Clinical Nutrition, said that children are likely to have greater brainpower if their mothers ate fish during pregnancy. An earlier study showed that the consumption of fish during pregnancy was associated with a higher verbal IQ in children tested at eight years of age. The researchers focused on omega-3 and omega-6 fatty acids, given that they are key components of cells, and in particular the cell membranes of the brain.

Eat Greens and Fruits Eating vegetables and fruits is good for your brain as well as your body. Research proves the brain-healing properties of brightly-coloured fruits and vegetables. These contain high levels of antioxidants, reputed to prevent oxidative stress to the brain caused by free radicals. Many mental illnesses are linked to oxidative stress in the brain. This often leads to physical destruction of brain tissue, which is believed to trigger cognitive decline and low-level inflammation. For example, a string of studies from Tufts University in the US shows that spinach, blueberries and strawberries, are particularly effective in slowing cognitive decline.

Moderate your intake of alcohol as too much alcohol kills brain cells, and accelerates the development of memory loss and even dementia. Eating sensibly and drinking moderately will also shed excess pounds and keep you fit and healthy

The Brain Loves Physical Exercise Physical exercise induces the body to produce an array of chemicals that the brain loves. These include endorphins, serotonin, dopamine, epinephrine and norepinephrine. These chemicals are also produced in the heart which demonstrates the mind-body connection. Endorphins are the brain's own opiate like substances, manufactured by the body to reduce stress and relieve pain. Serotonin is a chemical in the brain which helps keep us happy and calm; helping us to sleep, calming anxiety and relieving depression. Dopamine is a neurotransmitter that helps control the brain's reward centres, and fuels the emotions of pleasure and desire. It helps regulate movement and emotional responses, and helps us identify and pursue rewards. Dopamine deficiency results in Parkinson's disease.

Epinephrine, which is also known as adrenaline, is a hormone and a neurotransmitter. Among other things it increases heart rate, opens up the airways in the lungs, and helps in the fight or flight response. Similar to epinephrine, norepinephrine is a hormone and a neurotransmitter. Norepinephrine or noradrenaline is the fight or flight chemical in the brain which is triggered in response to stressful situations. It increases heart rate, blood pressure and narrows blood vessels in non-essential organs, enabling the body to perform well in stressful situations. In a hospital setting norepinephrine is used to restore blood pressure in emergency situations.

In addition, two recently discovered compounds, brain-derived neurotropic factor (BDNF) and nerve growth factor (NGF) promote cell health and development in the brain, stave off the ravages of aging and stress, and keep the brain in good condition. These chemicals are released when the brain cells are active, such as when we think or problem solve over something. Nothing stimulates the production of BDNF and NGF as robustly as physical exercise, whether just walking, or working out in the gym. This explains why those who exercise regularly experience sluggishness if they miss their exercise, and the brain boost it gives them for a few days. Our brains are the ultimate adaption machines eager to learn from new experiences.

Inspiration

"You know you've got to exercise your brain just like your muscles."
Will Rogers

Emotion

Without love, affection, appreciation and positive thinking, the brain will wither and die. On the other hand, studies show that stress kills brain cells particularly in the hypothalamus. Premature babies especially need love and affection. Babies kept in incubators where there was a policy of no touching failed to thrive. Researchers found that premature babies who were held lovingly, caressed, stroked and shown affection thrived. Stress hormones declined, and the secretion of growth hormones increased, so that the babies doubled their growth rate.

Satisfying emotional needs is essential at any age. It is well known that a rich emotional, relaxed and loving environment enhances brain development and learning. Research shows that ageing rats given some tender loving care live longer than ignored ones. Similarly, young children institutionalised in a Romanian orphanage, deprived of love and affection, were stunted mentally and physically. This suggests that the limbic system or emotional centre and the cortex, work in harmony for the wellbeing of the whole person.

A Happy Brain is a Healthy Brain

This is recognised in the contribution of emotional intelligence to success in life, and the role of genuine praise in making people feel positive, and even in improving job performance. In the brain, praise is usually accompanied by the release of dopamine, a transmitter linked with pleasure and well-being. Being happy and maintaining a positive outlook, is good for your brain. Happiness releases dopamine, which is a regulator of mood and self-esteem.

Google is a company that knows a relaxed and fun work environment encourages creativity, and facilities new learning and high productivity. If employees need a nap, it's okay for them to do so, and then resume working afterwards. Instead of productivity going down, it has gone up. Google is a fun, brain friendly work environment for a good reason. They know that a relaxed and challenging workplace and having fun with col-

21

leagues is good for your brain, and that workers produce top quality creative work in such circumstances. They employ the best people from all generations, and encourage them to be cooperative and happy, and have fun at work so that their brains are relaxed and creative.

The Positive Effects of Meditation

Experiments show that the region of the brain linked with emotions, such as compassion, shows considerably higher activity in those who practise meditation over the long-term. These discoveries suggest that humane qualities can be deliberately cultivated through mental training. Meditation has been shown to have a positive influence on mental health.

It appears that you don't have to be highly trained to benefit from this, as 20 minutes of daily meditation can contribute significantly to a reduction of anxiety, stress, and the tendency to become angry. It is claimed that 30 minutes a day over eight weeks results in improved concentration, and a strengthening of the immune system. In addition, it speeds up the healing of psoriasis, and decreases arterial tension in people suffering from hypertension.

Evolution and emotion

Many of our fears are emotional, instinctual, and subconscious, and have been instilled over time through the process of evolution. Fear of heights is a useful self-preservation mechanism, which is even seen in young babies. Claustrophobia, or fear of confined spaces, developed as a survival mechanism, when we lived in dark caves to protect us from possible predators. Xenophobia (fear of strangers), and racial bigotry evolved from millions of years of militant tribal relationships, where any difference in colour or personal appearance spelled potential danger.

What most of us do not realise is that rational decisions are influenced by our emotions. For example, Professor Antonio Damasio, of the University of Southern California, has shown that subconscious and emotional drives are paramount in our decision-making process. The link between the rational and emotional has a long historical lineage, going back to the ancient Greeks and earlier. Plato described peoples' emotions as like driving a chariot drawn by two horses - reason and passion.

Wishful thinking

Emotions also affect our memory, perception of risk, and our propensity for wishful thinking. When people become sad they tend to recall sad memories making them feel sadder. When people are angry they feel less threatened by risk, while when people are sad they feel more threatened. People are good at persuading themselves that what they would like to happen is what will happen.

Quack remedies for desperately sick people, and get-rich-quick scams, are undoubtedly aided by the human propensity for wishful thinking. Computer scams, telling people they won the lotto, with the proviso that all they have to do is to give their bank account number to get the cash, is a case in point. Wishful thinking may also explain high rates of business failure, speculative trading in financial markets, under saving, and low rates of provision for education.

Fixed & Growth Mind Sets

Psychologists have discovered two types of mind sets namely fixed and growth. A person with a fixed mind set believes that their IQ is fixed at birth, and therefore they can't do anything to influence it for the better. They believe that they are totally constrained by the natural talent they were born with. The result is they avoid challenges, new learning and developmental opportunities, and generally give up. They don't realise that expertise is acquired by hard work, focused learning, continuous practise, and perseverance. They often blame others for their failure, and don't seek help for self-improvement.

On the other hand, people with a growth mind set believe that IQ is not fixed, and that the brain expands with use. Increasingly, studies are showing that genius is more made than born. Expertise is acquired through 10,000 hours of specific dedicated practise, 3 hours a day or 20 hours a week, over ten years. Even though boredom may set in it is important to persevere, as it will lead to maximum benefits for you. It seems it takes this amount of time for the brain to assimilate enough knowledge and experience to become a true master.

Ability Plus Dedicated Effort Equals Success
The formula to remember is ability plus dedicated effort, equals success. Most people with average intelligence can achieve great things, provided they are motivated and put in the required time. However, there is no doubt that innate ability, and personal motivation and interest, count as well. You may never become a world champion, but you can become the best you are capable of becoming. So if you want to become a famous rock star keep on practising.

Evidence has now emerged that musicians are made more through training, rather than being born with a special gift. The brains of five to seven years old are structurally different after taking music lessons, but show no structural differences before taking lessons. This appears to confirm that most musicians are made and not born. The same applies to most occupations and professions, such as composers, basketball players, soccer players, rugby players, golfers, concert pianists, chess players, writers and master crafts people.

The Brain And Gender: Physical Differences

There are many physical differences between the male and female brain including the following:
- At conception, two XX chromosomes lead to a female, while XY chromosomes result in a male. Gender effects start shortly after concep-

23

tion, and extend throughout pregnancy. However, the XY will develop, and eventually be born looking and behaving like a male, only if the foetus, around the eight week after conception, generates sufficient male hormones. The hypothalamus controls sexual behaviour, and depending on the strength of testosterone the foetus will develop along male or female lines. These hormonal flows also affect other parts of the brain that collectively determine each person's priorities, attitudes and feelings, and their responses.

- In males the corpus callosum is relatively small compared to the female one. This makes cross-communication between the left and right hemispheres in males relatively difficult. Thus the male brain hemispheres tend to be more specialised, and the female brain more holistic and integrated. If damage occurs to one side of the male brain, it is likely to lose particular skills particular to the damaged side. However, such differences are much smaller in females. The female corpus callosum is far broader than it is in males, with very good communication between the two sides. Therefore, if one side is damaged there is less impact on the other side.

- Males have a thicker right hemisphere, which may account for their reported edge in visual and spatial tasks such as map reading. On the other hand, the female brain has a thicker left hemisphere, which may account for the female's edge in verbal fluency and language skills. Females are better at fine motor control, which would suggest that they would make superior surgeons.

- Men's brains are more specialised, and are more vulnerable to dyslexia and hyperactivity. There are more left-handed men than women, and boys with learning disabilities far outnumber girls. Boys are four times more likely to have autism than girls.

The Brain And Gender: The Senses

Men and women hear, see, feel, taste and experience the sensation of smell differently:

- Women generally have greater sensitivity in hearing, vision, pain, tactile sensation, taste and smell. For example, girls' noses, as well as their palates, are more sensitive. In addition, they are more attuned to sound – they hear better, they can sing in tune more easily, and discern variations in sounds more easily. It has been found that women can hear baby sounds that are inaudible to men.

- Women see differently: they have more rods and cones in the back of the retina, and are more sensitive to the infrared end of the colour spectrum. They see better in the dark and have better lateral vision, better depth perception, and greater ability to match shapes. Women have better visual memory, remembering landmarks and positions of objects. However, men cope better with bright light, and because they see more narrowly, are better able to focus on an object.

- Males are better able to focus and more adept at analysing patterns and systems. They know where they are spatially and can predict where others will be. They have a better-developed sense of direction. They are better at reading maps, while women are better at reading character. Men are more reluctant to ask for directions than women.

- Men can more easily manipulate three-dimensional objects, both physically and conceptually. Men are better at solving mathematical problems requiring abstract reasoning. They have a better sense of perspective and have better spatial skills.

The Brain And Gender: Social Differences

Men tend to be more aggressive than women. Women have superior empathy skills while men tend to ruminate less:

- Boys are more innately aggressive and competitive than girls. This is likely due to the high levels of testosterone that boys have naturally relative to girls. Even when small, boys prefer the rough and tumble of play more so than girls. Boys are more likely to be derogatory, or verbally aggressive, to achieve status or dominance with their male friends. Young men tend to express their hostility through physical violence, while women prefer dialogue to sort out their differences. Hence, men's keen interest in contact sports such as football and boxing. On the other hand, women secrete oxytocin, which encourages them to bond.
- The female brain is predominately hard-wired for empathy, encouraging them to share thoughts, feelings and aspirations. The male brain is predominately hard-wired for logic, facts and details. This is why females generally are more sensitive to others' needs, and better at interpersonal relationships than males. Girls like to socialise, while boys are more socially independent. From an early age, girls like to role-play parenting, and practise social roles. Females are far more socially oriented than males, and show more empathy towards their friends.
- From the first few days after birth, even though boys look at faces, they are equally fascinated by inanimate things. On the other hand, baby girls mainly fix on faces. Therefore, it is not surprising that women have a better memory for names and faces, and have greater sensitivity to others' preferences. Women also have better memory for verbal material. They spell better, are better at routine mathematical calculations and more dexterous than men.
- Girls maintain more eye contact, and smile and laugh more often than boys. They are better at body language and can manage situations more diplomatically, rather than engage in confrontations as boys tend to do.
- Imaging technology studies of men and women reading or thinking about words show differences. These studies have found that men generally use only their left cerebral hemisphere for processing language, but women use both hemispheres.
- Girls talk and read earlier, and handle grammar better than boys. Reading difficulties and stuttering is far more common in boys. Girls

Inspiration

"A man's sense of self is defined through his ability to achieve results. A woman's sense of self is defined through her feeling and the quality of her relationships."
John Gray

learn other languages more easily and are more proficient in their native language.

- Women ruminate about things that depress them, while men engage in distracting activities to deflect their minds away from problems. Women share their problems and anxieties with other women, while men tend to internalise them. This might account for the fact that men are more prone to commit suicide than women. On the other hand, women are more prone to depression than men.
- Males are more likely to be compulsive gamblers while females are more likely to be compulsive shoppers. Naltrexone, a drug that blocks the operation of opiate receptors in the brain, has been found to reduce the urge to gamble in men, while the same drug has been used successfully to treat compulsive shopping in women.

Our Brains Are More Alike Than Different

Many of the gender differences are learned rather than innate, and are due to expectation, upbringing, socialisation and culture. In fact, our brains are more alike than different, and neuroplasticity suggests that we can modify our brains through reflection, learning, education and experience. This would mean that boys can develop powerful linguistic skills and girls can acquire good spatial skills. In other words, there is no reason why women can't read maps despite claims to the contrary, and men can learn to empathise just like women. Women can acquire scientific skills just like men if they put in the same effort. Our brains are not hard-wired. Every skill, attribute and personality trait is moulded by experience.

The Brain And Age

There is no doubt that our body does decline with age. We slow down physically and our hearing, eyesight, muscles and reflexes deteriorate. For example, your muscles lose strength by 4 to 14 per cent per decade after the age of 30. Older people may get slower in processing and retrieving information, but superior experience and wisdom more than compensates for this disadvantage. Our digestive system is less efficient at absorbing the nutrients we need from food.

In addition, as we grow older our arteries may clog up due to plaque causing reduced blood flow to reach the brain. Brain cells are very sensitive to oxygen levels and a deficiency will cause the death of brain cells. However, the good news is that our brain is the last organ to decline provided we look after our general health. This is supported by recent research on the brain.

The findings of neuroscience suggest that there is no reason why your brain at 65 or older can't be just as good as when you were 25. It was once thought that older people lost thousands of brain cells each day but this has been contradicted by more recent studies. This would not have been news to thinkers such as Socrates, Copernicus, and Galileo. They were

Inspiration

"Very few women growing up in England in the late 18th century would have understood the principle of jurisprudence or navigation because they were denied access to them".
Joan Smith

Keep Learning into Ripe Old Age

still at the peak of their intellectual powers in their sixties and seventies, and even eighties. Similarly, George Bernard Shaw, Picasso, and Edison did some of their best work in their seventies and eighties.

Winston Churchill was exceptionally mentally active during his long life and went on to live until 90, despite lack of physical exercise, smoking cigars and drinking alcohol before, after and during meals. He served as Prime Minister of Britain for two terms and retired from office when he was over 80. It is not widely known that he won the Nobel Prize for Literature in 1953.

All these people were lifelong learners who knew that cognitive fitness is enhanced by challenging work, positive attitude, healthy diet and physical exercise, although physical exercise was not a priority for Churchill. There are always exceptions to every rule like Churchill, but this doesn't mean you should ignore the advice of cardiologists who recommend 30 minutes of moderate exercise five days a week.

If you keep mentally, physically and socially active you will be better at making decisions and solving problems. Recent research in neuroplasticity shows that brain cells and new pathways continue to develop throughout life. Every time we practise an old skill, learn a new one, or challenge ourselves mentally, existing neural connections are strengthened. Over time, neurons create more connections to other neurons and new cells can even be generated.

Training an ageing brain to learn and remember more effectively requires adherence to the SAR principle – Surprise, Attention, and Reward. These principles stimulate the production of chemicals called neuromodulators throughout the cerebral cortex. These help the brain to process information more effectively. Positive surprises and challenges release the neuromodulator norepinephrine, which is linked to alertness and motivation. When you focus your mind, your brain releases the neuromodulator acetylcholine. Loss of this chemical is linked to senility. When the brain is rewarded and expects a happy outcome, it releases dopamine, which regulates mood and self-esteem.

Surprise, attention and reward

A 2003 study found that people 75 years and older who danced, read, or played board games or musical instruments had lower rates of dementia. Using a personal computer, and keeping abreast of current affairs through newspapers and the internet, will stimulate your mind and keep it sharp. So keep engaged in doing something you enjoy for as long as possible. This could be paid or unpaid work. Going out and meeting people will keep you interested in life, and interesting work will keep you mentally challenged. Older people should reframe their attitude to ageing which should be seen as an opportunity for new challenges and beginnings rather than an endgame.

Unfortunately, many people as they get older get set in their ways, give up learning new concepts and new subjects, and so their brain's ability to learn begins to decline. Cognitive functions like memory, attention and learning will decline noticeably if you fail to keep mentally challenged and physically fit as you age. Continually challenging the brain makes its synapses stronger and improves cognitive performance. These changes can be seen in brain scans such as functional magnetic resonance imaging (fMRI). Something as simple as reading, walking, dancing and doing crosswords will keep your neurons firing on all cylinders. The phrase "use it or lose it" seems to be very true particularly in relation to the brain.

Summary of Chapter 1

As far as learning is concerned the brain's capacity is enormous. The cortex is the most recent part of the brain and is the seat of human intelligence. There are two hemispheres in the brain; right and left. The right is creative and holistic while the left is logical and analytical. Knowledge of how brain waves work will help you use your brain more effectively. The brain thrives on learning, oxygen, nutrition, exercise and emotion.

Psychologists have identified two types of mind sets, namely fixed and growth. A person with a fixed mind set believes there is little they can do to improve the capacity of their brain to learn. A person with a growth mind set believes they can grow and develop mentally throughout their lives.

There are differences between the male and female brain but they are more alike than different. Neuroplasticity suggests that differences can be mostly eliminated through purposeful learning, education and experience. People are capable of learning into ripe old age.

Inspiration

"If I had to live my life again I would have made a rule to read some poetry and listen to some music at least once a week; for perhaps the parts of my brain now atrophied could have been kept active through use".
Charles Darwin

Five Activities to Stimulate the Brain

1. Get out in the fresh air and walk for at least 30 minutes five days a week. The brain needs oxygen to stay healthy. Like the cardiovascular system the brain has blood vessels, so it follows that exercise will keep the blood vessels in the brain healthy. Take every opportunity to climb the stairs instead of using the lift. While watching television, during the advertisements, walk around the room to keep your circulation going. Even the simple task of brushing one's teeth with the left-hand can increase connections between the axons and dendrites in the brain. Get adequate sleep by making sure that you get 7-8 hours' sleep per night.

2. Take a daily multivitamin, and eat oily fish such as salmon and tuna or take an omega 3 fish oil supplement as a secondary option, and eat plenty of fruit and vegetables. Avoid sugary carbohydrates such as ice cream, cakes, fizzy-drinks and biscuits.

3. Moderate your intake of alcohol to prevent harming your brain cells and to stave off dementia. Research indicates that one or two glasses of red wine a day may be good for your heart.

4. Try to maintain a positive outlook on life. Positive thinking is good for you as it encourages the release of dopamine in your brain which is a regulator of mood and self-esteem.

5. If you want to excel at anything you must practise every day. Three hours a day, twenty hours a week over ten years is not unusual for those who acquire great expertise in their field. It requires a combination of ability plus effort to succeed in any occupation. You won't achieve much if you spend up to four hours slumped in front of the TV each night.

Inspiration

"Experience is food for the brain."
Bill Watterson

Chapter 2
Concentration

Concentration is directing attention on a single topic while ignoring irrelevant matters or blocking out distractions. It is the discipline of being totally absorbed in a topic to such an extent that you are unaware of anything else. The flipside to concentration is distraction. Psychologists have identified five principles of effective concentration. Being aware of the benefits of concentration will help you concentrate more effectively.

The blocks to concentration can be categorised into mental and physical. Mental includes lack of interest, procrastination and low frustration tolerance. Physical includes fatigue, lack of skill and having an unclear purpose and plan. In any area of life you can't achieve anything productive without exercising your powers of concentration. Better concentration can be achieved through mental and physical discipline.

What is concentration?

As children many of us were amazed at the awesome power and strength of a concentrated beam of sunlight. If you use a magnifying glass you could concentrate a ray of sun on a piece of paper and burn a hole through it. The beam would have to be carefully concentrated as the energy of a dispersed beam would be dissipated and not have the same effect. Similarly, mental concentration is directing attention on a single topic while ignoring irrelevant matters or blocking out distractions. Attention is like a spotlight, we notice only what we focus on. It is the discipline of being totally absorbed in a topic, to such an extent that you are unaware of anything else.

Concentration is intense interest in action. A person is focused when their thoughts and actions coincide. It is making the mind do what you want so that your energies are focused to the exclusion of everything else. It is a type of mental tenacity requiring perseverance and persistence in pursuit of a desired goal. Concentration gives us the single-mindedness to block out all distractions irrelevant to the task at hand.

WHAT YOU'LL LEARN
IN THIS CHAPTER:
- What is concentration?
- What are the principles of effective concentration?
- What are the blocks to concentration?
- What are the consequences of poor concentration?
- How can I achieve better concentration?

In sports, athletes are well aware of the link between concentration and success in their chosen field. For example, a golfer will regain concentration by just focussing on the shot, and forgetting about everything else around them, including the clicks of cameras and the shouts of spectators. Athletes who perform at their peak report that they focus only on things that are under their control, and information that is relevant to the task in hand. A testimonial to the value of concentration came from the British Open Champion golfer 2010 Daren Clarke. His career-best round of 60 in the 1999 European Open championship, coincided with a deliberate and sustained effort on his part to focus on only one shot at a time.

State of flow

To become the best they can be athletes must continually challenge themselves by stretching their capabilities and overcome obstacles. They often describe the process of achieving total concentration as being in the zone, or in a state of flow – a trance-like state in which time seems to slow down or even stand still, and where they are totally absorbed by and unaware of anything else but the task at hand.

Religious mystics describe the flow state as being in "ecstasy" while artists and musicians describe it as "aesthetic rapture". At a more mundane level, the rest of us can experience flow while working on an interesting project, dancing, playing bridge, conversing with a close friend, or reading an absorbing book.

Just like a sunbeam, flow is a source of mental energy that focuses concentration. Like most things it can be used constructively or destructively. Teenagers arrested for speeding, brawling, robbery or burglary will often justify their misdeeds for the intense adrenaline flow and feelings of elation they experience, while driving fast, fighting, stealing or breaking into a house.

The Flipside to Concentration – Distraction

Distractions can be neatly categorised into two types: internal and external. Internal distractions tend to be psychological, such as thoughts in your head demanding immediate attention, feelings, daydreaming or absentmindedness; and physical sensations, such as pain or fatigue, which impede our efforts to concentrate on the job at hand. You can control your thoughts and attitudes. You may not like what some people say about you, but it is your choice and yours alone if you decide to get angry and ruminate on it, or just ignore it and get on with your life.

Internal distractions

We are all subject to the ups and downs of life on a daily basis. The difference between successful and non-successful people is how they react to such events. It is important to remain positive. See setbacks as challenges to be overcome and mistakes as learning opportunities. Internal distractions can also include a negative attitude such as a belief that you are unable to concentrate. This is counterproductive as if you've made up your mind that you can't do something it is likely to become a self-fulfilling prophesy.

A graphic example of a very costly internal distraction happened to golfer Doug Sanders. He missed a putt of less than three feet which would have earned him victory at the 1970 British Open Championship, in St. Andrews, Scotland. Sanders had a lapse in concentration when his mind got distracted by thinking ahead about his victory speech, instead of focussing solely on the task at hand. Similarly, Sonia O'Sullivan, the Irish 2000 Olympic silver medallist in the 5,000 metres event in Sydney, allowed her concentration to slip in the 10,000 metres race. According to her interview after the event, the thought of the medal she had already won prevented her from focusing totally on the 10,000 metres race and may have cost her a medal.

External distractions

External distractions include environmental noises, the daily interruptions of phone calls, emails, text and tweets, and laptops looking for urgent attention. Unlike today, when I was growing up in Ireland in the 1950s there were very few distractions. Television hadn't arrived yet and only the wealthy could afford telephones. Our main sources of entertainment were stories by the fireside, playing cards, board games and listening to the radio. Personal computers, computer games, mobile phones and the internet were still in the distant future.

Distractions interrupt your momentum and it may take ten to twenty minutes to get your mind back on track again. In the work environment people spend about a third of their time dealing with unplanned interruptions. In relation to environmental noises, a camera click is reputed to have adversely affected Tiger Woods concentration and performance in the 2002 American Express World Championship, in Mount Juliet, Ireland.

In relation to mobile phones, users are often oblivious to the fact that phone interruptions ruin the rapport in a conversation, by showing a lack of respect and empathy to the other person. With regard to texts and tweets; a more disciplined approach, such as allocating special times during the day to deal with them, would eliminate this constant source of distraction. Email is probably one of the biggest distractions and time-wasters in modern life.

Browsing on the internet, rather than attending to work tasks, is a major source of distraction at work. Laptops can also be a source of distraction in college. Laptop usage in class has been associated with poorer learning outcomes, and students reporting feeling distracted by their own screen as well as their neighbours. Some students even browse online during

Inspiration

"All sport…is one of the few activities where young people can proceed along traditional avenues, where objectives are clear, where the desire to win is not only permissible, but encouraged."
Spiro T. Agnew

lectures. Unless we time manage these interruptions effectively they will take over our lives, and we may finish up not achieving anything worthwhile.

Dealing With Distractions

The following will help you deal with distractions:
- Stay positive and in control. A positive attitude will protect you from distractions.
- Look for the benefits in each situation. In life rather than focusing on the downside within every setback, look for opportunities for personal growth.
- Self-talk. Remind yourself that distractions do not have to absorb you. You can exercise control over your thoughts, and so you can refuse to be obsessed by them. You have the free will to change them, and to substitute positive for negative thoughts.
- Always have a plan B. Have contingency plans in place to deal with the unexpected, so that you are mentally and physically prepared for the unlikely. If you mentally and physically rehearse on how to handle the unexpected, you are less likely to get stressed on the day when you have to cope with them. Research shows that groups exposed to distractions during practice sessions do better than those who are not exposed to such situations.

Principles Of Effective Concentration

Psychologists have identified five principles of effective concentration. The acronym *FLASH* will help you recall the five principles:
1. **F**ocused Attention. Concentration requires mental effort and absolute attention. You must intentionally plan and prepare to concentrate, rather than hope it will happen by chance. We have all experienced daydreaming or mind wandering when studying. This problem can be overcome by writing down beforehand two or three specific questions, before you start reading a non-fiction book or studying a textbook or notes. This can also be achieved by using learning maps which are covered in chapter 4.
2. **L**ook for control. This is about mental discipline. Being in control means you are on top of your game. You lose concentration when you are focused on irrelevant matters or factors outside your control. These could be future events or past events not relevant to the task at hand.
3. **A**nxiety. If you are anxious or worried your concentration will be disrupted by negative thoughts and evaluations. Anxiety disturbs working memory with worries disrupting and impairing concentration. Anxiety may induce a negative psychological state, triggered off by obsessive thoughts and worries about imagined personal weaknesses, anticipated problems, and potential threats in the environment.

4. **S**pecific and relevant. You are focussed when you concentrate on actions that are specific, attainable and relevant, and under your control. Your mind is focused optimally when there is no difference between what you are thinking and what you are doing. This means that your mind is cleared of irrelevant thoughts, and the focus is centred only on what is important at that specific moment.

5. **H**ave only one thought at a time. You can only consciously focus on one thought at a time. Our short-term or working memory is limited. This means that multitasking is a major source of distraction despite claims to the contrary.

Benefits Of Concentration - Mindfulness

Knowing the benefits of concentration will help you concentrate with more focus and effectiveness. It will also give you a reason and motivation to acquire the skills of concentration. Concentration is essential for anyone who wants to succeed in life.

Mindfulness will improve your concentration, and help you live in the present moment, and get rid of distractions. It doesn't mean you live for the moment. Rather it means that you live the moment. Mindfulness can best be described as an awareness of our inner and outer worlds, including thoughts, emotions, sensations, actions, feelings or surroundings as they exist at any given moment. Briefly it can be described as the ability to observe your brain in action. It is easy to forget that we exist only in the present moment, with no direct experience of either the past or future.

How To Become More Mindful
The following will help you become more mindful. Just think of the acronym *SLIM*!

*   **S**top thinking about your performance to improve it. Thinking intensely about what you're doing actually makes you worse. When dancing if you think you have two left feet you are likely to fall over yourself. Focus more on what's going on around you, rather than the mental self-obsessed chatter going on in your mind. This will help you become less self-conscious, and stop you from self-evaluation. You are part of humanity rather than an isolated individual. Learn to focus on other people rather than on yourself.

*   **L**ose track of time by becoming totally absorbed in what you are doing. This is known as flow where your concentration is so focused that you forget about the passage of time. To reach the state of flow you need to set a goal that is challenging, but not impossible to achieve. The challenge will motivate you, but if it is too difficult you will get disheartened and give up. The task should be in line with your capabilities, so that you do not feel unduly stressed, while at the same time not so easy that you get bored. You should get direct and immediate feedback, so that you can adjust your behaviour and learn from your mistakes.

Inspiration

"What do I mean by concentration? I mean focusing totally on the business at hand and commanding your body to do exactly what you want it to do".
Arnold Palmer

- **I**nhabit the present moment in order to avoid worrying about the future. Often we are so engaged with thoughts about the future and the past that we forget to enjoy what we are experiencing right now. Relish or savour what you're doing at the present moment, such as walking in the countryside, sipping a cup of coffee, savouring your food, enjoying a pastry or taking a shower. If you live in the moment you are more likely to be happy, as negative thoughts usually concern past or future events. Mindfulness decreases your ego so that you are less likely to feel slights to your self-esteem, and more likely to accept things at face value. It also makes people feel more connected or empathetic towards each other, and thus improves relationships.
- **M**ove towards what is bothering you. It is better to accept a problem rather than run away from it. We naturally try to resist unpleasant thoughts, feelings, and sensations. When we are heartbroken, because of a failed relationship, we resist our feelings of heartbreak. As we get older we try to recapture our youth, rather than growing old gracefully as evidenced by the mid-life crises where people often do silly things. However, in many cases, negative feelings can't be avoided and trying to do so only magnifies the pain. For example, if you feel sad, you can accept the feeling, label it as sadness, put it aside and then direct your attention to something else. You can dispassionately observe your thoughts, perceptions, and emotions go through your mind without getting involved. Thoughts are just thoughts; you don't have to believe them or do what they say.

Inspiration

"Mindfulness can be summed up in two words; pay attention. Once you notice what you're doing, you have the power to change it."
Michelle Burford

Other Benefits Of Concentration

The acronym APSIS will help you remember the other benefits of concentration:

- **A**ccomplish goals. Good concentration will help you stay on course, complete a task on time, and achieve your goals. This will give you job satisfaction, and you may impress the boss! Remember it is important to enjoy the process of getting there, so enjoy the completion of stages on the journey to your goals as well.
- **P**roductivity. Concentration helps you get things done more efficiently and effectively, with less mistakes and savings in time. At work you should concentrate solely on getting one task done at a time rather than jumping like a grasshopper from one thing to another.
- **S**tudying. Good concentration will help you improve your comprehension and retain more in formal studies or at work. This will help you to study more effectively by learning more in less time and pass exams.
- **I**nventions and works of art. Concentration has its uses as meticulous attention to detail is required in many fields such as accountancy, finance, economics, law, quality control, computer programming, science, engineering, architecture and artistic endeavour. We would not have electric light, and the electronic revolution which followed, if great scientists like Edison had not been so focused and persistent

in his work, which led to his invention of the electric bulb in 1879. Similarly, we would not have penicillin, and the medical revolution which followed, if Fleming had not noticed the mould in a dish in his laboratory in 1928. Great composers like Mozart and Beethoven, would not have spent so much time in perfecting their pieces of music if they hadn't great powers of concentration. Great poets such as John Milton, W. B. Yeats and Robert Frost would not have spent months perfecting their poetry, often spending weeks searching for the most expressive word, if they hadn't exceptional powers of concentration. Great artists would not have produced masterpieces if they hadn't spent weeks and weeks perfecting the tiniest detail of their paintings, sculptors and architectural designs.

- **S**kill. You are a work in progress. When you've finished learning one skill, be sure to start learning a new one. Life is all about having new challenges to continually stretch yourself. Learning something new will challenge your powers of concentration as well as developing your brain. Always try to engage in self-directed learning as you go through life.

Blocks To Concentration - Mental

One of the ways of improving our powers of concentration is to become aware of the blocks to concentration so as to take action to counteract them. Some of these include:

- Fatigue, stress, anxiety or poor health. It is widely known in psychology that anxiety impairs attention and adversely affects performance. If you are in poor health and in pain, the associated worry, anxiety and discomfort is likely to adversely affect your physical energy levels and powers of concentration. In fact, you may be unable to think of anything else except health related issues. If you are working all the time, without taking the opportunity to take breaks for rest and recreation, it is likely that you will become mentally and physically fatigued. Obviously, if you are tired all the time for no apparent reason, you should consult your medical practitioner. It is well known that depressed people obsess about their worries, and find it difficult to concentrate.

- Procrastination. This means continually postponing tasks that you should be attending to right now. Human nature encourages us to do the enjoyable and pleasant tasks first, rather than the difficult but critical and relevant tasks which are postponed. Procrastination diverts you from high priority tasks with the delusion that you will be able to tackle the task more effectively tomorrow, or that the sun will be brighter, things will be better, and you will be happier. The 21st century has facilitated the process of procrastination because of the variety of distractions available 24/7, such as mobile phones, emails, and the social internet networks such as Facebook and Twitter. Psychologists maintain that the real elephant in the room is a low tolerance for frustration. You avoid the task because of a negative perception and

Inspiration

"One reason so few of us achieves what we truly want is that we never direct our focus; we never concentrate our power. Most people dabble their way through life, never deciding to master anything in particular."
Anthony Robbins

a feeling that you can dodge the discomfort through postponement and diversion.

- Lack of interest. If you are inherently interested in something you will find it absorbing, motivating, effortless, and a pleasure to do it. On the other hand, if you are disinterested in something you will find it difficult to focus on it, and will look for an excuse for not doing it. Thus interest and motivation are strongly interlinked. An intense focus on specific interests or goals induces a flow state, which in turn elicits feelings of achievement and well-being.

- Inappropriate learning style. There are three basic learning styles: visual, audial and tactile, or in more down to earth terms; seeing, hearing and doing. Most people have a preference for one style over another, although we all use a combination of styles from time to time. Some people like to read books and study notes. Some like to learn from lectures, demonstrations and actual practise. Some like to listen to CDs and lectures, while others like to view DVDs and look at diagrams and pictures. Use the learning style that you feel most productive and comfortable with.

- Low frustration tolerance. Some people have grasshopper minds, jumping from one thing to another often craving constant stimulation. They are unable to practise the skill of delayed gratification, or the ability to do without in the short-term so as to benefit in the long-term. This is part of the instant gratification and spend mentality on which modern consumerism is built.

- Personality. People with attention deficit disorder (ADD) have exceedingly short attention spans, and are easily distracted and restless. The good news is that once properly diagnosed and treated ADD can be controlled and successfully dealt with.

- Short-term memory. Our short-term memory can only hold between 5 and 9 or even less items at a time. This means that when it comes to concentration that we only have a limited amount of working space in our memory. Thus if we want to concentrate effectively we must learn to focus on relevant cues. For example, it has been found that sprinters trained to use race plans with interim times for stages run faster than those without this training.

Blocks To Concentration – Physical

- Lack of training and practise. Concentration is not a natural capacity that we are born with. Like any other skill it must be diligently learned, practised, acquired and nurtured. This will take persistent effort over 20 days until it becomes an automatic unconscious habit. The brain changes in line with where you place your attention. So if you practise concentration a part of your brain will become specially activated to do so. It is better to acquire the good habit of concentration, rather than the bad habit of inattention. Replacing bad habits of concentration with good habits involves four stages: - recognition, replacement, repetition and retention. First recognise your bad habits, and replace them with good habits. Then repeat this process until the good habits are firmly retained and the bad ones replaced. As bad habits are created over a considerably period of time, it will take a similar period of time to replace them with good habits.

- Multitasking. Despite conventional wisdom, multitasking slows you down, and the divided concentration involved facilitates mistakes. The mind can only concentrate on one thing or thought at a time. Research at Stanford University compared the effectiveness of multitaskers with non-multitaskers. It found that multitaskers performed poorly at recognising changes in their environment, and filtering out irrelevant information. Moreover, the multitaskers took longer to switch between different tasks, and were less efficient at juggling problems. This suggests that our attention span is finite. When you multitask you prioritise the execution of one task at the expense of another. With routine tasks you may not notice any fall off in performance. However, when a task involves significant brain power, it's impossible to sustain both at high levels of performance. Multitasking is almost always less efficient and more error-prone than performing the same task alone. This is why it is illegal to use a mobile phone while driving.

- Unclear purpose or plan. Purpose provides a focal point for your concentration while a plan provides a systematic route for its accomplishment. Pursuing excellence in any field of human endeavour requires you to focus on the goal you want to achieve. As the saying goes: "If you don't know where you're going you're liable to finish up somewhere else" and sometimes in a place that you don't want to be.

- Alcohol. As anyone who has tried to study after taking alcohol knows; alcohol adversely affects concentration making it almost impossible to stay focused and study effectively. Also, excessive drinking kills off valuable brain cells diminishing your future capacity to concentrate and learn effectively.

Inspiration

"I never could have done what I have done without the habits of punctuality, order, and diligence, without the determination to concentrate myself on one subject at a time."
Charles Dickens

Consequences Of Poor Concentration

You cannot achieve anything worthwhile without exercising your powers of concentration. I couldn't write this book if I hadn't the ability to plan, research, think and concentrate. When writing I concentrate on one chapter at a time. Within chapters I concentrate on perfecting each section. Sections should follow on logically from each other. Within sections I concentrate on perfecting each paragraph, and making sure that paragraphs are pertinent to the section and in a logical sequence. Within each paragraph I concentrate on getting each sentence right. I try to make each sentence as reader friendly as possible. For each sentence I try to pick the most suitable words in order to get my meaning across clearly and concisely.

I couldn't have successfully studied and passed examinations for degrees and professional qualifications without the ability to focus my concentration for long periods of time. I couldn't surf the net, drive long distances, find my way around, or hold my own in a conversation without the ability to concentrate. Indeed, I couldn't even enjoy a movie, book or play, or get a job done without being able to concentrate. A lack of concentration has caused sports people to lose tournaments and games with personal, career and financial consequences.

Car and plane accidents caused by lack of concentration

Many mistakes and accidents are caused by a lack of concentration. Lapses of concentration are a major cause of car accidents. Distractions can be classified into two types: - physical and mental. Physical distractions include eating, drinking, conversing, and fiddling with the radio and CD player while driving. I recently witnessed an accident where a young lady driver crashed into a parked car. She leaned down to get her handbag and momentarily lost control of the car causing considerable damage to the parked car. Recently, on a stretch of road on the way into the picturesque village of Adare in Co. Limerick I was rear-ended. The young motorist who did the damage said that he was daydreaming at the time.

A major physical distracter is using the mobile phone while driving. Studies indicate that driving while using the mobile phone shows similar impairments as motorists who drink-drive over the limit. Some studies show that a person using a mobile phone is 40% more likely to crash while those texting while driving are 60 times more likely to crash. Consequently, the use of the mobile phone while driving has been banned in many jurisdictions.

Mental distractions include loss of focus due to work or family concerns, children fighting or arguing in the back of a car, or inattention created when a driver gets angry over the perceived dangerous driving of other drivers. Tempers flair and drivers may be tempted to engage in more aggressive and dangerous driving. Another is when a driver is running late and engages in inappropriate and dangerous manoeuvres to make up for lost time.

Similarly, aeroplane accidents are sometimes caused by a lack of concentration in the cockpit. Murphy's Aviation Law dictates that pilots get distracted at the most inopportune times. For example, a business pilot taxing his plane along several rows of aircraft reached down for his checklist momentarily interrupting his line of sight. During this momentary distraction, he struck three other aircraft causing considerable damage. Thankfully, nobody was injured. On the farm and in the workplace accidents lead to loss of productivity, injuries and even deaths. Health and safety legislation tries to prevent accidents from happening.

Reflection and focused attention

People who lack concentration are unable to reflect and learn from past mistakes and find it difficult to visualise and plan for the future. Reflection is possibly our greatest source of learning. People should learn how to organise their time so that they can actually spend some time thinking. We need time to think on how we could do things better and work more safely and effectively. Focused attention is needed for success in any area of life. Even the greatest person would not achieve much if they lacked concentration and effort.

Companies that diversify too much away from their core business often end up bankrupt. Those who concentrate on what they are really good at doing, or stick to the knitting, are usually more successful. The graveyards of business are full to capacity with the corpses of those companies who failed to abide by this principle.

Better Concentration - Visualisation

- Mental practise or visualisation. Mentally practise what you want to do in your mind before you actually do it. When you do it your concentration will be more focused. Imagery will help you prepare in advance for hypothetical scenarios, thereby ensuring that you won't be distracted by unexpected events. Visualisation can help you focus on what's relevant in a particular situation. Sports people often practise their moves in their minds before they actually do them on the pitch. Using visualisation, a golfer can decide where the ball is going to land before he strikes it. He may evoke a technicolor image of its flight and a physical expectation of how it will feel to send it flying to its target. He is using the pre-frontal cortex of the brain, where conscious plans are made to send instructions to the more primitive cerebellum and motor cortex, which automatically control the muscles.
- Timed imagery. Some of the best athletes have even put a stopwatch on their imagery to ensure that their timing and pacing are exactly what they want. For example, in preparation for the Olympic Games, Alwyn Morris, gold bronze medallist in canoeing at the Los Angeles Olympics in 1982, and Alex Bautmann, double gold medallist in swimming at the Los Angeles Olympics in 1984 and world record holder in swimming, did timed imagery. More recently, Aaron Rodgers the famous American football quarterback for the Green Bay Packers and AP Male Athlete of the year 2011 attributes his success to visualisation. To quote from Rogers 'A lot of those plays I made in the game, I had thought about. As I lay on the couch, I visualised making them'. Similarly, a business person can practise the pacing and timing of their presentation in their head before doing it. Remember mental rehearsal is almost as effective as actual practise.
- Self-talk, trigger words and actions. Psychologists recommend that trigger words should be concise, concrete, vivid and phrased posi-

Inspiration

"Great entrepreneurs focus intensely on an opportunity where others see nothing. This focus and intensity helps to eliminate wasted effort and distractions. Most companies die from indigestion rather than starvation, i.e. companies suffer from doing too many things at the same time rather than doing too few things very well."
Naveen Jain

tively to yield maximum benefits. Self-talk and trigger words are used by athletes such as golfers and tennis players and is said to enhance concentration. Trigger words, which are a fast-track meditation technique, are a signal to the brain that attention must shift to a state of present focus. This trigger can be anything like tugging on your shirt or scratching your nose. Practised faithfully, whether you're at the driving range, or on the last hole of the golf course, it will stimulate a memory of what it's like to be focused and at ease, no matter how tense the situation. Tennis players often use trigger words such as "split" and "turn" which they claim leads to improved performance and enhanced concentration on court. Surveys of athletes report that they use trigger words for staying focused. For example, Serena Williams, the world renowned tennis player, uses trigger words to help her concentrate effectively while on court.

Better Concentration - Focus

- Divide and conquer. Concentrate on one step at a time. How do you eat an elephant? One bite at a time! This is also known as chunking. You can improve your short-term memory by grouping long numbers or long lists of data into smaller chunks. This is a well-known technique for remembering anything including telephone numbers.
- Stay focused. Avoid distractions such as gossiping with colleagues, interrupting yourself continuously to attend to email, surfing the internet, using Facebook or YouTube while at work, and answering phone calls. Organise your time by designating a certain time of your day for looking at emails and attending to phone calls.
- It is easy to concentrate on a subject that you are passionate about. Enthusiasm and interest creates motivation. Marie Curie (1867-1934) was totally dedicated to physics and went on to win two Nobel Prizes. From 1922 she concentrated on finding practical medical applications for her radioactivity which today is used to treat cancers. Ironically, she died in 1934 from the effects of radioactivity exposure endured over a dedicated working lifetime.
- Think about it all the time. Andrew Wiles when recalling the degree of focus and determination that eventually yielded the proof of Fermat's Last Theorem said: "I carried this problem around in my head basically the whole time. I would wake up with it first thing in the morning, I would be thinking about it all day, and I would be thinking about it when I went to sleep. Without distraction I would have the same thing going round and round in my mind."
- Concentrate on what you want rather than what you don't want. Psychologists have found that when we focus on not wanting something to happen, we are actually making it more likely to happen. For example, just try not to think about a pink elephant and see how difficult it can be! Psychologists believe that if you are told not to think or do something the unwanted thought or action is exactly what happens. In one experiment with Australian Rules footballers, players became

more aware of the umpires when told not to pay attention to them. Clearly, this finding raises doubts about the effectiveness of asking athletes not to worry about an important forthcoming sporting event or outcome. In fact, it is likely to be counterproductive as telling them not to worry is likely to make them worry more.

- Choose to concentrate. Intentionally choose to concentrate in order to focus more effectively. You can take a horse to water but you can't make it drink! If you really want to concentrate you must first choose to do so. Michelangelo (1475-1564) was a renaissance sculptor, painter and architect, a man of genius comparable to the great Leonardo da Vinci. Michelangelo had a remarkable ability to concentrate his thoughts and energy to the task at hand. Often while working he would forget to attend to his personal needs. He would eat very little, would sleep on the floor besides his unfinished painting or statue, and continue to wear the same clothes until he finished his work.

Better Concentration - Psychological

- Create a challenge. If something is too easy it kills motivation because it doesn't present a challenge. You need to create a challenge so that your capabilities will be stretched and your interest engaged. It is the difficult things that really develop us and spurs us on.
- Think benefits instead of difficulties. What's in it for me? (WIIFM). Answering this question will help you create a positive attitude of mind. More importantly, what will you lose if you don't settle down and concentrate on getting the task done? This might include a failed exam, a missed deadline, loss of money or professional prestige. Having an emotional reason for concentration will help you to concentrate better.
- Perseverance and concentration go together. You must focus your attention on what you need to do until you accomplish your goal. Persistent people never take their eye off the target and are determined to succeed despite repeated failures. They are not afraid to make mistakes but learn from them and keep on going. Giving up half-way through is not an option. Winners are not quitters.
- Meditation. Meditation means paying attention in a particular way and is something we are all capable of doing with the right approach and practise. Just paying attention to your breathing for a few minutes is a simple way of meditating. Most of us take our breathing for granted. But as an experiment clamp your thumb and forefinger over your nose, close your mouth and see how long it takes before this becomes very uncomfortable and you have to stop. It doesn't take very long to realise how breathing is so important to our lives. The mind and body are interconnected.
- Train your mind to control your thoughts. Whereas many of us train our body to do various things we seldom train our minds to control our thoughts. Our thoughts tend to be scattered, jumping from one thing to another. When we try to focus our attention on one thing

it tends to drift to something else, so that we find it extremely difficult to reach a state of mental calmness. Meditation is a discipline for training the mind to develop greater calm, concentration and focus. In contrast, Buddhist meditators have developed the techniques of mediation over 2,500 years, and it is only in relatively recent times that the West has started to catch up. Buddhists know how to control the flow of their thoughts. We can do likewise if we choose to modulate our moods, regulate our emotions and increase our ability to use our brain power more productively. Meditation is just not for reducing stress in our lives, but will also help us to improve our relationships, be happy, kind, more creative and to concentrate more effectively. Imagine the difference it could make to your life and relationships if you learned to pay more attention to the important people around you!

Better Concentration – Study

- Study. When studying prime your mind with questions that you seek answers for. This gives you a reason and a purpose for reading. We learn best when seeking out answers for pertinent questions. In addition, make sure the study environment is comfortable, free from distractions and conducive to learning. Decide whether you prefer to study on your own or in a group. You may prefer to study with others. Studying with others may refresh your interest, and spark off new ideas, and see things from new perspectives. Take short breaks every half hour or so to recharge your batteries, and maintain your concentration level. Take a short walk in the open air to refresh your brain.

- Music. It has been found that background music enhances the efficiency of individuals who work with their hands. For example, in a study of surgeons it was found that background classical music increased their alertness and concentration. It did not cause distraction because music and skilled manual work activates different parts of the brain. Similarly, classical background music aids learning and concentration in the classroom and in the workplace. On the other hand, it has been found that stimulating music can be a source of distraction. It seems to be a case of different strokes for different folks as some people find any kind of music a distraction when learning.

- Circadian rhythms. Each of us has a unique biological clock as regards levels of concentration and tiredness which varies throughout the day. Some of us are larks - more alert in the morning, while others of us are owls - more alert in the afternoon. In addition, larks tend to be introverts who are conscientious, introspective and driven, while owls are more often impulsive outgoing extroverts. In the morning larks have higher levels of the stress hormone cortisol than do owls, which may account for their energy. In comparison, owls' heart rates are higher in the afternoon, which perhaps is the reason they are mentally sharper and more energetic as the day goes on. Teenagers and young adults tend to be owls, as any parent will testify to when they endeavour to get their offspring off to college in the morning. On the other hand, because of hormonal changes and adherence to strict early work starting and routines times, most people become larks as they get older. Determine your own biological clock, so that you can pick the appropriate time of day when it is best to study or do complex work, requiring mental energy, stamina and focused concentration.

- Targets. Have a start and finish time as that which can be done at any time is usually not done at all. Deadlines concentrate and focus the mind. Remember Parkinson's Law which states that work expands to fill the time available for its completion. This suggests that you will spend more time than necessary to complete a job if you haven't strict time constraints and guidelines for getting it done. The Law of Inertia states that a still body tends to stay stationary. On the other hand, the Law of Momentum states that a body in motion tends to stay in motion. Getting started and keeping up the momentum is often the most difficult part of getting any study or job done. So just do it! Get going and do it now!

- Students can learn to concentrate more effectively in examinations by taking mock exams beforehand in simulated conditions, and practising doing likely examination questions. However, there is one proviso. You cannot replicate completely what will happen in a competitive situation, or dealing with the unlikely and unexpected question that pops up in the examination. Nevertheless, careful planning and anticipation is better than not being mentally and physically prepared.

- Prioritise. Create a "to do list" which prioritises tasks that you need to study or do during the day. Categorise your list into "must do", "should do" and "nice to do". Tackle the "must do" items first, the "should do" items next and the "nice to do" items last. This will concentrate your mind on what's important and needs to be done on an urgent basis.

Better Concentration — Physiological

- Sleep. A good night's sleep will help you to concentrate better. The average person needs 8 hours sleep per day and this is equivalent to spending a third of our lives asleep. Margaret Thatcher, the former Prime Minister of Great Britain, thought that sleep was a waste of valuable time and is reputed to have only slept for 4 hours each night. President Kennedy believed in taking naps in the afternoon to refresh his mind and restore his energy. Many people suffer from a sleep deficit, resulting in problems ranging from fatigue, drowsiness, gloomy moods to impaired decision making, reduced creativity, reckless behaviour and paranoia. Healthy sleep must contain REM periods – times in which you dream. This is why alcohol-induced sleep is not restful because it interferes with the REM pattern. Paul McCarthy of the Beatles dreamed the song Yesterday, woke up and wrote it down. It became one of the best selling songs of all time. Dreams may help us integrate and consolidate knowledge and inspire us to achieve great things. During our sleep, our brains are making sense of the world, discovering new links and associations between existing memories, looking for patterns, formulating rules, and even solving problems. Some people have a Eureka moment shortly after waking up from sleep. Many inventions are said to have been inspired by such moments.

- Listen with your right dominant ear to improve your concentration. Your right ear is connected to the left side of your brain which is the language centre. This means that your hearing is superior in the right ear so try to use this for listening. When you are listening to some-one, give them your total and undivided attention. Don't let your eyes wander elsewhere while the other person is talking. Apart from an-ything else this demonstrates courtesy and respect. Concentrate on what the person is saying and give no heed to anything else. Do not interrupt and do not finish the other person's sentences. You should keep the conversation going by asking intelligent questions that show you are paying attention to the speaker. It is much easier to talk than to listen. Listening will improve your concentration skills and in the process you may make friends and learn something new!

- Practise thought stoppage when distracted and refocus quickly on your original task. Say to yourself "Stop" to redirect your thoughts when they are straying and then bring them back gently to where you want them to be. Keep doing this until your concentration is restored.

- State. Get in the right physical, psychological and emotional state. It is difficult to concentrate when you are cold, worried, anxious or upset. As well as preventing obesity and keeping your heart fit, simple ex-ercises like walking daily, will improve your circulation, memory, at-tention and concentration. Many top class athletes engage in pre-per-formance routines to get them into the right mental state before they perform key tasks. For example, tennis players tend to bounce the ball a preferred number of times before serving. Similarly, rugby place kickers like to adopt a unique physical stance, and go through a sys-tematic personalised series of steps before kicking the ball for a pen-alty shot to block out any distractions from the crowd. These routines help sports people to concentrate on the present moment rather than on past or future events.

- Simulation. Psychological experiments have proved simulation or do-ing a dress rehearsal works. Athletes can learn to concentrate more effectively and deal with distractions in real-life pressure situations by simulating them in similar conditions. Many adverse, unsettling, or unexpected conditions, can be overcome if they have already been simulated and experienced in practise beforehand. Earl Woods, the father and initial coach of Tiger Woods used simulation techniques on his son when he was a very young boy. Today Tiger Woods claims he still benefits from the strategies and tactics of dealing with distrac-tions that his father taught him as a child. Even astronauts prepare carefully for their trips in space by undergoing simulated training, which mimics the conditions they will experience in space.

Inspiration

"When you write down your ideas you automatically focus your full attention on them. Few if any of us can write one thought and think another at the same time. Thus a pencil and paper make excellent concentra-tion tools."
Michael Laboeuf

Summary of Chapter 2

Concentration is like a spotlight; we notice only what we focus on. Concentration is intense interest in action. A person is focused when their thoughts and actions match. Concentration gives us the single-mindedness to get rid of all distractions irrelevant to the task at hand. You lose concentration when you are focused on irrelevant matters or factors beyond your control. Knowing the benefits of concentration will motivate you to concentrate more effectively.

One of the ways of improving your powers of concentration is to become aware of the blocks to concentration, so that you can take appropriate action to counteract them. A lack of concentration has resulted in students failing examinations, companies going bankrupt and sports people losing tournaments and games with personal, professional and financial consequences. You can achieve better levels of concentration through mental and physical approaches.

Five Activities to Improve Your Concentration Skills

1. Always have a clear purpose or plan. Purpose provides a focal point for your concentration while a plan provides a systematic route for its accomplishment. Intentionally plan and prepare to concentrate rather than hope it will happen by chance.
2. A simple everyday technique of improving your concentration is to listen more attentively. By focusing on what the other person is saying you will improve your listening and concentration skills and win friends and influence people.
3. Practise the technique of mental rehearsal or visualisation. Sports people practise their moves in their minds before they actually do them on the pitch. Students practise their examination technique by going through the actions they will perform in the examination room. Business people practise their presentation skills through mental rehearsal before they speak in public. It has been discovered that mental rehearsal is almost as effective as actual practise.
4. Practise thought stoppage when distracted by irrelevant matters, and factors outside your control to refocus quickly on your original task. Say to yourself "Stop" to

redirect your thoughts when daydreaming or mind-wandering and then bring them back gently to where you want them to be. This means that your mind is cleared of irrelevant thoughts and the focus is centred only on what is important at that specific moment.

5. Simulate what you will actually go through in practise. Athletes learn to concentrate more effectively and deal with distractions by physically going through the process that faces them, provided it mimics as closely as possible the conditions in which they will perform.

Chapter 3
Reading Skills

The SQ4R is an effective reading technique applied to serious reading matter, and stands for Survey, Question, Read, Recall, Record and Review. It is used for studying textbooks and non-fiction books. Speed reading provides a number of powerful techniques to help people get a quick overview of material. They can then decide if they want to read further or otherwise. The techniques of speed reading include skimming, scanning and skipping. The reasons why people read slowly include small recognition spans, regressing and sub-vocalisation. There are seven ways to improve your reading skills. There are different reading strategies you can apply to different types of reading material.

SQ4R

SQ4R is an elaboration of the SQ3R reading technique developed by Professor Frank Robinson, a psychologist with the Ohio State University in the USA. Although this technique was designed for students studying textbooks, it is equally of use to people who want to develop a systematic approach to reading non-fiction books. It gives readers a mental framework to organise facts correctly, and discriminate between what is important, what is less important and what is irrelevant. The SQ4R technique is not only suitable for students, but is relevant for senior managers as well who must handle large amounts of reading matter as part of their job. Even workers need to be able to read efficiently and effectively when they are faced with very technical material, like manuals for car mechanics and technicians, to succeed in their jobs.

The SQ4R technique will prime your prior knowledge, and help you integrate and understand the text to follow. Prioritise your reading on a 'must know', 'should know', 'nice to know', and needn't know' basis. The 'must know' needs to be studied carefully, the 'should know' needs to be skimmed, the 'nice to know' can be scanned through, while the 'needn't know' can be ignored. Before you start establish the purpose or reason why you are reading the book. What do you want to know

WHAT YOU'LL LEARN
IN THIS CHAPTER:
- What is the SQ4R technique?
- What are the techniques of speed reading?
- Why do some people read slowly?
- How can I improve my reading skills?
- Where can I apply different reading strategies?

after reading it? For textbooks, you usually want to learn, remember, understand and apply the content of the book.

The acronym *ADMIT* will help you recall the advantages of the SQ4R technique:

- **A**nswer questions. The question part of the technique encourages you to formulate questions so that you will learn more purposefully, actively and effectively. These will also help to activate prior knowledge.
- **D**ifferentiate between main ideas and details for greater understanding and retention, by creating a mental hierarchical framework in which you will fit facts correctly. You will separate important information from irrelevant data.
- **M**emory. Makes the best possible use of your memory by getting you to recall and fill any gaps in your knowledge, while adopting a systematic review plan.
- **I**ncreased concentration and comprehension. You will concentrate on key points and concepts and ignore superfluous information.
- **T**arget. You read actively with a purpose. Reading with specific objectives in mind, such as certain questions to be answered, directs attention and facilitates comprehension of relevant information. Once you establish a purpose, you then read with that purpose continually in mind.

Let's now look at the SQ4R technique in more detail.

1. Survey the book

The purpose of surveying is to get an overview of the topic, discover key points, and identify the relationship between the parts and subtopics. Psychologists experimenting with rats running a maze found that learning was more efficient when the rats could see the whole maze before starting. Survey is in fact a reconnaissance of the unfamiliar terrain of the book, to enable you to build up reference points or landmarks in advance.

The survey stage is at two levels: at the book level and at the chapter level. We will concentrate on the book level first which will give you an overview of the book. At this level, you want to find out what the book is generally about, how the book is organised, and what the major topics of the book are. This stage will give you the organisational framework of the book, will alert you to the key points, and will arouse your curiosity and help your concentration. It will also give you the motivation and momentum to get down working, overcoming any inertia you may feel. It is important not to get bogged down in details at this early stage.

Look at the cover of the book. Take note of the title as this will tell you what the book is about. Take a mental note of how many pages there are in the book, so that you have an idea of the task facing you. Read the front and back cover and take particular note of the author's bibliography. This will tell you why the author is qualified to write on the topic. Read the copyright page, and take particular note of the date of publication, which tells you how current the book is. The material in some books can be out of date by the time they are published, particularly in scientific and technical areas.

Browse through the list of contents and the index. If you are familiar with a topic in the index, go to the text and check out how the author has dealt with it. This will give you an idea of how competent the author is to deal with the topic. Read the preface as this will give you a quick overview of the book and may tell you why the author wrote the book. Has the author a particular audience in mind? Study the glossary of terms if provided. This is most important if the subject matter is new to you, as your reading progresses and comprehension will be hampered by unfamiliar terminology. The size of your prior knowledge and working memory capacity are also important in determining the extent of your comprehension.

Study the chapter titles. Read the introduction and the summary or conclusion to each chapter. If chapter objectives are provided, read these carefully as they highlight important points. Now study the chapter headings and subheadings. Notice the relative size of headings, or classification system, used for clues as to the importance of ideas, organisation and structure. After this stage you may form the opinion that the information provided is not what you want, and you may decide not to go any further.

Survey the chapters

The survey of the chapter is similar to the survey of the book but is done in more depth. First take a mental note of the number of pages in the chapter. This will give you an idea of the scale of the current reading task which is facing you. The survey of the chapter will tell you how the chapter is organised, what the chapter is about, the major topics covered in the chapter and the key words and ideas. Study the chapter title, headings and subheadings. Read the introduction and summary.

Read the first and last sentences of each paragraph. The first sentence is usually the topic sentence while the last sentence is the conclusion or the flow into the next paragraph. Study the chapter objectives if provided and pay particular attention to the questions, if any, at the end of each chapter. These questions cover what the author considers to be the key concepts of the chapter. If these are not provided, make up your own questions covering the key concepts of the chapter.

Study the visual and verbal signposts which provide clues as to the importance of ideas. The *visual signposts* include photos, diagrams, graphics, maps, charts and illustrations. The author has included these because they illustrate important and often difficult concepts, where words alone would be inadequate. If preparing for exams, bear in mind that the ability to illustrate points by including diagrams, drawings, models or graphs wins valuable marks from the examiner. Other visual signposts include

Inspiration

"The worth of a book is to be measured by what you can carry away from it."
James Bryce

51

bold face, bullet points and italics. These may be used to show emphasis, enumeration, indication of cause and effect or conditions. These signposts and others alert readers to what is coming next and that, in turn, will allow you to decide if you want to carefully study or skim the text.

Figure 6
Visual Signposts

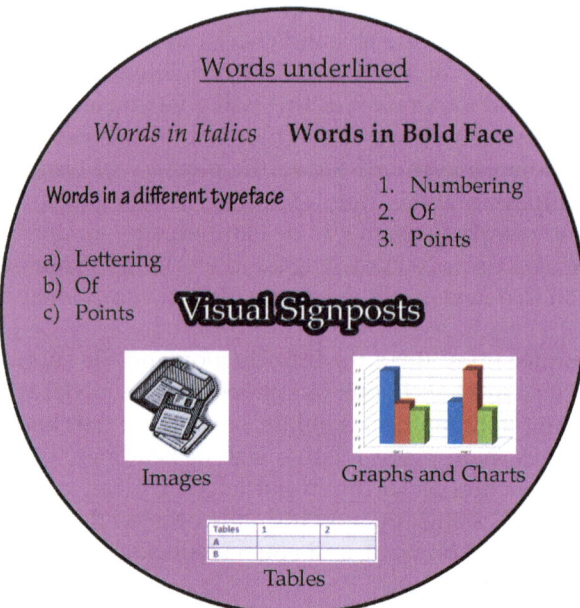

Authors often use *verbal signposts* to make transitions moving from one idea to another or to change direction. The ability to anticipate what has not been seen is vital to reading, just as the ability to anticipate what has not yet been heard is vital in listening. If you look for verbal signposts you will be able to predict what is coming next. This will help you navigate the material rapidly with anticipation and in a discriminating manner.

To add a thought authors may use 'but, yet, nevertheless, regardless, although.' To give an example, they may use 'for instance, that is to say, since.' If an author is about to qualify a point they use 'however,' which signals that some exceptions to what has been stated will follow. Pay particular attention to sentences introduced by phrases such as 'most importantly' and 'therefore'. The first indicates that the author is about to say something of great significance while the second means that they are about to arrive at a conclusion.

A cause and effect statement signals to the reader the need to look for two related descriptions, circumstances, or fact. For example, 'because I slept late, I missed my bus and was late for work.' When a writer wants to summarise, he or she will use such words as 'finally, in conclusion, in short, in summary.'

Depending on your purpose, completion of the book survey, or chapter survey stages, may meet your needs without going any further. For example, if you only need an overview of a topic these stages may be sufficient. We are now ready to go forward to the next stage: question.

2. Question

Before you start the formal questioning process set down your level of prior knowledge. This will highlight areas to be explored, representing gaps in your existing level of knowledge and questions you need answered. Ask yourself what you wish to learn from the chapter. Use the knowledge gained from the survey stage to help you formulate questions. Turn chapter objectives or learning outcomes into questions. Turn headings and subheadings into questions. If headings are missing look for the topic sentence in each paragraph and turn this into a question.

For each section of the chapter ask the questions: Why? Who? What? When? Where? How? Why? means that you are looking for reasons, conclusions, deductions, inferences, implications and opinions. Who? means you are looking for information about people. What? means that you are looking for events, actions and things. When? means that you are looking for dates. Where means that you are looking for a context, place or location. How? means that you are looking for a system, method or process.

Try to determine how different sections of the chapter relate to each other. In general, do not passively accept what the author says, but instead actively question statements made and challenge ideas presented. This will turn the reading process into a critical thinking exercise. Many business books and textbooks have questions at the end of each chapter. Use these to explore the key issues as exam questions are often based on these. The questions are in fact the author's method of highlighting important points essential to the proper understanding of the subject.

Questions prepare the mind for the reading stage, create anticipation, conditions for reflection, and improve comprehension. When your mind is actively searching for answers to questions you are reading with a purpose, which helps your mind engage with the learning process. Questions create a curiosity and tension which will only be satisfied and relieved, when you discover the answers to the questions. In the meantime, your powers of concentration are enhanced by the tension caused by the unanswered questions. In fact, the better the quality of questions you ask, the better your level of concentration. They also help you decide what information you need to look for and learn. Questions prepare you for the next stage – reading.

3. Read

Put your book on a bookstand as reading at an angle of 45 degrees under incandescent lighting reduces glare. It will also improve your reading speed and prevent eyestrain. Read actively to get answers to your questions. As you read evaluate ideas, remember the key points, and mentally

Inspiration

"Nothing is worth reading that does not require an alert mind."
Charles Dudley Warner

note the supporting details which explain the main ideas and show relationships between ideas in the section. Differentiate facts from opinions and assumptions.

Visualise the important information, and make links and associations to make it more meaningful and memorable. The more connections that you can make with a reading the more meaningful it becomes. Relate your own experience and knowledge to the writer's statements and examples, to test the validity of the writer's point of view. If you haven't direct experience of the topic try to think of people that you know who have, and substitute this for your lack of experience.

Inspiration

"Every reader, if he has a strong mind, reads himself into the book, and amalgamates his thoughts with those of the author."
Johann Wolfgang von Goethe

Use a pencil to put light check marks on the margin alongside important ideas. You can easily erase these later on and maintain the integrity and resale value of your book. Reread difficult sections if necessary and restate in your own words. Put question marks alongside parts you don't understand for further investigation. In any event the material further on may explain more adequately the problem causing the stumbling block.

The worst thing you can do when you come to something you don't understand is to get discouraged and give up. In any learning situation you will have periods of rapid progress, slow progress and no progress. This is known as the learning curve and periods of slow progress and no progress are called learning plateaus. There is nothing unique or unusual about your situation, as this happens to all learners. The main thing is to persevere. Stop at the end of each section to see if you can answer satisfactorily the questions you formulated from the survey stage. You may have to revisit areas you are unsure of to fill in gaps in knowledge.

Read material in phrases, chunks, or thought units, usually two to three words long. This will enhance your concentration and comprehension. We read for meaning and understanding and so the correct reading speed is the one that accomplishes that purpose. So vary your speed in line with the importance and difficulty of the text. Reduce your speed for difficult passages, and speed it up for material that you are familiar with. Skip material that you know already. Use context cues for unfamiliar words, and if this doesn't work look the word up in a dictionary. Carefully study charts, graphs, tables and pictures for new information, or to clarify and bring together difficult concepts. This brings us to the next stage: recall.

4. Recall

Can you recall the answers to the questions that you formulated? Close the book and try and recall in writing what you've read, concentrating on key facts and concepts. Check your answers and restudy parts of the text if necessary to fill any gaps in your knowledge. Remember the following advantages of recall:

• Recall gives you an opportunity to discover any gaps in your knowledge requiring remedial action. This is the learning principle of knowledge of results and feedback. Feedback combined with corrective action is a vital element of successful learning.

- Recall is an active rather than a passive method of study. By summarising your knowledge you are actively engaged and getting to grips with the subject.
- If you recall mentally and in writing, you are engaging the three senses of learning: seeing (your notes), hearing (verbalising and paraphrasing), and doing (writing).

Mentally recall the main ideas and key concepts at the end of each section. Recalling at the end of each paragraph would disrupt the flow and continuity in reading. How much time should you spend recalling? Approximately half your time should be spent in recalling what you have read to maximise your retention. Generate images for key words as you recall and reflect. People remember pictures better than words and visual memory lasts longer than verbal memory. Try and visualise models, diagrams, charts and pictures in your mind's eye. With constant practise your ability to do so should improve considerably. These exercises bring the right or imaginative side of the brain into play. By using both sides of your brain you will enhance your ability to learn effectively. In an experiment with students, psychologists found that those who visualised images linked to the sentences, scored 40 per cent higher on comprehension than those who read the same story without visualisation.

Inspiration

"To read without reflecting is like eating without digesting."
Edmund Burke

Reflect means to think deeply, thoughtfully, critically, carefully and calmly about something. Reflection is an integral part of recall. The brain needs time to think about, evaluate, consolidate, make sense of, and understand information. Plato said, 'The life which is unexamined is not worth living'. Learning begins when we think and reflect on what we have read. The purpose of education is to acquire wisdom by reflecting on important issues and questions. Reflection is the second stage of the learning cycle of 'do something, think about it, conclude, and then do something differently'. Reflection helps us to think about how we are going to use the information, and clarifies what else we need to learn.

It is important that when you recall information that you reflect on its context and significance. Think of concrete examples and areas where you can apply the knowledge. It is easier to remember information that makes sense, and conclusions that are supported by the facts. Reflect how the information relates to any prior knowledge of the topic that you have, and how it relates to other information within the chapter. People learn by linking and associating new knowledge to what they know already. The good learner quickly integrates prior knowledge and experience to text information. During the recall and reflect process record your thoughts in writing. Remember that recall, recitation and paraphrasing mentally and in writing, is a great way of imprinting information on your mind.

Figure 7
Overview of SQ4R

5. Record

The best way of recording your recall and reflection is by using learning maps which are covered extensively in chapter 4. A learning map is a type of graphic organiser which gives you the big picture and a permanent record for review. It shows key concepts and main points with supporting detail and visually displays how ideas are linked. It thus identifies the overall themes and relationships between concepts. For each chapter use a learning map to record the answers to your questions and the main ideas and key concepts recalled.

The hierarchy of ideas in the chapter will help you compile your learning maps. The main idea of the chapter is the chapter title; the supporting ideas are contained in the section and subsection headings, while the first and last sentence of each paragraph should give you the main idea of the paragraph. Make one-word summaries of each paragraph and integrate these into your learning maps. If you invent mnemonics for key points you will be able to remember them better.

From individual chapter learning maps, prepare a master learning map for the whole book. You will now have an overview learning map of the book, supported by learning maps for each chapter. This will facilitate efficient and effective revision. Students who need to memorise certain things for exams, like to reserve a column on the learning map on the right hand side for definitions, rules, principles, and formulae and so on. Research shows that the act of writing notes makes them more memorable and clarifies understanding.

6. Review

You forget very easily if you don't review. In fact you may forget up to 80 per cent of what you read in just 24 hours if you don't review. Within a week you will forget 90 per cent, and eventually you will forget almost everything if you don't review. These facts highlight the importance of adhering to a systematic review plan. If you review immediately and then within 24 hours and after that periodically, you will ensure that key concepts and main points will go from your short-term into your long-term memory.

Begin learning maps at the recall stage and complete them at the reflect stage. Four or five readings of textbooks are normally required before their contents are in any way familiar. If you use the learning maps for review these re-readings are not required. In fact the permanent record you have created in your learning maps is now more useful to you than the original text. However, you may like to cross-reference points on your learning map to the text. This will facilitate the process of looking up relevant points in the book if you need to revisit them for clarification. Use your powers of visualisation to review your learning maps.

As part of your review plan, put the learning map aside and see if you can draw it from memory. Compare your efforts with the original learning map and see what gaps arise in your memory. Keep doing this exercise until you can draw the original learning map from memory. This is a great way to strengthen your memory, particularly if you need to remember things for exam or career purposes. An effective way of reviewing information is to teach it to somebody else as you quickly find out what you do and don't understand and what others find difficult to follow.

This completes the SQ4R approach which is a systematic, slow and studious, but effective way of studying text or non-fiction material. You will need to practise the SQ4R approach for about a month before it becomes an ingrained habit. We will now look at some general reading strategies that can be used separately or in combination with the SQ4R approach.

Inspiration

"What we become depends on what we read after all the professors have finished with us."
Thomas Carlyle

Speed Reading

The main reason for adopting speed reading strategies is information overload. The average executive is bombarded with more written information than ever before such as business magazines, minutes, reports, proposals, brochures, texts and emails. Similarly, for people involved in formal learning, or continuous professional development (CPD), speed reading provides a set of powerful techniques to help them get through large volumes of reading.

Speed reading saves time, is more efficient, keeps you mentally sharp, broadens your mental horizons and keeps you current. It gives you choice as regards what you should read carefully, what you should skim and scan, and what you should ignore. Reading is one of the most effective and economical ways for a person to learn and develop. Through reading you can benefit from the knowledge and experience of others, and by adopting strategic approaches to reading you can do so quickly and more productively.

If you are given a large report you may not need to read it all as reading the management abstract may be sufficient to meet your purpose, if all you need to know is an outline of the subject. If you choose to go further speed reading can help you overview the report, using skimming, scanning and skipping techniques. These are practical techniques that help you get the gist of the information that you need. It has been established that with training you can read considerably more strategically and faster without any loss of comprehension.

Average reading speeds
The speed at which you read depends on your purpose and the level of comprehension you want to achieve. The less detail you need to remember, the faster you should read. Conversely, the more detail you need to remember, the slower you should read. The average reader reads at a speed of 250 words per minute (wpm), with a comprehension level of about 70 per cent. The reason for this is that this is approximately the rate at which people speak, and most people when reading say the words to themselves internally, which restricts the speed of their reading to the speed at which they speak. For example, US president, Franklin D. Roosevelt spoke at the rate of 136 wpm during his famous 'fireside chats' on radio given between 1933 and 1944.

As most people subvocalize or use inner speech when reading this process constrains the rate at which they read. You should learn to read with your eyes instead of your ears. With the help of appropriate techniques reading speed can be improved, with a little training, to 360 wpm. With sustained effort and plenty of practise you can achieve 600 words when reading easy material, such as newspapers, while it is likely to be considerably less when reading unfamiliar, difficult material, such as textbooks or legal documents. Some things like legal documents, contracts and insurance policies have to be read very carefully. Here you should be satisfied with a speed of 300 wpm or less. President Kennedy is reputed to have had a reading speed of over 1000 wpm. Lady Thatcher, former Prime Minister of Great Britain, read at a similar speed. Senior business executives usually have good speed reading skills to help them cope with high volumes of paperwork.

The average resting heart rate is 60 beats per second. Most books have about 10 to 12 words per line. A reading speed of one line per second results in both a rhythm of 60 beats per second using the hand as a pacer, and allows the eye to read between 600 and 700 wpm. Make this speed your objective for general material. For more difficult material, or where you lack a conceptual background, and in order to maintain satisfactory comprehension levels, you should be satisfied with a reading rate of between 300 to 400 wpm. However useful a technique speed reading is, remember speed without comprehension is counterproductive!

Constraints on Reading Speed

Most experts consider a comprehension rate of 70 per cent or above to be adequate. On the other hand, according to research studies, there appears to be a minimal reading speed of 200 wpm, below which the reader may fail to process the meaning of text effectively, and thus suffer a significant loss in comprehension. The connection between reading speed and comprehension can be understood by reference to a movie film. A movie film is made up of still images flashed in rapid succession so that the eyes see it as continuous. If you slow down the film, frame by frame, its movement, coherence and meaning are lost. Similarly, when you read word by word you are not reading efficiently. Just like a conversation you need to group words together so that they coalesce into ideas. Reading below 200 wpm apparently reflects inefficient, word-by-word reading, not conducive to integrating and comprehending text in a meaningful way. The only time it pays to read slowly is when you are trying to understand very difficult material.

Research has also shown that when the term reading is interpreted in the sense of comprehending most of the words on a page, it is physically impossible, because of visual and short-term memory capacity and processing limitations, to read faster than 800 to 1000 wpm, and that comprehension suffers above a speed of 400 wpm. If the eyes transmit faster than the brain can absorb the material, you won't remember what you've read. Of course, higher speeds can be achieved when methods such as skimming, scanning and skipping are employed, but these approaches should be distinguished from genuine reading. It should be remembered that skimming, scanning and skipping, while useful time saving approaches in certain circumstances, are no substitute for thinking, reflecting and absorbing which take considerably more time.

An incredible reading speed

Therefore claims of people reading thousands of words a minute are incredulous. There is only one person who could read at these phenomenal speeds. His name was Kim Peek (1951-2009) and he had the ability to read two pages simultaneously, one with each eye, with 98 per cent retention. He could simultaneously read, in about 3 seconds, two pages of a book at once, the left page with the left eye, and the right page with the right eye, and could recall them perfectly. Nobody knows how he did it so we can't learn from his example, but we do know that he was born without a corpus callosum, the bundle of nerves that connects the right and left hemispheres of the brain.

According to the New York Times he read as many as 12,000 volumes in his lifetime and more remarkable could remember what he read. He read a book in about an hour, and could recall vast amounts of information in subjects ranging from history and literature, geography, and numbers to sports, music and dates. The Oscar winning film 'Rain Man' starring Dustin Hoffman was based on his life and it was after this that he came

Inspiration

"Reading is a means of thinking with another person's mind; it forces you to stretch your own."
Charles Scribner, Jr.

to the attention of the public. Early in his life, doctors said he had mental retardation and would never be able to do much. Despite this and poor motor skills he achieved great things in his short life. He was a popular speaker and travelled almost 3 million air miles, and talked to nearly 60 million people which is an amazing legacy to leave.

Recognition span

Intuitively we feel that our eyes move smoothly across the page when reading. In fact, the eyes move with a jerky, intermittent motion and then stop. The eyes can only read when they stop. These stops are called fixations giving your eyes a chance to transmit the meaning of the words to the brain. This means that you can read only when your eyes momentarily stop. To be a faster reader therefore, you must increase your recognition span by taking in more words at each fixation. Physically the recognition span is only about three to four words depending on their size. Reading for ideas by chunking words means that you will have fewer fixations, taking in larger groups of words with a faster reading speed. For example, if you are reading a page that has twelve words to a line, and you stop at each word, you will make twelve fixations, each of which takes a fraction of a second. However, if you can read four words with each fixation, you will make only one-third of the stops, and thus considerably increase your reading speed.

A significant constraint on reading speed is caused by texts that are poorly laid out and written, or you might find that for some reason the author's style is difficult for you. The solution is to find another text on the same topic more suited to your needs and that is more clearly written and better laid out. Sometimes a clearer explanation of the same topic is all it takes to make an incomprehensible subject accessible and understandable.

Common Reasons Why People Read Slowly

- They have small recognition spans with many eye fixations. Each fixation is of longer duration than that used by good readers. In addition, they read each word individually which makes the flow of their reading disjointed and hinders comprehension. Try to read a whole phrase instantaneously. You think in thought units and therefore, you should read in the same way.
- They regress or progress. Their eyes drift back to reread words and phrases. This shows a lack of confidence in their reading ability, as it is more than likely that they have absorbed what they have read. This habit destroys concentration and the momentum of the rhythm that the reader has built up. The cause of regression may be due to your eyes losing their place on the page which can be prevented by using a pacer. Progression refers to the habit of jumping forward in the text for no apparent reason.
- They vocalise or talk to themselves. This is a hangover from early schooldays where we were taught to verbalise words when learning

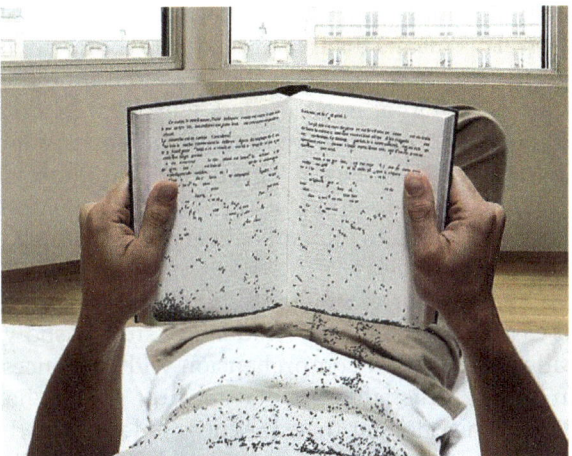

Figure 8
Avoid the common pitfalls that cause you to read slowly

how to read, and as a consequence speed and quality of reading suffer. In certain circumstances, such as revision for exams, vocalising can aid memory. Although the minority of readers vocalise, the vast majority subvocalize, i.e. say words internally, some even moving their lips when doing so. Although it can be very difficult to eliminate this habit you can speed up your reading by not subvocalizing structure words, such as 'and,' 'the,' 'to, 'and so on. Structure words are a significant proportion of any reading matter. The Pareto Principal is the law of the significant few and the trivial many. Applied to reading, it suggests that large proportions of words such as structure words are superfluous and redundant, and are not needed for an understanding of key concepts. For example, it is very unlikely that you subvocalize full stops, commas or indeed road signs such as 'Stop'. Regardless you still understand the sentence. However, subvocalizing key words such as nouns and verbs have been proved by psychologists to aid memory.

- They do not vary their reading speed in line with their purpose, level of prior knowledge, and the novelty and difficulty of the reading matter. The effective reader is flexible and adjusts his speed, while the ineffective reader is inflexible and uses the same speed for all types of reading material. Even within the same article you can slow down for difficult parts, and speed up for easy parts, while still maintaining an acceptable speed for the whole article. Obviously, you can scan, skim and skip material that is already familiar to you or that you don't need to know. Good readers see more in less time, and vary their reading speed in line with their purpose, and the difficulty and novelty of the text.

- They fail to integrate prior knowledge and experience with text information, and do not apply critical reading skills such as analysis, synthesis and evaluation to the written text. We learn by reflecting on and linking new information to what we know already through previous learning and experience.

- They may have a small working memory capacity, and consequently less capacity for holding previous information while absorbing new information. This means that when reading a long sentence, they will have forgotten the start of the sentence by the time they get to the end. On the other hand, good readers with a large working memory should be able to retain more of a text in working memory while processing new text, so their integration of the information may be more thorough. Even if you have a good memory, you may overtax your memory by trying to remember everything you read, rather than remembering selectively.

- Studies show that shorter sentences with shorter words are easier to read and easier to understand. Readability studies show that the average reader has the best comprehension with sentences of about 16 words in length. This suggests that most of us will have difficulty following sentences longer than 16 words in length, and this difficulty will be compounded if the sentence contains unfamiliar words, or technical jargon.

- They have a limited vocabulary. This means that they have difficulty understanding text. Some have to stop reading to look up certain words in a dictionary. This will slow up and interrupt the process of reading considerably. Good readers have a huge working vocabulary which they continually add to throughout their lives.

- Slow readers have poor powers of concentration. Efficient readers are able to exclude distractions, and read at times of the day when their powers of concentration and body rhythms are best, and read in environments conducive to good concentration. They are also aware that they should read in short sessions, preferably not more than 30 minutes, to maintain effective concentration levels. They realise that multitasking inhibits good concentration and so they focus their powers of concentration on one thing at a time.

- Slow readers often lack purpose and motivation. This means that they have no clear goals to aim for when they read, and do not think of the advantages they get from their increased learning. In addition, slow readers concentrate on surface rather than *deep learning*. Deep learning is intrinsically motivational – readers try to understand the meaning of their reading, the context of new ideas and concepts, and how they relate to each other and how they can apply them. Deep readers relate ideas to prior knowledge, and evaluate the text by examining the logic of the argument. They examine conclusions to see if they are supported by the evidence. On the other hand, *surface learning* tends to be rote learning without having a purpose or reading strategy. Surface readers fail to distinguish principles from examples, and focus on individual points rather than integrating ideas. The emphasis is on memorisation rather than comprehension.

- They lack self-belief in their ability and capacity to acquire speed reading skills. Speed reading is as much about mental belief as about physiology. Some people believe they need to read one word at a time to maintain comprehension. They don't realise that with practise they can significantly improve their reading speed without any loss

Inspiration

———————

"Life transforming idea have always come to me through books."
Bell Hooks

of comprehension. Like any other skill the more you practise the more proficient you become. A positive attitude and an acquired habit of reading will go a long way to achieving your aim to become an efficient and effective reader.

Reading Techniques

Use to your benefit the different techniques of speed reading, skimming, scanning, skipping and reading slowly. Match and mix and vary your speed depending on you purpose. For example, you might be reading for enjoyment, information, or to complete a project. If you are exploring or reviewing, you might decide to skim a document. If you're searching for information, you might scan for a particular word. If you are already familiar with something you may decide to skip it. To study, you might use the SQ4R approach for careful and reflective reading.

Skimming

Develop speed reading skills by applying the VERTIGO system (discussed in the next section). You could employ rapid or speed reading to advantage with a novel or not too difficult text. Obviously with light material you can follow the story line without reading each word carefully. In bygone days when milk was delivered to homes, many people skimmed the cream off the top and used it to enhance the flavour of pastries and desserts. The same principle applies when you use skimming as a strategic approach in your reading. You remove the best information and ignore the information of little consequence.

Skimming means selective reading; reading what is important, and deliberately ignoring what isn't. Skimming is done at a speed of 1000 wpm, or three to four times faster than normal reading. Skimming is a preparation for detailed reading rather than a substitute, and may be used when you are looking for an overview of main ideas, issues, arguments, theoretical perspectives and so on. Skimming is where your eyes cover certain pre-selected sections of the text to gain a gist of what the text is all about.

Use skimming if you want to narrow down your reading to useful and relevant texts. It is also useful when you want to revise something that you have previously read in detail. College students do this automatically before they enter the examination room, as they have covered the material in detail previously. To survey a book employ the skimming technique, by reading first and last chapters, first and last paragraphs in each chapter, headings and subheadings, first and last sentences of each paragraph and chapter summaries. Vary the depth of your survey in line with your purpose.

Some texts contain superfluous examples and illustrations. Since these are included to clarify ideas, skip over them if you feel they are not needed for your understanding. Sometimes detailed explanation and elaboration are not needed, and if so skim over them quickly. Stop skimming when you have an overview of the information, or when you have found the material that you need to read.

Scanning

Air traffic controllers use radar to scan the skies to locate incoming and outgoing aircraft. Similarly scanning is reading systematically and quickly to locate specific information in a text. To become an effective scanner, you should first decide what you are looking for, and what form it will take. For example, if you want to know when something happened, you would look for a date. If you want to find out who did something you would look for a name. If you want to illustrate a point you will look for an example. If you keep in mind at all times what you are searching for, it is likely to stand out more clearly than the surrounding words, and thus becomes easier to locate.

Scanning can be done at up to 1500 wpm. While scanning readers ignore all other information, concentrating on only finding what they want. It usually involves moving your eyes quickly down the page, seeking specific words and phrases. Pay particular attention to words in bold type or italics. Scanning could be used when researching for specific information, such as locating information in an index, telephone directory, timetable or finding a specific word in a dictionary. Scan your reading material until you find the information you want, then read only the part containing the relevant information that provides the answer to your question.

Scanning can also be helpful if you want to check that a book or article does contain the specific information that you want, and you want to quote it for research purposes. Scanning usually comes before skimming. Once you've scanned the document and found what you wanted then you may decide to study it in more depth and skim it to extract the important ideas and information that you need.

Similar to scanning, if you are reading for specific information, as in research, you should skip that matter not essential to your purpose. Use the list of contents, or the index at the back of the book, to locate what you want rather than aimlessly flicking through the pages. Research has found that shorter, more frequent, and more predictable words are read faster and are skipped more frequently.

Finally, with difficult texts you must read slowly for comprehension. Slow reading, such as that involved in the SQ4R approach, is normally suitable for studying where you need a detailed knowledge and understanding of the subject. But remember; vary your style of reading in line with your purpose. Read quickly material that you are already familiar with. Read slowly material that is new or that you find difficult. When reading for pleasure, you may decide to appreciate the literature by savouring the words and the language that the author uses. Some people feel compelled to read everything, even material that they know already or that is unrelated to their purpose. This is a waste of time.

Poor Readers

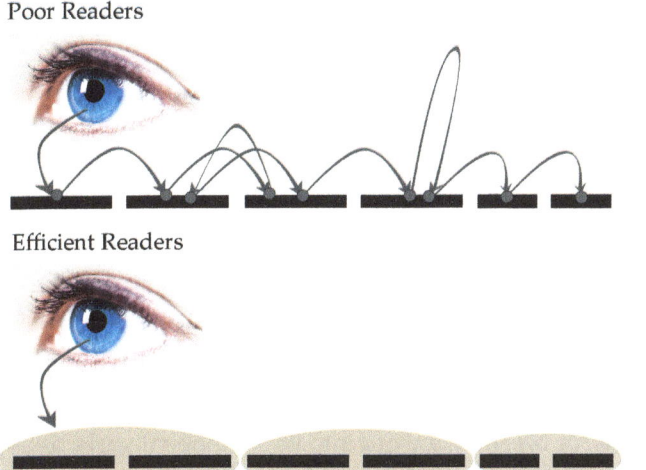

Efficient Readers

Figure 9
Efficient Readers are effective scanners

Seven Ways to Improve Your Reading Skills

Use the acronym *VERTIGO* to improve your reading skills. VERTIGO stands for vocabulary, eyesight, regression, talking, ideas, guide and operating speed.

V = Vocabulary

You can read faster and maintain a constant speed if you possess a wide and comprehensive vocabulary. Being unable to recognise the meaning of words will slow you down considerably, although context and inference may provide cues as to meaning. Actively build up your vocabulary by following these rules:

- Read widely. If you read 15 minutes a day you would read 18 books in a year reading at an average reading speed. If you develop a habit of reading you will become more confident and self-assured in your ability to comprehend and understand all sources of information. In addition, your writing skills will improve. Reading is the foundation on which all academic skills are built. So develop an insatiable appetite for acquiring knowledge through reading.

The more knowledge you possess the easier it is to acquire more knowledge. A good background of general knowledge and experience will help you tackle material of greater difficulty, and help you grasp things quicker. The wider your reading and the more you know the easier it is to learn and gain more knowledge. The old saying that knowledge is power is true.

- Learn some of the common Latin and Greek roots to English words. Study common prefixes and suffixes. A prefix is one or more syllables added to the beginning of a word to qualify its meaning, while a suffix is added at the end. For example, in the word 'premeditated', the prefix is 'pre' meaning 'before', 'meditate' means to think, and 'ed' is the suffix which refers to the past tense. Similarly the word 'phobia' means fear. Hydro means water and therefore hydrophobia means fear of water. Other phobias include 'claustrophobia' fear of enclosed spaces, 'acrophobia' fear of heights, and 'agoraphobia' fear of foreigners. Word analysis, or breaking a word into its component parts, as above, is a useful strategy to adopt for understanding words without referring constantly to a dictionary.

- Watch out for new words and look up their meanings in a dictionary or Google 'Onelook,' a comprehensive online dictionary. For greater comprehension and to make them more memorable look for synonyms and antonyms, and examine origins and usage of the word. Synonyms are words that mean the same, and antonyms are words with the opposite meaning. Record the new word on cue cards for reference and memorisation. File the cards alphabetically and review periodically. Alternatively carry them with you and review during spare moments of the day. As you commit the words to long-term memory you can file away the cards for future reference if needed. There are calendars available organised around the concept of learning one new word each day. They consist of 365 sheets, with the date and relevant word – one for each day of the year. Buy one of these and you can improve your vocabulary by 365 words in a year, which means that you would learn 3,650 new words over a ten year period. Use new words you learn at every available opportunity. Integrate them into your everyday conversation, and thereby commit them effortlessly to long-term memory. Better still when you get an opportunity; use them in your writing.

- Compile a glossary of technical terms in your speciality or, better still, if available, buy one of the specialist dictionaries in your chosen field. If a glossary of technical terms is provided in the book, photocopy it and keep it beside you as you read. Use this approach to build up your technical vocabulary in your specialist subjects. This will help you progress in your career. Remember there are words which are part of your everyday vocabulary, but have a specialised meaning in a particular subject area. An example is 'principal' which means the teacher in charge of a school. In a finance context it is the capital sum of money which is borrowed at interest.

E = Eyesight

Wear spectacles, if your eyesight is bad and adversely affecting your ability to read. Amazingly, many people neglect wearing spectacles because of vanity or inertia. During reading sessions rest your eyes occasionally by focusing them alternately on a near and distant object. This will relax and refresh your eyes and prevent fatigue from setting in. If you have recurring and persistent problems with eyestrain or headaches, you should consult your optician or doctor. After all the most important reading tools are your eyes, so it's important to look after them!

R = Regression and progression

As a general rule, stop regressing and progressing and develop a rhythm for reading. Don't go back over words you think you don't understand. More often than not the meaning will become clear because of context, structure and elaboration as you continue reading. Readers also regress because they lose their place on the page. Progression is jumping ahead when reading for no apparent reason. However, there are exceptions to every rule. In practice, any reader, no matter how efficient, will make strategic regressions when they are confronted with unfamiliar or complex material. In addition, readers are inclined to spend more time rereading and reflecting on text relevant to their goals.

T = Talking

If you find yourself vocalising, stop! However, there is one exception to this. When you are trying to understand a complex concept it is often a good idea to speak the material aloud for better impact and retention. Speed up your reading by avoiding subvocalizing structure words. In fact, the faster you read the less subvocalizing you will be capable of doing.

I = Ideas

Read in thought (idea or concept units). Increase your recognition span, while taking in more words, and spending less time on each fixation. For example, when reading the newspaper, position your eyes on the centre of each sentence of a column. With practice your eyes should be able to take in the beginning and end of the sentence automatically. The columnar structure of newspapers facilitates this process. Chunk words in groups of two or three at a time when reading text as this is the size of the perceptual span. You may also find that you can increase your perceptual span by holding the text a little further from your eyes. The greater your perceptual span the greater your reading speed. Good readers attend primarily to the meaning of the text, while poor readers attend more to it surface characteristics.

G = Guide

Use a visual guide such as your index finger, a pencil or pen, to help your eyes move smoothly across the page as they cannot do so on their own. Alternatively, you could use an index card, which will prevent you from regressing to previous lines of print. Unlike other gadgets, an index card is cheap, is easy to carry around with you, and can double as a bookmark! Run the visual guide under the line you are reading without touching the page. Vary your speed in line with your purpose, and the difficulty of the text as you progress.

This technique focuses your attention and thereby improves your concentration. Using the hand as a pacer allows you to see and read groups of words at a time and helps to reduce subvocalization. It adds rhythm to reading involving the right side of the brain. Also, two senses are involved, vision and touch, thus increasing your command and retention of the reading material.

You may experience slow recovery, the time it takes to move from one line to the next. Consciously speed up your index finger to minimise recovery times and speed up reading. Move in one word on each line and read to the penultimate word to take advantage of your peripheral vision. Anticipate page turning so that you accomplish it in a smooth and efficient way. Always maintain an upright but relaxed posture. The desk you are reading at should be of a suitable height. Research shows that the distance between your eyes and the book should be between 15 and 24 inches. Obviously, using a guide is only appropriate for serious reading – for leisure reading the emphasis is on relaxation, and savouring and enjoying the text.

O = Operating reading speed

Benchmark your current reading speed so that you know where you are starting from, and will be able to gauge your progress over time as you adopt the various speed reading techniques. It is easy to determine your existing reading speed. Time the reading of a page of an article. Then count the number of words in the page. Divide this number by the amount of time in minutes it took to read it, to arrive at an average reading speed in words per minute. If you have an average (250 wpm) or below average reading speed, there is no reason why you can't improve it by between 50 and 100 per cent without any loss of comprehension.

However, claims of reading speeds in excess of 1000 wpm without any loss of comprehension are not true. It is not possible to read extremely fast without sacrificing understanding and innumerable research studies have confirmed that this is so. Practise reading faster, straight away! Use the daily newspaper for practice sessions. More importantly, apply the rapid reading technique to your study material or business books as appropriate. Compete with yourself. Make each reading a step towards more effective reading.

It is a good idea to improve your reading by practising one of these skills at a time. When you are satisfied that you are proficient in that one, move on to the next. By this process you will build up your speed reading skills on a gradual but permanent basis. For more effective and permanent learning distribute your practice over a period of time, as spaced learning is the most effective. Remember, practise makes permanent and practise makes perfect.

Inspiration

"The greatest gift is a passion for reading. It is cheap, it consoles, it distracts, it excites, it gives you knowledge of the world and experience of a wide kind. It is a moral illumination."
Elizabeth Hardwick

Reading Strategies

Vary your reading speed with your purpose. We read for numerous reasons including to learn, to answer questions, to solve problems and help us make decisions, to self-inform, to critically review, to enjoy, summarise, to research and to proof-read. For example, note the following types of purpose driven approaches and use them as appropriate. The acronym *SCRIBE* may help you recall the reading strategies.

- **S**pecific. You may research a topic of interest to you, or to obtain specific information, say for a particular problem, or exam question you want to solve. Similarly you may want to find the meaning of a word, the biographical details of a famous person, or what a particular writer has to say about a topic that you are interested in. Use the list of contents or the index at the back of the book to guide you to the particular section that interests you, or will answer your specific question, and then read the section carefully. When researching a topic, use the search engine 'Google' to get you started. If looking for research articles on topics use 'Google Scholar' as it contains papers that have been cited by experts in the topic area. This is an example of reading with a purpose saving you considerable time and effort.

- **Critical.** Critical reading involves making inferences, assumptions, deductions, interpretations, predictions and evaluations. Increasingly people are suffering from the Google syndrome. They accept what they read online as fact when it may not be, rather than viewing and cross checking the information critically. Socrates believed that only the examined word – and the examined life – was worth pursuing. When reading critically you are looking for merits and faults in order to reach a balanced judgement on a piece of writing. Critical reading is essential when reading business books especially books which appear daunting due to their complexity and size. You must learn to discriminate between what is important and what is not. Is it relevant or irrelevant? Is it supported by the argument or not? Do you agree with it? Does it support or contradict other material? Is it based on solid research or hearsay? How does it add to what you know already? Apply higher level thinking skills such as analysis, synthesis, and evaluation to the written text. To support your critical reading apply a creative reading strategy. Creative reading involves synthesis, integration, application and extension of ideas. It means making the reading your own and getting more out of it than is actually there.
- **R**evision. Revision reading confirms and reinforces your knowledge and helps you to retain it in your long-term memory. It is the type of reading students do coming up towards exam time. Use learning maps for this purpose to familiarise yourself thoroughly with all the main concepts. Scanning, skimming and skipping can be used with advantage here especially when reading texts. There is no point in reading material that you are confident that you know already.
- **Informational.** Additional reading is essential for most subjects to give you familiarity and broad background knowledge. It is especially important for students at advanced stages of their degree programmes. Reading around your subject will give you different perspectives, and a greater insight and understanding of the topic. It will also build up your store of knowledge so that gaining additional knowledge is made easier. When researching a topic for a book or a project, this is the type of reading that may help you develop ideas and themes.
- **Browsing.** Lunchtime often presents opportunities to visit a bookshop or library to browse at your leisure. Browsing can be a very educational, enjoyable, relaxing and rewarding pastime, and can form an integral part of your effective study time management system. Many of us have discovered the pleasure of serendipitous discoveries made while browsing that are highly relevant to our information needs, though found in surprising places and situations. By browsing in an unfamiliar field, we may discover new ideas that have not been applied to our own area of interest, or gain new perspectives to apply to our work. Browsing on the internet, with the facilities provided by hyperlinks, can be enjoyable as well as productive. Look at any book that interests you; books that will help you progress in your studies or your career. Practise scanning, skimming and skipping techniques as

appropriate, reading only those sections that you consider important to you. This familiarity will help you when you are looking for useful resources for research or other purposes.

- **E**njoyment. Of course, we all read for relaxation and pleasure. As you know, when reading a novel it is not necessary to read every single word to get the gist of the story. Apply speed reading techniques with effect here, using skimming, scanning and skipping as necessary. Alternatively, you may just want to slowly savour the content of the book to appreciate its literary style.

Proof-reading is one method not obviously applicable to your needs, but very useful in a business context if called on to check a document or report. However, a variation on the theme, such as reviewing or check reading your own work, should be your approach on completing a letter, report or thesis. Check it for grammar, punctuation, misspellings, sense, logic, flow, clarity and neatness. Does B always follow A, and have you demonstrated it? In practice this simple procedure is often overlooked or neglected. It is surprising the amount of damage that can be done to a company's image by poorly conceived and written communications.

Reading Different Material

Newspapers, books, magazines, letters, memos, e-mail and reports are just some of the reading matter that you will encounter on a daily basis. Most of us have a desire to read these in an efficient and effective manner. Part of President John F. Kennedy's legend was his ability to speed read through four or five newspapers every morning.

Newspapers
Newspapers are usually organised in sections such as home and foreign news, and sections devoted to leisure and business. If you are a regular reader of the newspaper you will know which sections are useful for your purpose, and which can be skipped altogether. Pay particular attention to the front page of the newspaper, as it will contain the issues of the day which the editor considers to be the most important. The major story of the day will be placed in the most prominent position.

Read the headlines to get an overview of the newspaper and to determine what articles to read. Read the photo captions to get additional information. Photo captions often serve as an intermediate between the headline and the actual story, because they give you some details but not everything. Prioritize your reading by interest, and determine purpose. Use the 'must know', 'should know' and 'nice to know' approach. Read all the 'must know' material. For 'should know' material, speed read the first few paragraphs and the last paragraph. For 'nice to know' material, prioritize on an interest basis, and skim quickly through the rest.

Typically material in newspapers is organised on the basis of an inverted pyramid, with the most important information presented in the first few paragraphs. Reading the opening paragraph will give you the gist of what the article is about. This should help you decide whether the article merits further attention. Reading the first three paragraphs will give you the most critical information, with anything after that interesting detail, but unlikely to be essential to your purpose.

Newspapers are laid out in columns giving you an opportunity to practise all the techniques of reading: scanning, skimming, skipping and reading slowly. Newspaper columns are narrow and you can train yourself to get the meaning from them with about two fixations per line. At first your understanding may suffer, but if you continue to push yourself your comprehension will soon return to their previous levels.

Three main types

Articles in newspapers tend to be of three main types:

1. News articles. Journalists use the questioning formula to organise their articles, answering the questions who, what, when, where, and how first, while background information comes later. This means that in news articles the most important information is presented first, with the information becoming less critical as the article progresses. Reporters present 80 per cent of the key information in the opening paragraph, followed by the detail elaborating on the key points. The rest should only be read on a need to know basis. When reading news, skip what you already know, and concentrate on the new information, or what you want to find out. Read with a purpose, as a strong purpose will increase your reading speed, and improve your comprehension.

2. Opinion articles such as the editorial present a point of view. The introduction at the start, and the summary at the end, contains the most important information, with the middle containing supporting arguments. It is important to remember that editorials are opinions and not objective reports

3. Feature articles. These provide entertainment or background on a popular subject, in areas such as sports, health, lifestyle, education, books and authors. Typically the most important information is contained in the body of the text.

Non-fiction books

You will apply an active reading approach to non-fiction books. This combines reading with critical thinking, learning and decision making, while annotating and note-taking. Most non-fiction books, like technical writing, are well structured and thus lend themselves to the SQ4R method. Non-fiction writers usually put the key sentence of the paragraph first and then elaborate on the key point. State, then elaborate, is the general rule. Therefore, we can get the gist of what the author is making by just reading the first sentence of paragraphs.

Prioritize by interest or on a need to know basis. What sections are essential to your purpose? Determine purpose on a 'must know', 'should know', 'nice to know, and 'needn't know' basis. Vary your reading speed in line with your purpose. You may need to read all the 'must know' material, survey the 'should know' material, skim through quickly the 'nice to know' material, and skip the material not relevant to your purpose.

Novels

You will apply a passive reading approach to novels. These are read for pleasure where you get absorbed in the flow of the narrative and its content. Novels are great for practising your speed reading skills on and for expanding your vocabulary. With the knowledge you now possess about reading techniques, you have the choice of a variety of approaches when reading a novel. You can read slowly to savour the content, or scan, skim and skip material as you please. Preview the novel by reading the front and back covers and read the author's biography or foreword.

Now read the first page. If this grabs your attention continue reading the book. If it doesn't grab your attention consider whether the book is of interest to you or not. Skim through the rest of the book reading the first few sentences of each chapter and picking up the odd key word. If the book still doesn't catch your imagination you can always decide not to continue reading it. Alternatively, if you think it's going to be a good read, you can read it at your own pleasurable pace so that you can relish, savour and appreciate the writing.

Magazines

To see what interests you, overview the list of contents. Then browse through the magazine to find out what is in it and where it is located. Notice the layout of the articles and how the information is presented. Prioritize articles by interest or need. Determine your purpose on the same basis as previously discussed. Actively read in search of answers to your questions.

Read all the 'must know' articles and apply scanning, skimming and skipping techniques to the others. Magazine articles tend to be well structured and thus lend themselves to the SQ4R approach. You may decide to photocopy articles which you feel may be of help to you in your studies or professional career.

Typically magazine articles only concentrate on the most interesting and spectacular aspects of a topic. This helps to sell the magazine. They may often ignore less interesting information, essential to a full understanding of the subject, which nevertheless might be critical to your needs. You may need to search elsewhere for this information.

Letters, memos, e-mail

Letters that are not for your attention should be redirected to the proper source. Letters and memos usually start and close with formalities. The early and late middle paragraphs tend to carry the most important information and this is where the reader will want to focus their attention. Prioritize your reading by interest or need.

Pre-read quickly to discard, delegate or read for more detail and action. Some will go straight into the bin. Those requiring action, decide on the response or follow-up activity required. File those that don't require a reply. By looking at the sources of the e-mail and the topic you can judge whether it is junk mail or not. Delete the junk mail before reading it. Your objective should be to handle mail only once.

Reports

The style of reports varies with the subject matter and the target audience. Adopt the following approach to reading reports.

- First survey the report to see how it is structured and organised. There may be a lot of background material of no immediate concern to you.
- Second, look for the theme, scope, development of ideas and conclusions by reading the cover title and management summary at the start of the report.
- Third, read the table of contents and examine the appendices. Then read the findings, conclusions and recommendations. If you need more in-depth reading preview the report, marking those sections of particular significance and which you may need to study in detail. If you prepare a learning map summary of the report it may save you time later when you need to review the content quickly.

Summary of Chapter 3

SQ4R stands for Survey, Question, Read, Recall, Record and Review. The purpose of the survey stage is to get an overview of the topic, discover key points, and identify the relationship between the parts and the subtopics. The survey of the chapter is similar to the survey of the book but is done in more depth.

Questions prepare the mind for the reading stage, and improve learning and comprehension. When your mind is actively searching for answers to questions you are reading with a purpose. As you read evaluate ideas and identify and remember key points. Try to recall the answers to your questions, and write down your answers. The best way of recording your recall is by using learning maps. Adopt a systematic review plan as otherwise you will not remember what you have learnt.

The main reason for adopting speed reading strategies is information overload. Speed reading gives you choice as regards what you should read carefully, what you should skim and scan, and what you should skip and ignore. Most of us can significantly increase our reading speed without any loss of comprehension. The reason why some people read slowly

Inspiration

"Every man who knows how to read has it in his power to magnify himself, to multiply the ways in which he exists, to make his life full, significant and interesting."
Aldous Huxley

includes small recognition spans, regressing, poor vocabulary and subvocalisation.

VERTIGO is an acronym reminding you of the seven ways of improving your reading skills. It stands for vocabulary, eyesight, regression, talking, ideas, guide and operating speed. Reading strategies can be recalled by the acronym SCRIBE which stands for specific, critical, revision, informational, browsing and enjoyment. Approaches to reading newspapers, non-fiction books, novels, magazines, letters and reports were discussed.

Five Activities to Improve Your Reading Skills

1. Memorise the SQ4R approach and apply it to the next textbook or non-fiction book that you read. Adopt this approach to all serious reading matter that you need to learn, comprehend and recall.
2. Apply the speed reading techniques in the chapter to everyday reading tasks like newspapers and magazines.
3. Improve your vocabulary by looking up words in a dictionary that you don't understand. Commit the words to long-term memory so that they won't be an obstacle to your understanding when reading in the future. Remember if you commit one new word a day you will learn 365 words in a year.
4. Increase your recognition span by reading two to three words at a time. Over time gradually adopt the other ways to improve your reading speed.
5. When reading textbooks or non-fiction books use a visual guide to help your eyes move smoothly across the page. This will prevent you from regressing and speed up your reading.

Chapter 4
Learning Maps

Learning maps are tree-like, radiant, nonlinear ways of organising in-formation by showing the connection between a central idea, and sup-porting relevant related information. They provide a simplified over-view of complex information, allowing learners to better understand relationships, and find new connections. They can be produced indi-vidually or by groups. They can be made by hand or by a computer software program. Learning maps combine a textual and visual way of recording information to engage the dual processing capabilities of the brain.

There are now millions of people using learning maps throughout the world, for brainstorming, note taking, writing, project planning, prob-lem solving and decision making. For instance, the mind mapping tool FreeMind is downloaded over 150,000 times a month, and a software mind mapping package called MindManager is used by over 1.5 million people. Learning maps have stood the test of time, and have now been used in various formats for more than fifty years. They have evolved from, and borrowed ideas from, flow charts, organisation charts, dia-grams and visual metaphors.

Visual metaphors, when one element of experience is described in terms of another, can be used to convey complex concepts and to increase uniqueness and memorability. For example, an iceberg is often used to show the strong role of the unconscious mind governing our actions compared to the conscious mind. The conscious mind is seen as the tip of the iceberg, supported by a vast subconscious mind submerged below the water, which plays a major role in influencing our behaviour.

Learning maps have gone through various incarnations, such as seman-tic maps, knowledge maps, concept maps, spider diagrams, mind maps and idea maps. Some of these techniques such as concept maps start with the central idea at the top of the page and work down, whereas learning maps start in the centre and work out. One of the main dif-ferences between concept maps and learning maps is the liberal use of

WHAT YOU'LL LEARN
IN THIS CHAPTER:
- What are learning maps?
- How do I make learn-ing maps?
- How are learning maps used?
- Why use learning maps?

images and colour in learning maps. Concept maps are mainly used in science and education whereas learning maps are mainly used in business but are becoming increasingly popular in other areas as well.

I prefer the term learning maps which emphasises their unique quality to enhance learning effectiveness in a variety of contexts including business, study and education. One way to grasp the essence of a learning map is to compare it with a map of a city. The city centre represents the main idea, the main road leading from the city centre represent the main branches or key ideas, and the secondary roads represent the sub branches or supporting thoughts. Special images, icons, symbols or shapes can represent landmarks of interest, or particularly significant ideas.

Figure 10
An Example of a Learning Map

History

Mankind has used pictures, images and symbols to record information, and leave their mark on the world for thousands of years. Evidence for this has been found throughout the world in the form of prehistoric cave paintings, in places such as France, Australia and South America. Images have evolved into written languages such as Egyptian hieroglyphics and Chinese characters. The ancient Egyptians created an entire language in 3000 BC, using words and images. The oldest known geographic map was produced by a Chinese cartographer in about 1100 AD. The Chinese characters and language has evolved over time from hieroglyphics and pictograms. In more recent times the great brains of history such as Leonardi da Vinci, Michelangelo, Darwin and Einstein used pictures, images and symbols to clarify their thinking before they produced their great inventions, masterpieces and theories.

Inspiration

"Mind maps can be used for almost anything – from planning the day, to taking notes, to organising a presentation or simply exploring one's own thoughts."
Janet Mason

Maps of various types are used in many areas of industry with the capacity to bring complex topics to life making them understandable and accessible to a wider audience. Schematic wiring diagrams help engineers and electricians understand how electricity networks operate. System flow charts help systems analysts design computer based systems. Flow process charts are used by industrial engineers to improve movements and methods in the workplace. One of the most famous flowcharts was created in 1933 by Harry Beck. His flowchart of the London Underground is still in use today and has influenced the depiction of transport systems worldwide.

Critical path analysis is used to monitor and control large construction projects. Fishbone diagrams help managers identify and solve complex business problems. Cycles, such as the product life cycle and working capital cycle, show how ideas are related in a circular manner. Decision trees are widely used in financial and management accounting, and show the options available when making decisions. Organisation charts show the management hierarchy within a company.

Inspiration

"A properly prepared flowchart is like a road map. It can be used to plan important steps in your thinking. It can be used to help you remember how you arrived at a certain point in your thoughts. Sometimes a flowchart will help you find a better way to solve a problem."
Mc Quigg and Harness.

Today the majority of our communication is still done through the written word but images are beginning to play a more significant role. Modern advertising on billboards and television means that our senses are continually bombarded by colourful and stunning visual images. The advent of computers and smart phones has given a new impetus to the role of visuals in cartography (the art, technique, or practice of compiling or drawing maps or charts) and in communication generally.

GPS (global positioning systems) are now used routinely in cars to help us plan our journeys, and Google maps are now part of our lives. Unfortunately our ability to map knowledge is not as sophisticated. However, the integration of computer technology and telecommunications has improved our ability to map knowledge, and we can now routinely draw learning maps illustrated with clip art images. As our work has become more complex we need charts, diagrams, graphs and learning maps to record it and make it more comprehensible to ourselves and others.

How to Draw Learning Maps

It is comparatively easy to draw learning maps, but they do require practise over time to become proficient in their use. They go against our natural instincts to construct things from the bottom up or the top down. In the West our education has taught us to write in a linear way; starting in the top left hand corner of the page and working out and down. Instead learning maps start in the centre and work out in a radiant fashion. This goes against everything we were taught to do as school children and so takes some time to get used to.

An example of a learning map is shown figures 10 and 11. For a visual metaphor of a learning map imagine an octopus with lots of tentacles. Like a clock, learning maps are drawn and read from 1pm going clockwise giving them clarity and order. Learning maps mimic the network organisation of major systems in the world, such as electricity, telecommunications, water, roads, railways and airlines. Learning maps are as unique to a learner as finger prints and so are idiosyncratic to each individual. Different people will produce different learning maps for similar ideas.

Guidelines for drawing learning maps

The following is all you need to know to hand draw a good quality learning map:

- Blank sheets of paper. Take an A4/A3 sheet of good quality blank paper and place it in a landscape position so that you have plenty of room for your work. Blank paper provides a limitless and free thinking space.
- Key words. Put your key word in the centre and branch out in a radiant way. This is in contrast to linear notes that start at the top left-hand corner of the page and work down. It is also in contrast to concept maps which start at the top of the page and progress down. Use single words on branches, as these are more likely to creatively trigger off further relevant ideas connected to the main idea. Minimum use of text makes it easy for the reader to scan for a word or get the gist very quickly. In addition, this prevents 'map shock' or confusion caused by clutter or putting too much text on the map.
- Hierarchy of ideas. Use a hierarchical structure to show the importance of ideas. Ideas go from the general to the specific as you move from the centre out. Use bigger letters for words nearer the centre than for words further out. In addition, use the thickness of lines or colour to emphasise structure and importance; those near the centre will be thicker than those branching out. The lines should be curved and should be the same length as the word. Curved lines give rhythm to the map and make it more interesting to look at. In addition they will help you to keep all your words upright and easy to read.
- Images. Use images instead of text, or in addition to text, to make the information more memorable, and to appeal to both sides of the brain. The images must be a visual metaphor for the idea that it is meant to reinforce or convey, so that when you see the image the idea comes readily to mind.
- Supporting detail. Attach key words on branches to the centre. These in turn should be supported by supporting words on sub branches. All branches should lead back to the central keyword. Words chosen should be concrete nouns, strong verbs or adjectives because these are easier to remember. In normal writing key words make up only 5 to 10 per cent of the text but convey most of the meaning. For emphasis, print words, larger at the centre, and smaller as you radiate out.

The large letters and thicker lines emphasise the hierarchy and significance of ideas, by making them more distinctive and visible and thus more memorable.

- Make it unique. Use colour, images, symbols, icons, abbreviations, and acronyms so that your learning map looks as unique and artistic as possible. Colour further enhances learning maps making them more interesting, fun, unique and outstanding thus improving retention and recall. Colour should be used to differentiate or emphasise ideas, rather than used arbitrarily, which can create confusion rather than clarity.

- Abbreviations. Use personalised codes and well-known abbreviations as a type of shorthand, just as you do for texting on your mobile phone. For example, 'mgt' for management, 'ctee' for committee, 'u' for you, ? for question mark, and so on. This saves space and speeds up processing, encoding and registration of information. Personalised codes using colours, arrows and asterisks add a fourth dimension to learning maps. In addition, well-known mathematical symbols such as < (greater than), > (less than), = (equal to), + (plus), % (percentage) and so on can be used to save space on your map.

Inspiration

"Everything is connected to everything else."
Leonardo Da Vinci

Education Uses

Learning maps are now used in many areas of life, such as education, business, science and personal development. People who use them attest to their effectiveness as learning tools. They encourage active hands-on-learning by engaging the senses of the learner such as visual and touch. They are a means to an end rather than an end in themselves. They will help you to learn more efficiently and effectively, but they are no substitute for hard work. Learning requires long hours, concentration, positive thinking, motivation and persistence. Without these attributes you are unlikely to succeed in any endeavour.

Learning maps improve concentration because they promote the interaction and engagement between learner and text. They force the learner to decipher the precise relationship between concepts, link ideas to other ideas, and determine the hierarchy of the ideas. They encourage learners to make explicit tacit knowledge which often they don't realise that they possess. However, learning maps will only make the job a little bit easier, but will not do the learning for you. You must do this yourself. Let's now look at some of the applications in education and training and development for learning maps.

Applications in education, training and development
Learning maps have a long history in formal education, and training and development. They are a powerful tool for teaching and learning and can be used for, curriculum design, training needs analysis, and training evaluation. They can be used to involve relevant parties in curriculum development, such as fellow educators, trainers, learners, professional bodies

and employers. Learning maps show how all the theories and knowledge in a syllabus fit together. They can be used to organise learning material for individual courses or for entire curricula.

They can be used to identify the relevant knowledge a learner possesses before or after training. A comparison between the before and after should determine the amount of learning that took place as a result of the training. In a corporate setting learning maps can be used to capture expert knowledge, so that it can be preserved and shared with others. They have even been used to record and analyse the variety and complexity of tasks involved in a trainer's and teacher's job, so that a comprehensive job description can be compiled.

Inspiration

"The mind is like a parachute - it only works when it is open" *Old Saying*

Learning maps can be used for note taking as when taking notes at a lecture and note making as when summarising the main points of a chapter or book. Students can also use them for recording, organising and sharing complex research. They help students integrate and see the connection between their prior knowledge and new information. They also help students realise that they may not know how two ideas are related, and this leads them to develop new questions to investigate and explore. Macro maps can be used to summarise a complete book while micro maps can be used to summarise a chapter supporting the macro map. Creating one huge map with everything on it can quickly become unmanageable so that the need for supporting maps becomes apparent.

Learning maps have been found to be useful when planning essays, particularly in examination conditions where strict time constraints operate. When doing essays in exams students need to keep their answers relevant, clear, logical, organised and sharply focused on the question. It has been found that planning an essay, in the form of a learning map, can help students answer essay type questions more effectively. It also aids the recovery of information from a student's memory banks of prior knowledge in an exam context. This means that the time spent doing a learning map, before getting down to the essay, is worthwhile as it will be reflected in a better thought through essay.

Business Uses

Learning maps have a wide application in business. They are used by companies such as Boeing, Disney, Microsoft and NASA to help them plan their business activities. They have been used by banks to capture knowledge, and make it available to other employees. Charles Jennings, global head of learning of Thomas Reuters, uses them to keep track of the different aspects of their training throughout their organisation. These aspects include course content development, course workbooks, trainer training, training delivery, and assessment of outcomes. Jennings maintains that learning maps play a central role in every aspect of their learning and development work; from training needs analysis to brainstorming around course development and delivery, through data capture and performance charting. The maps can be exported to programs such as Microsoft, PowerPoint or Project, enabling the manager to monitor and control the individual projects of employees.

In human resource management interviewers use them when preparing for selection interviews, and to record the proceedings of the interview. At the end of the interviews they have a good overview record of the proceedings for selection comparison purposes, rather than relying on memory. On the other hand, candidates for the job can prepare for their interviews using a learning map to plan their research on the company, clarify their thoughts, anticipate likely interview questions, and plan their approach and answers to likely questions during the interview. Negotiators can use learning maps to give them the competitive edge when negotiating. They use them to plan their negotiations, identify players and goals, compare strategies, and clarify options while focusing on the big picture.

Learning maps can be used in strategic planning to think through such useful techniques as SMART goals (specific, measurable, attainable, relevant and timely), SWOT (strengths, weaknesses, opportunities and threats) and PEST (political, economic, social and technological) analysis. For example, a SWOT learning map can be drawn up to identify competitive threats, and exploit the company's strengths and most promising opportunities to deal with them. In marketing they can be used to flush out the 7P model (product, price, promotion, place, people, process and physical evidence).

Marketers' have used them to create marketing plans, brainstorm product improvement, and new product developments. Sales people have used them to create their sales plans and make their annual sales presentations. They have even been used to demonstrate how marketing can be used to promote the arts. Tax consultants have used them for client financial planning. Learning maps can be used to clarify complex ideas in business management, management accounting, law and marketing.

Taking notes and making presentations
Learning maps can be used to plan meetings and draw up an agenda. During the meeting they can be used to record the main conclusions and decisions made, and draw up the minutes after the meeting. People responsible for agreed outcomes and actions are recorded, so that there is no doubt as to who is going to do what and when. At the next meeting the completed actions and outcomes can be accounted for. This means that things decided at the meeting are followed up and done.

They have been used by law lecturers to make business law more accessible and understandable to students, by making the relationships between key concepts transparent and visual. Just like for lectures and training sessions, learning maps are great ways to plan, prepare and deliver presentations. They help many overcome the fear of public speaking and writers' block when preparing their speech. Learning maps will keep you on track and in time. They can be used to plan and structure communications, such as email, letters, memos and reports.

These maps have been used by librarians for teaching and other presentations, researching and writing, brainstorming, and project planning and management. They are particularly useful when brainstorming in groups. Ideas can be captured as they come up, without worrying about where they fit in the scheme of things. Once all the ideas are captured, they can be grouped, analysed, debated and prioritised.

My Own Experience Using Learning Maps

Inspiration

"Few processes are more complex than negotiations, but there is no better way to model a negotiation than with mapping. All this complexity becomes accessible."
Clive Lewis

In my career as a training manager, financial controller, training consultant, lecturer and writer I have used learning maps extensively. I also used them at a personal level when studying for professional qualifications and university degrees.

Lecturing

As a part-time lecturer of over thirty years I used learning maps to prepare and present my lectures in such areas as business management, marketing, costing, management accounting, strategic planning, finance, and human resource management. On the other hand, I encouraged students to use them for note taking and most of them found them useful: there is some resistance to change at the start as it is often a question of getting used to the unfamiliar. However, experience has shown me with some training, students adapt to them readily.

Sometimes I would build up a learning map on the flipchart or whiteboard, and students found this better than the usual talk and chalk approach, as it encourages active learning in the form of exploration, discussion and participation. When discussion leading I used them to record points of view and debate their validity. I also gave out skeleton learning maps for students to complete and customise as the lecture went on. This gave them 'hooks' to hang their new learning on. They found this very useful as it gave them the opportunity to customise the learning map to their own needs. This was in response to student requests, as I always emphasised that from a learning point of view it was better if they prepared their own learning maps. Nevertheless, they found the skeleton frameworks useful as a starting point. In fact, the more personalised the learning map the more effective they are for learning. Most of the learning is in the making and preparation of the map.

Training

During my career as a training manager in the Electricity Supply Board (ESB) I ran learning maps workshops for all grades of staff, including clerical, administrative, accounting, information technology, marketing, human relations, legal, supervisory, technical and engineering. The feedback from these workshops was very positive, and the variety of applications of the technique was diverse. I also ran study skills workshops, including a session on learning maps, aimed at staff doing university degree and professional qualifications part-time. Most participants of these workshops went on to use learning maps extensively in their formal studies, work lives and even in their personal lives.

Similarly, I used learning maps to research, prepare and present my lectures. I also encouraged course participants to use them. I found them to be an excellent tool in collaborative learning particularly when analysing business case studies, and in facilitating brainstorming and creativity. They are a great technique for capturing group composite thinking, while at the same time developing individual and team skills and group morale and confidence. Group members learn to present debate and defend their ideas, listen to other peoples' point of view, and learn from the diversity of thinking, experience and knowledge within the group.

I took early retirement from the ESB in 1994 and set myself up as a freelance training consultant, part-time college lecturer and writer. In this role I have used learning maps to design, prepare, and deliver training and educational programmes in a diverse range of private and public sector organisations. I have used them to design course syllabi and course schedules. When making presentations, learning maps help me to maintain eye contact with the audience – a most important aspect of making effective presentations. They also allow me the flexibility to stay within time, as I can easily customise the presentation to fit within time constraints while still covering the main ideas. Using learning maps as a presentation tool will help your presentation to be free-flowing and natural, rather than histrionic and formal.

Writing
From experience I have found learning maps to be a great antidote to writer's block. Their open ended structure helps me to be creative in brainstorming ideas, and exploring issues when writing. When you use them to record your existing level of knowledge they mirror what you know at a particular point in time. They help me to identify gaps in my knowledge and alert me to areas that I need to do further research. The research and writing process may take place over many months and even years, during which time I can be distracted by other work. However, once I have made the learning maps it is a permanent record to return to again and again and the writing flows seamlessly from them. Learning maps help me to stay focused and I can return to them and resume my concentration even after interruptions of many weeks or months.

Visual outlining tools such as, learning maps, diagrams and flow charts are very useful to writers in helping them organise their ideas while providing a stimulating framework for their writing. Learning maps help me organise my notes in a systematic way when researching a particular project. As the author of over 20 books on personal development, management, learning and study skills, I have used learning maps to research and integrate my material from various sources. Learning maps help me to organise my knowledge, ideas and thoughts in a structured and logical way. They have helped me produce well written and structured books, in less time and with fewer drafts, significantly increasing my productivity. So far any book that I have written has been published. They have also helped me get articles published in various professional journals over many years.

Personal Development Uses

At a personal level learning maps can be used when problem solving or decision making. For problem solving they can be used to clarify interpersonal relationship issues, generate alternatives, and suggest appropriate solutions. The biggest long term financial decision you will make in your life is when you decide to buy a house. It becomes even more complicated when you have an existing house to dispose of. Buying a house, while selling an existing one, can be a traumatic time and needs careful consideration and planning because of the variety of professionals you need to deal with, such as mortgage providers, auctioneers, surveyors and solicitors. For everyday short term financial planning and budgeting, learning maps can be used to set out your daily, weekly, monthly and yearly sources of income and expenditure so that you know exactly where your hard earned money is coming from and how you are spending it.

Learning maps can be used as a tool for lifelong learning when keeping up-to-date in your particular field. In the modern world where knowledge is exploding at a phenomenal rate and innovation and creativity is highly valued, it is very important to keep up to speed in your particular area of expertise. Learning maps can also be used to clarify your life vision, plans and goals so that you know where you are going and have a road and purpose to follow in life. At a more mundane level, people have used learning maps to plan their holidays, outings and birthday parties.

I have also found them very useful when studying for professional and university degrees such as the Chartered Institute of Management Accountants (CIMA) and the M.Ed (training and development) with distinction from the University of Sheffield. I used learning maps to summarise the content of management accounting and management texts. I was a prize winner in the CIMA exams and I attribute my success to the use of learning maps. I used learning maps when planning my assignments and thesis for the M.Ed degree which I passed with distinction. Just like many others, I found them a useful way of condensing, integrating, digesting and overviewing information from many sources, including research, experience, observation and reflection.

Learning maps helped me structure assignments and my thesis in a systematic, holistic and logical fashion and condense large amounts of information on a single page. They helped me reflect on my level of knowledge and understanding, thereby providing me with feedback, so that I could monitor and identify my learning needs and address my weaknesses. However, as I said before, learning maps are only a tool which will help you on your way. They are no substitute for concentrated study and hard work, but they will increase your efficiency and productivity.

Science Uses

Learning maps have proved their usefulness in areas such as economics, law, accountancy, social science, engineering, health, medical science and even polar exploration. Learning maps helped accounting students integrate and clarify complex materials better than just relying solely on the textbook. I taught accounting, costing, and management accounting to CIMA students over many years at night classes and during exam revision courses and they found them very useful as a learning aid.

Learning maps support learners to think in conceptual and theoretical terms. Learning maps are used routinely by students in medicine, nursing, science and mathematics. Medical students learning physiology gained deeper meaningful knowledge, and exhibited more critical thinking when they used learning maps. Critical thinking has been defined as the ability to link data, knowledge, and insights together from various disciplines to provide information for decision-making.

Social science students learned more effectively when using learning maps. The reason for this seems to lie in the manner in which learning maps integrate students' prior knowledge with new information. In one case race relations were explored through the use of learning maps. It was found that the maps enhanced students' critical thinking skills by visually connecting social, historical, and economic factors to ideas about race relations.

It is believed by some researchers that learning maps may be better suited to qualitative research because they provide more flexibility than concept mapping. Some reflected that learning maps were a useful way to record experience, were easy to make, and helped them see things in a new light. Some suggested that this was because learning maps helped them remember events from years ago, and helped them organise their thoughts about their experience systematically. Others suggested as a visual aid learning maps helped them put the experience in context and provided a clear view of what happened. Many were not novices in the use of learning maps, as over the years they used them to focus on key experiences, concepts and connections.

Jim McNeil, polar explorer has been using a software package called

Inspiration

"The real strength of the Mind Map approach comes when you combine your notes from various sources into one map giving you an overview of your accumulated knowledge in any topic."
Dan Butler

MindManager since 2004 to help him draw up logistic plans for his expeditions. He uses this to plan the routes the team will take, the fuel they will use, and to anticipate safety issues. He used a notepad and pen before, but as his missions became more complex and the conditions more severe, the need to quickly model and modify simulations with the rest of the team became more urgent. He has used the tool to visualise, brainstorm and plan for different scenarios that may arise on their expeditions through the Arctic.

Why Use Learning Maps?

The short answer to this is because they are of practical use, and have proved themselves to help people learn more effectively and productively for more than fifty years. A multitude of peer-reviewed articles have been published in reputable academic journals on their application and use in the social sciences, engineering, business and science. They are indirectly supported by research on the brain, memory and learning theory, in addition to personal testimony and anecdotes. Briefly, they promote active, meaningful, and reflective learning. Despite being initially labelled by some as quack psychology, they have now quite a substantial following, and body of research, supporting their use. Let's now look at some of the scientific evidence supporting the use of learning maps.

Brain research

Our brains do not work in a linear fashion. We have numerous thoughts, images and impressions that occur simultaneously. Conventional outline notes can't keep pace with the complexity of our thoughts but learning maps can. The centre of the learning map and its radiant organisation reflects how the brain is structured, wired and interconnected. Use images and colour in learning maps because the old Confucian saying 'a picture speaks more than a thousand words' applies to both memory and creativity. Colour is known to stimulate the brain, and our ability to remember images is better than our memory for words. In psychology this phenomena is known as the picture superiority effect.

The linked nature of learning maps reflects the associative and connective nature of the brain with its network of neurons, dendrites and synapses. Some psychologists maintain the human memory is a vast, intricately interconnected network. According to such models it is not letters, syllables, or words that are recorded in the brain, but a mental model of the world or concepts. The concepts are thus related in various ways to other concepts, forming an associative network.

The act of encoding or recording something on the brain is simply forming new links and associations in the network. Learning maps mimic the organisation of the brain by showing the links and relationships between key concepts giving users an overview and a greater insight and understanding of the topic. Learning maps are designed to replace conventional note taking by reflecting the way the brain actually connects information.

Two sides of the brain

Due to the work of Nobel prize-winning researcher, Professor Roger Sperry, we now know that the human brain consists of two hemispheres, connected by a large structure of 300 million neurons called the corpus callosum. Briefly the left hemisphere of the brain deals with words while the right hemisphere handles images. Although the brain is bi-functional, the most creative and productive intellectual functioning occurs when the two hemispheres are talking to each other. Thus integration and creativity can be encouraged through the use of learning maps. It is noticeable in the great scientific advances throughout history, that people like Da Vinci and Einstein, combined imagination and intuition with careful reasoned analysis to boost their creativity.

The left hemisphere controls the right side of the body, and a stroke to this side of the brain may impair speech ability. On the other hand, the right hemisphere controls the left side of the body and a stroke to this side of the brain may impair spatial awareness. Hence the conclusion that the left hemisphere is more verbal and logical, while the right hemisphere is more spatial and creative. However, it has been discovered that hemispheric specialisation is not as clear cut as it is sometimes made out to be. It has been found that reports of deficits of imagery, for example, were just as likely to follow left hemisphere damage as right hemisphere damage.

Furthermore, more recent research on left brain/right hemispheres shows more integration and plasticity than was previously thought. Some psychologists compare our memory to a tree. The more branches on the tree, the greater the possibility for new branches to grow. The open ended nature of learning maps, mimics the plasticity and synaptic networks of the brain, and encourages links and associations and the identification of relationships.

Memory

Miller's magical number 7 plus or minus 2 rule in memory suggests that main branches on the learning map should not number more than 9. Some experts even suggest that our memory store is limited to only four pieces of information at a time. Learning maps chunk information on branches into meaningful groups by a process of segmentation. In most practical situations there are seldom more than seven or eight main branches, so that the material on a learning map can be organised into a number of easily remembered chunks to facilitate recall.

Each main branch can in turn be divided into seven or eight sub branches, to keep them within the short-term memory capacity of nine items. Learning maps thus capitalise on Miller's memory law, by careful organisation and grouping of words within segments to maximise learning and recall. In addition images, diagrams and colour, are more easily stored in mem-

Inspiration

"Our education system, as well as science in general, tends to neglect the non-verbal form of intellect. What it comes down to is that modern society discriminates against the right hemisphere."
Prof Roger Sperry

ory than text.

People remember things better if they are unique and outstanding. In psychology this is known as the Von Restorff effect. Hence learning maps are constructed to print key words in colour and to make them two dimensional for greater emphasis. The connecting lines are also made thicker near the centre and less so as they radiate out; so that lines and words have a hierarchy of thickness signifying the importance of ideas. In education, learning maps have been found to be better in promoting knowledge retention, than attending class lectures, reading, or participating in class discussion.

Studies in psychology show that it is far easier for people to remember information if it is personalised. Personalised codes on learning maps using colours, arrows, symbols and abbreviations add a fourth dimension to learning maps. They enhance the learner's ability to analyse, define, structure, organise and reason. Most words are still recognisable if vowels are dropped providing a unique form of shorthand giving more space on learning maps as needed.

Your short term memory is remarkably fickle. Recently presented material, if unrecorded and unrehearsed is usually soon forgotten. Ideas externalised in a learning map can be studied, explored, extended, enhanced and experimented with. The structure of learning maps, with review, facilitates storage in long term memory. In educational psychology the three 'R's' of memory are registration, retention and recall. Every form of learning involves information encoding, storage and retrieval.

Acronyms and mnemonics

A learning map processes information by making it meaningful through its spatial radiant organisation, and its links and associations. It is in fact a major mnemonic device. It is also an external record that can be studied and reviewed as needed. After a number of reviews the information on your learning map will be registered in your long-term memory. Psychologists have long established that up to 80% of textual material is forgotten within 24 hours, unless reviewed. The learning map is an ideal instrument of speedy review. Learning map summaries of complete texts can be reviewed within 5 minutes. A systematic review plan spaced over a period of time will ensure registration in long-term memory.

We make information more memorable in learning maps by inventing acronyms for key points. Mnemonics such as acronyms have a long track record as memory aids. They go back thousands of years to Greek and Roman times when philosophers and scholars recognised their usefulness for remembering key points when making presentations. The method of loci is one of the oldest mnemonic devices that memory experts use. Learning maps are a method of loci, with their unique shapes, using the branches as main locations, and the sub branches as more specific locations. The locations can be used to associate a series of ideas to be learnt and to put them into context.

Today school children use mnemonics without prompting, and they are the secret weapon behind stage mnemonists who amaze their audience with their memory feats. These memory experts recall vast quantities of information by forming idiosyncratic verbal and visual associations for the information they want to remember. They realise that words converted into images are more easily memorised than those that are not. Similarly, it has been found that students who express their learning visually had a 40 per cent higher retention rate than verbal learners. In fact, learning maps are a major visual mnemonic device.

Learning theory
Many of the theories of learning may support learning maps. Gestalt and Freudian theories are classic examples of holistic approaches in psychology. Gestalt psychology puts forth the view that context, organisation, and meaning, are important factors for perception, learning and memory. Freudian theories emphasise the importance of the subconscious in learning because of its vastness, and impact on our behaviour. The basic concept of a holist position is that a complex phenomenon cannot be understood by an analysis of the constituent parts alone. To understand we must perceive the 'big picture' rather than dwell on individual elements of an idea, concept or picture. Learning maps are based on the principle of holism, giving the total picture made up of many parts.

Many new educational programmes around the world now focus on how to improve the mind's operation through 'learning how to learn skills'. In a rapidly changing world, with new techniques coming on stream frequently, it will be more important for people to know how to learn. Most people now change careers and jobs several times in a lifetime, and often have to acquire new experience and learn new knowledge and skills to equip them for their new roles.

It is thus essential to learn new skills efficiently and effectively. Learning maps are one of the visual learning techniques that will enable people to achieve this goal. Peter Drucker, the late great management guru, realised this when he said that the business executive of the future must be someone who is able to 'learn how to learn'. In medicine, science and technology, particularly information technology, a graduates' knowledge is out of date within a few years. So if you want to keep up to date you must engage in purposeful lifelong learning.

Deep versus surface learning
It is now known that the probability of learning something effectively is a function of the depth of processing. Words processed only in terms of their superficial visual appearance are poorly retained. Words categorised in terms of their sound and visual associations being somewhat better

recalled. The best learning tends to be associated with richer word encoding. This means identifying key words in terms of the whole picture while making connections between theories, concepts and prior knowledge. Learners should concentrate on key issues, concepts and principles rather than getting bogged down in detail. Learning maps encourage rich word encoding and deep rather than surface learning.

Many scientists have come to the conclusion that the key to more effective learning may lie in the limbic system within the brain. The limbic system controls the emotions, and engaging the emotions is the most effective way to create attention, interest and motivation which are key ingredients to successful learning. The novelty, fun, aesthetic and entertaining quality of learning maps may activate the limbic system by appealing to the emotions and thus help learning.

High level learning involves comprehension, making relationships, synthesis, evaluation, application and analysis. Learning maps bring together information from various sources on a single page enabling the mapper to critically analyse and make sense of the information recorded. This process encourages deep rather than surface learning.

Learning simply by listening passively to presentations or lectures is more likely to result in rote learning whereas students who produce their own learning maps are more likely to engage in deep learning. This is so because learning maps help students to actively learn by linking new information to what they know already, rather than relying on memorisation and cramming. In addition, people who become proficient at using learning maps for note taking, claim they are a great way to take more organised notes in real time, because they're inherently structured and endlessly flexible to handle additions. Encouraging students to compare and contrast learning maps with fellow students is an additional activity that can promote and encourage meaningful learning.

Learning styles
The Dual-Coding Theory in learning claims that learners encode information in two distinct information processing systems, one representing verbal information, and the other representing visual information. Learning maps present a visual image as well as verbal information and therefore presumably taps into this dual-coding system.

The basic learning styles are visual, verbal and touch. Learning maps engage all three styles. Visual in the form of the text and images recorded. Verbal when the information on the learning map is rehearsed, revised and reviewed. Touch when the learning map is created with all its branches, sub branches and interconnections.

In a lecturing context auditory learners are well catered for by the traditional verbal presentation. However, visual learners need additional support, and tactile learners need to do things to learn, so that if they construct learning maps it will meet these needs. In addition, in line with the theory of multiple intelligences learning maps will help to engage your verbal, visual, spatial and creative intelligences.

Kolb's learning style inventory has four dimensions: active experimentation (doing), abstract conceptualisation (thinking), reflective observation (watching), and concrete experience (feeling). It has been found that students with a 'doing' learning style learn more effectively from constructing and using learning maps.

People learn better in groups by sharing ideas and learning from each other. Collaborative learning maps facilitate this process, and also encourage idea generation and creativity.

Software Packages for Learning Maps

Over the past 20 years software packages have been developed and refined to facilitate the drawing of learning maps individually or in groups. They have been used in various areas such as business, education, science, information technology and engineering. Such programs overcome the limitations of hand drawn maps, which are time consuming to create, inflexible, cumbersome, and difficult to revise. In addition, they can often look aesthetically unattractive, messy, and difficult for others to follow.

These software packages will quickly produce learning maps of a consistently high quality appearance and standard. Some of the reasons why some people shied away from learning maps are because they claimed they were too difficult to create, and that they lacked the artistic abilities to draw the images and icons to support the ideas. With software packages these problems are overcome.

One of the great advantages of software packages is their flexibility. Learning maps can now be easily created on screen. Branches, sub branches and words can be manipulated and moved around at the click of a mouse in seconds. It is easy to modify and customise the map as your knowledge expands, and your thinking evolves. Font sizes can be created bigger nearer the centre, and smaller as you move outwards to differentiate the importance of ideas. Branches can be created in different colours to create emphasis and interest. Items such as icons and branches can be dragged and dropped around the screen as you desire.

The modern networked computer environment facilitates individual or collaborative learning through the sharing of learning maps. People can collaborate remotely with others in creating group learning maps. During their construction people engage in critical debate about the topic they are learning. Learning maps provide support for that thinking as well as for subsequent reflection, review and knowledge revision. Some software

93

packages have built-in internet conferencing features, allowing users to view one or more learning maps at the same time, and the leader of the conference can give the other users permission to make changes. Some of these software packages are so flexible that you can make learning maps almost as fast as you think.

Libraries of icons and clip art images

The packages come with libraries of icons and clip art images, which mean that you no longer need to be artistic to create visually stunning maps. In addition, photos, images, icons, cartoons, graphs, videos and text can be imported from the internet. Hyperlinks with your learning map can connect to other files, web sites or supporting topics. Learning maps have been used to plan and design web pages on the internet.

Learning maps can be saved and imported into Power Point presentations, or published as web pages. You can send your learning map to others as an attachment to email, and revise them later in line with their comments. Hundreds of books, blogs and websites have been created about learning maps, in their various incarnations, so that there is plenty of information about them on the internet.

Figure 11

A Learning Map about Learning Maps!

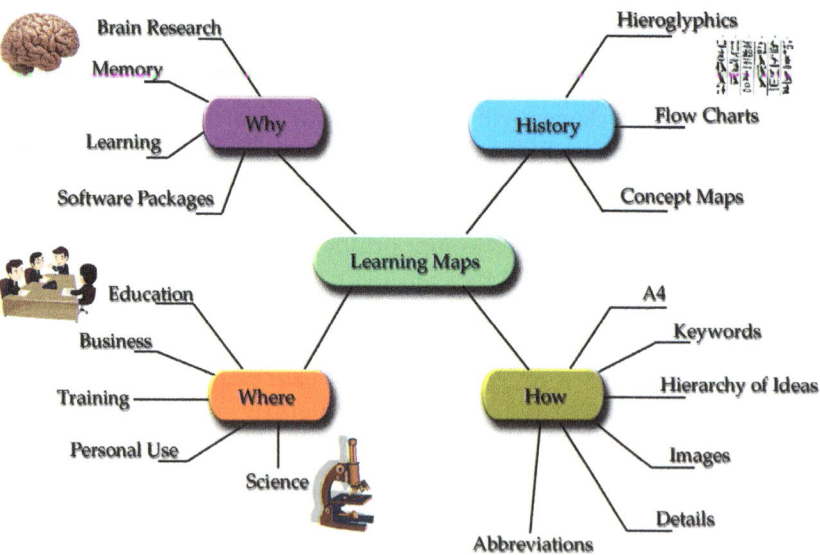

Summary of Chapter 4

Learning maps are tree-like, radiant, nonlinear ways of organising information by showing the connection between the central topic, and supporting information. Visual methods of displaying information have existed for thousands of years. Some languages have even evolved from hieroglyphics and pictograms.

You will find it easy to draw learning maps if you follow the rules set out in the chapter. Learning maps are now used in many areas of life such as education, business, medicine, science and life planning. Evidence supporting the use of learning maps can be drawn from research on the brain, learning and memory. They are also supported by personal testimony and anecdotes and articles supporting their use have been peer reviewed in reputable academic journals.

Over the past 50 years they have been adopted by millions of people throughout the world and many leading corporations use them. Over the past 20 years sophisticated software packages have been developed to facilitate the drawing of learning maps individually and in groups.

Inspiration

"MindManager is a visual thinking tool designed to enhance a user's productivity by transforming the linear text of traditional brainstorming and planning sessions into colours, graphics, and icons that enhance creativity and innovation, establish key relationships between ideas, and ultimately speed up project implementation."
Massue Mirelle

Five Activities to Improve Learning Mapping Skills

1. Follow the rules set out in the chapter under how to draw learning maps so that your learning maps are of a high quality and understandable to yourself and others.
2. Support the text by visual metaphors such as clipart to make your learning maps more memorable. Pictures and images can be used to trigger off words and ideas.
3. Practise using learning maps in all areas of your life including business, career, study and personal planning.
4. Use a software package so that your learning maps are cleaner, neater and more aesthetically appealing.
5. Do a micro learning map for each chapter of the next non-fiction book that you read and a macro learning map for the complete book. These will help you to review the book quickly if necessary. Use your spare time to practise doing learning maps and slowly introduce them into your daily and lifelong learning activities.

Chapter 5
Learning from Mistakes

Humans are fallible and are therefore prone to making mistakes. Pride is one of the reasons that people don't admit to their mistakes. We often lack the knowledge, training, skills and experience to do tasks satisfactorily and thus make mistakes. In the business world people are rewarded for success and penalised for failure. Mistakes are often due to system failures, inefficiencies and inadequacies. In addition, businesses may be operating to out-of-date and incorrect models and theories.

Mistakes happen in all areas of life including personal and business. The medical profession can learn a lot from the aviation industry, in their quest of thoroughly investigating and learning from their mistakes, and doing everything humanly possible to stop them from happening again. In fact the medical profession are prone to close ranks and cover up their mistakes.

A simple way of preventing mistakes is through improved communication. On a personal level living within our means will help us avoid the pain and shame of bankruptcy. In a corporate context, systems and controls can be designed to highlight and prevent mistakes from taking place. Low staff and management turnover can help reduce the incidence of business errors. Simulators can be used in training to help build proficiency in vital skills and confidence so that mistakes are less likely to happen. Knowledge management systems will help a company learn from its past mistakes.

If we fail to learn from our mistakes we will go on making them, resulting in lost opportunities, lost business, lost customers, lost time and lost productivity. Most successful people will tell you that they learned more from their mistakes than from their successes. Making mistakes may expose us to legal claims from those seeking compensation for harm caused.

Because of the scandals in all areas of private and public life people no longer have any hesitation in questioning authority figures to make

- Why do people make mistakes?
- Where do mistakes happen?
- How can we prevent mistakes?
- What are the consequences of mistakes?
- What lessons can we learn from mistakes?

them accountable for their mistakes. With a loss of trust came a loss of deference. People now place a high value on traits such as honesty, integrity, and fairness, in their personal and business dealings with others.

Why do People Make Mistakes?

We make mistakes because of human fallibility. We tend to be irrational and have low values and standards. Sometimes we lack the required knowledge and skills to do a task satisfactorily. Often we fail to follow the rules. Success is incentivised and failure is penalised. Organisations may experience system failures, or adhere to inappropriate models. People are more likely to make mistakes when stressed or tired.

Human Fallibility

The source of some mistakes is human behaviour. We are prone to error with a fallible human memory; we tend to be forgetful, and are easily distracted with limited powers of concentration. Our decisions are often based on incomplete information and can be flawed. We do not have the precision of machines, but instead we all have unique competencies, different strengths and weaknesses, different attitudes, behaviours and ways of doing things. In most areas this is not critical, but in areas like medicine and aviation it can be a question of life or death.

We are poor communicators, tend to be self-obsessed and therefore are not great at listening to what others have to say. We can easily misinterpret information and events, and we perceive things uniquely and often inaccurately. We can be anxious, worried, frustrated, stressed and preoccupied with our own thoughts and problems. All of these individually and collectively can result in us making mistakes.

Many mistakes are due to hubris, arrogance and pride, and consequently we are unable or unwilling to admit our mistakes. Other common human failings include anger, greed, deceit, and wishful thinking. In Greek mythology hubris was considered a major personality defect and the gods punished it mercilessly. Achilles died during the Trojan War because he didn't realise he had a weak spot which was his heel. Throughout history generals have lost battles and died because they didn't recognise their limitations, or acknowledge the strengths of their enemies. In business the downfall of many companies, like Enron and Arthur Anderson, had their genesis in arrogance, where any officer or partner was able to do what they liked, with few checks and balances, and little regard to the overall corporate welfare.

We Tend to be Irrational

There is a difference between intelligence and rationality and they do not always go together. Very intelligent people do stupid things. We overestimate our abilities and underestimate what can go wrong. We tend to think we are cleverer, better and more competent than we actually are, and we sometimes take on more than we can handle. We often jump to conclusions without considering alternatives. We look for evidence that supports what we believe. Our decisions are influenced by self-interest and emotional attachment, and we tend to be overoptimistic about outcomes. We are influenced more by a good story than by facts. We're convinced that we are not affected by biases like other people are, and don't realise that we are just as prone to stereotype.

People invest in Ponzi schemes on the prospect of getting huge returns quickly, which sound too good to be true and they are. Ponzi schemes are fraudulent investments with unreasonably high returns are actually paid out of the investors own capital. This human tendency to accept people at face value and do stupid things has now become known as dysrationalia, or the inability of people with adequate intelligence to always think and act rationally and independently, even in the face of insurmountable evidence.

Low Standards

Low morals and ethical standards can cost people huge reputational damage and monetary loss and cause them to do stupid things. We are all aware of President Bill Clinton's sexual escapades with Monica Lewinsky and his subsequent embarrassing lies and deceit when attempting to cover up his misrepresentation. In 2009 we heard about Tiger Woods multiple illicit sexual affairs. Within a year his wife divorced him and Tiger paid her $750 million in settlement.

We tend to be greedy and never know when we have had enough. Any business that doesn't recognise its weak spot, or Achilles heel, is prone to die because of it. In the recent past many entrepreneurs have become insolvent because they became greedy and invested in areas outside their expertise and destroyed their core businesses. An example is Sean Quinn, the Irish former multi-millionaire, who made his fortune in building materials, but lost it all when he diversified into insurance and banking. In 2012 he was declared bankrupt.

Low standards in high places such as poor corporate governance and ethics, and a failure of governments and central banks to regulate made a bad situation worse. Banks lost the run of themselves, and became like casinos gambling clients' deposits, on financial instruments like derivatives, hedges, forward contracts and contracts for difference, which nobody but an inner clique understood. They thought they could make money out of fresh air, but unfortunately it imploded like a house of cards, bringing the whole financial system down and governments as well, who were faced with the task of bailing them out with taxpayers' money.

In 2012 JP Morgan's chief investment officer resigned over a €2 billion loss on a portfolio of credit derivatives. The portfolio included layers of instruments used in hedging that became too complicated and too big to unravel. At the end of the day all this kind of stuff is just recklessly betting with other peoples' money.

Low Competency
On a personal level we often lack the knowledge, skills and experience to complete tasks satisfactorily. Once a skill is developed it must be maintained through practise, repetition and experience, as over time our proficiency in the skill will be degraded and eventually lost. This is why we all need up-to-date experience, training and continuous learning, to make us less prone to mistakes, attention slips and memory lapses.

Rules and Procedures
Many mistakes are caused when people do not follow designated rules and procedures. Ignorance of the law or indeed policies, rules and regulations may cause us to make mistakes. However, ignorance is not a defence in law and even in business ignorance of policies, rules and regulations is not accepted. Car accidents are often caused when people don't obey the rules, exceed the speed limit, or engage in prohibited acts, like using a mobile phone while driving, driving while intoxicated, or tailgating or speeding in built-up areas. Similarly, in the workplace accidents may happen when people do not abide by the health and safety laws and rules, or the procedures laid down by the company.

In the financial world laws were broken with impunity and contributed to the economic recession. Even in aviation pilots have been known to violate the rules even though this is very rare. Violations would include operating aircraft with known deficiencies, performing hazardous manoeuvers such as low-altitude flight, flying with insufficient fuel for contingencies, and flying knowingly into adverse weather conditions. Cases where pilots have turned up for duty intoxicated have been reported in the media from time to time.

In aviation there are very specific procedures to be followed at virtually all stages of the flight. Unfortunately, on occasion these procedures are misapplied, or inappropriately applied, for the circumstances encountered, often culminating in an accident. Pilots may be subject to perceptual errors, especially at night, or in challenging weather conditions. In such conditions they are confronted with acting on inadequate information, and run the risk of misjudging distances, altitude, and descent rates, as well as responding incorrectly to a variety of visual illusions.

Failure is Penalised
In business we are rewarded for success and penalised for failure. On the other hand, we learn more from our mistakes than from our successes, because we have a greater personal incentive to put things right after failure. Organisations and bureaucracies, in particular, tend to have a blame culture rather than accept that mistakes are a natural part of life, and should be seen as learning opportunities rather than sources of shame and blame.

We are thus reluctant to admit our mistakes as there is no incentive or culture to do so.

In a business context managers are often reluctant to abandon projects, even when it is obvious that they are no longer financially viable. This is particularly so if they have a significant psychological investment in the project, in the form of time, commitment, money and resources. Thus people stick with a project when the sensibile thing to do would be to conclude it and cut their losses. This is known as the sunk cost fallacy, where decisions are made on the size of the previous investment, rather than on the size of the expected return. We throw good money after bad even though we intuitively know that the project is uneconomic and should be discontinued.

Similarly, Research and Development (R&D) projects are often kept going much longer than is justified economically. As humans we have a tendency to be overoptimistic and hope for the best and avoid failure at all costs. Failure is part and parcel of the R&D process. As Albert Einstein said, it would not be called research if we knew what we were doing. It's when you don't know when to stop is the problem.

Managers may make strategic errors when drawing up their corporate plans and may make tactical errors when implementing budgets and operational plans.

System Failures

Mistakes are often due to system failures and inadequacies. Poorly designed or maintained systems, equipment, products and structures may facilitate mistakes. This is often compounded by deficient planning, coordination, monitoring and control. Poor quality controls and poor internal controls will see minor mistakes become major problems, because they are not picked up and put right on time. An effective internal control system is one of the best defences against business failure. Our systems need to have appropriate limits, checks, monitors and reviews built in so that errors are discovered quickly and rectified.

In 2012 RTE (the Irish National Television Network), was fined €200,000 following an investigation which showed that the 'Mission to Prey' programme, falsely and maliciously claimed a Fr. Reynolds had sexually abused a young girl and fathered her child, while a missionary in Kenya. The report was critical of supervisory and journalistic standards, and found that there was a significant failure of editorial and managerial control within RTE; that note-taking was inadequate and that in some cases gossip was treated as fact. There was a lack of scrutiny and challenge within the department to such an extent that they drifted into a groupthink mentality. In summary, they failed to establish the facts.

Inspiration

"The most fruitful lesson is the conquest of one's own error. Whoever refuses to admit error may be a great scholar but he is not a great learner. Whoever is ashamed of error will struggle against recognising and admitting it, which means that he struggles against his greatest inward gain."
Goethe, Maxims and Reflections

101

Inappropriate Models

Businesses may be operating to incorrect models and theories. Yesterday's paradigm may not be applicable today. The efficient market hypothesis, widely adhered to in the recent economic and financial collapse, is thought to be one of the reasons for the recession. It believed that there should be no constraints put on the free market system. In other words, demand and supply should be allowed to operate without artificial regulatory interventions or controlling mechanisms.

Moreover, overreliance on econometric models in banking, and automatic systems to approve mortgages increased the bank's exposure to risk. If they had stuck with traditional banking practices and common sense and judgement, they would not have created the present crisis. No forecasting model predicted the present economic crises and it caught most economists and business people by surprise. Those few economists who forecast an impending recession were ridiculed as harbingers of doom and gloom. We should bear in mind that theories are provisional and incomplete because they will eventually be proved to be false, and be superseded by better ones as knowledge and understanding advances.

Stress and Fatigue

Medical staff often works under stressful conditions, with long hours, a fast tempo and poor staffing. This can have an adverse effect on performance and result in medical mistakes. Doctors in particular often work excessively long shifts in the accident and emergency area. Research studies show that an individual's judgement and ability to react are reduced as a result of overwork, sleep deficiency and fatigue. In addition, modern health care can place high demands on medical staff due to the expertise needed to operate technically advanced apparatus and monitoring equipment.

At the same time fewer opportunities exist for further education for some health care staff, especially those lower down in the hierarchy, such as nursing assistants. An additional risk occurs due to the graduate education of nurses. Newly graduated nurses may not have the practical clinical skills necessary and thus be more prone to error. During changing shifts, errors can be made when the outgoing physician or nurse fails to inform the incoming physician or nurse of information about the patient's condition that he should know.

Where do Mistakes Happen?

Mistakes occur in all aspects of personal and business life, including information technology. Some well-known mistakes have happened in the car industry and politics. Mistakes in the aviation industry and medical care can cost lives.

Personal Life

In the personal realm people overspent on credit cards and took out mortgages which they could ill afford. Interest rates were so low that many re-mortgaged their homes to fund their extravagant life styles. When the recession came they found themselves in negative equity. Worst still many lost their jobs and found they were unable to pay their debts. This was compounded by the fact that most people didn't save during the prosperous years and didn't live within their means.

Writers like me will tell you that despite proofreading a script several times, you will still find errors in the published book. In the business world mistakes are made in all areas of corporate life including information technology, finance, marketing and human resources management.

Information Technology

Probably one of the most bizarre mistakes took place in 1983 in the UK, when a project to equip an RAF Nimrod aircraft, with computerised air-defence early-warning systems was abandoned. It was discovered that the computers were too heavy for the purpose-built nose section of the aircraft, resulting in about £800 million of taxpayers' money being wasted. A lack of foresight and planning was to blame.

Look before you leap

E-voting machines were hailed by politicians as the way to bring Ireland out of the pencil and paper age. In 2002 E-voting machines were piloted in a number of constituencies in Ireland. Plans to roll out the machines nationally in 2004 were abandoned after an independent report raised concerns about their reliability. A lack of a paper trail and security issues, suggesting they could be open to hacking and manipulation, meant they could not be used.

In 2009 it was decided to scrap the system because it would cost too much to upgrade. Finally in 2012 the infamous machines were sold for scrap for €70,000. From the outset the project was poorly conceived, planned and delivered, and eventually cost the Irish taxpayer €55 million.

Test out your project thoroughly before you go live. In November 1992 the chief executive of the London Ambulance resigned after problems, in the ambulance computer aided despatch system, led to three hour delays in reaching emergency patients. The repair bill came to about £9 million with the likelihood that people died because ambulances failed to arrive promptly.

Investigations unearthed numerous errors. The system had been implemented against an impossible deadline, and neither software nor hardware had been properly tested. Employees both in the central control teams and ambulance crews were inadequately trained. In addition, management had underestimated the difficulties involved in changing the deeply ingrained culture of the service.

How not to manage a project

The PPARS (personnel, payroll and related systems) computer system commissioned by the Irish Health Service Executive (HSE) was a shambles and a comedy of errors, and another example of gross inefficiency, and a waste of taxpayers' money. The initial estimated cost of €9 million ballooned to over €220 million, and the system was only able to do a fraction of the work intended. It was hoped it would provide detailed information on its 136,000 staff for human resources as well as draw up rotas. However, it is only capable of paying 30,000 staff and storing information on 70,000.

A review into the project showed up a litany of problems, and is a case study on how not to manage a project. Unsatisfactory pilot results in two hospitals were ignored. The project was poorly planned, managed, co-ordinated, controlled, monitored and budgeted for. Budget and project times were seriously underestimated. The project team was incompetent, which led to the hiring of multiple outside consultants at enormous cost. There was a lack of leadership. Project managers were given a job to do, but were not given the necessary authority to do so. There was a failure to make managers accountable for staying within budgets and achieving deadlines.

A basic principle of successful management is to impose limits, checks and balances with independent monitoring and reporting. This obviously was not done with PPARS. The old maxim is relevant here: when you fail to plan, you plan to fail. The solution, of course, is to spend adequate time thinking through your project in advance, anticipate problems, and have contingency plans to deal with them.

Car Industry

In the car industry, some of our well-known brands such as Toyota and Mercedes Benz made mistakes, which they unsuccessfully tried to cover up making a bad situation worse. Toyota ran into trouble in the autumn of 2007 when the company recalled 55,000 cars. The floor mats had a tendency to slide forward and trap the gas pedal. It became a major public concern when in August 2009; a 2009 Lexus suddenly accelerated, hit another car, fell down an embankment and caught fire. By January 2010 Toyota had recalled about 4.2 million vehicles for the pedal problem, and an additional 2.3 million vehicles for the accelerator problem. Thirty four deaths were alleged to have been caused by the pedal problem over the 10 year period to 2010.

Despite the media attention Toyota management failed to acknowledge the malfunction of its vehicles, be open and transparent in its dealings with the press and public, and so the problem escalated into a product safety and public relations disaster. It could no longer claim with any credibility that it had the best built cars in the world. During the crises Toyota showed poor communication with the public and displayed little compassion or concern for their safety. This happened despite Toyota's philosophy of transparency, continuous improvement, and learning from mistakes. Obviously one should be seen to walk the talk, or a loss of credibility will occur!

The launch of the Mercedes-Benz A-class in 1967 was greeted with enthusiasm by the international motoring community, until tests showed it was prone to overturn when cornering. Rather than attending to, and solving the problem, Mercedes-Benz adopted a policy of silence when confronted by the media. In response to this, motoring journalists took the car for further tests themselves with similar results. Mercedes-Benz could no longer deny the problem. However, it chose to scapegoat Goodyear tyres for the problem, rather than acknowledging that it was its own problem. If Mercedes Benz had adopted a more open, honest and proactive approach to its dealings with the public, instead of stonewalling and scapegoating, it could have saved a great deal of time, money and embarrassment.

Politics

One of the most infamous cases of wrongful convictions was the sentencing to life in prison of the Birmingham six in 1975, for the Birmingham pub bombing which killed 21 people. They were just six Irish people in the wrong place at the wrong time with the evidence against them invented and purely circumstantial. Nevertheless the legal authorities including judges, lawyers and police convinced themselves that they were guilty. They needed to get scapegoats quickly for the bombing to satisfy the British public. They were convicted on the basis of forced confessions, and fabricated and suppressed evidence. Their convictions were declared unsafe and unsatisfactory, and the forensic evidence was judged to be wrong by the Court of Appeal in 1991. The six men were awarded compensation ranging from £840,000 to £1.2 million.

The Bay of Pigs fiasco is often attributed to group think. This is a phenomenon where members of a group tend to reinforce each other's assumptions, rather than test them out logically. In April 1961 an invading Central Intelligence Agency (CIA) trained force of Cuban exiles, was defeated by the Cuban armed forces within 3 days. After the failed Bay of Pigs invasion, President Kennedy decided to learn from his mistakes, and split his policy advisor into a blue team and a red team. The blue team would list down all the reasons why a particular decision would succeed while the red team would identify the likely reasons why it would fail. This balanced two side of an argument approach, is credited with the successful stand-down of Russia during the missile crises of October 1961, thereby preventing a major war from happening.

The Aviation Industry

The aviation industry has a good reputation of thoroughly investigating and learning from mistakes. Flying is in fact one of the safest forms of transportation. You are 30 to 50 times more likely to die in a car accident than in a plane. Even when flying a pilot will tell you that a jet is off course, 90 per cent of the time. However, the crew is constantly correcting and aligning the flight plan, based on prevailing conditions, thereby preventing possible mistakes from happening.

Being in a hurry can cause a disaster
The worst aviation disasters ever, the March 1977 collision of two Boeing 747s, on a foggy runway at Tenerife in the Canary Island, which killed 583 people, was directly caused by time pressure. The KLM flight crew was concerned about returning on schedule to Amsterdam, and about the possibility of the fog worsening resulting in further delays. Under time pressures, checklists, paperwork and safety measure are often relegated to second place status to save time. James Reason, the world's leading researcher on human error, found that time pressures increased the chance of human error eleven-fold.

Relatively minor mistakes can have dire consequences
In April 1988, the Aloha Airlines Flight 243, a Boeing 737-297, suffered extensive damage after a decompression explosion. It managed to land safely at Kahului Airport on Maui. One flight attendant was killed and another 65 passengers and crew were injured. The incident has had far-reaching effects on aviation safety policies and procedures.

The US National Transportation Safety Board's (NTSB) report concluded that the accident was caused by metal fatigue. The root cause of the problem was failure of a resin adhesive to bond the aluminium sheets of the fuselage together, when the plane was manufactured. Water entered the gap where the two surfaces had failed to bond properly, and started the corrosion process. The aircraft was 19 years old, and this was a key factor in why the corrosion had been so severe. As a direct result of this incident the US Federal Aviation Administration instituted additional, and more thorough mandatory checks, for aging aircraft.

For want of a screw the plane was lost
In September 1991, Continental Express Flight 2547 crashed as it was approaching the runway for landing, killing all 14 people on board. The NTSB discovered that missing screws on the horizontal stabiliser led to the crash. The bolts had been removed during maintenance the night before the accident and, following a shift change, the screws were not replaced. The maintenance and inspection personnel had failed to adhere to proper maintenance and quality assurance procedures. The crash of Flight 2547 was a turning point for safety culture in the US. The corporate culture of the company failed to prioritise safety, and consequently it is

now a key issue in aviation.

Ignore warnings at your peril

In aviation they have learned to train across disciplines to make sure that breakdowns in communication do not happen. On 9 March 1989, an Air Ontario Fokker F-27, was preparing for take-off from a small airport in Northern Ontario. While the jet waited for take-off clearance, several passengers noticed an accumulation of snow on the wings. One of them brought it to the attention of a flight attendant in charge, who assured them that there was nothing to worry about.

The flight attendant did not think it was appropriate to bring it to the attention of the pilots. The aircraft took off, and then crashed in a nearby wooded area because of the snow on the wings. Twenty four people died in the crash. During the investigation, when asked why she didn't alert the pilots to the problem, she said she didn't feel it was her job to do so. This demonstrates an undue deference to authority and a lack of team-work.

Sometimes mistakes line up and combine to cause major accidents

In another incident involving a British Midlands 737-400, which crashed near Kegworth in Leicestershire on the 8 January 1989, killing 47 and seriously injuring 74. The accident report stated that three cabin crew said that they saw flames coming from the left engine but failed to alert the pilots. The pilots had mistakenly shut down the right engine instead of the malfunctioning left engine. In addition, the pilots did not check the vibration detectors, because those on previous planes they had flown were notoriously unreliable. The pilots had received no simulator training on the new model, as no simulator for the 737-400 existed in the UK at that time. The engine had only been tested in the laboratory and not under actual flight conditions.

A lack of openness and transparency can lead to disaster

The Space Shuttle Columbia disaster occurred on 1 February 2003. It disintegrated during re-entry into the Earth's atmosphere, with the loss of all seven crew members. The primary cause of the accident was a piece of foam insulation which came away during the launch, and damaged the Space Shuttle's external tank. This had catastrophic consequences on re-entry. A secondary cause was the bureaucratic culture operating within NASA. Management were aware of the foam insulation problem but decided that it was an acceptable risk. A rigid hierarchy and schedule-obsessed culture meant that engineers were afraid to voice their safety concerns.

Medical care

The high incidence of mistakes in hospitals and medical care facilities has come under scrutiny, and the culture of secrecy, denial and cover-up within the medical profession is no longer acceptable to a more aware and better educated general public. The types of mistakes that happen are too numerous to list comprehensively. However, some typical errors include:

* misdiagnosis,
* mixing up test results,
* giving the wrong type blood,
* removing a healthy kidney instead of a diseased one,
* unnecessarily removing healthy breasts from a woman,
* adverse drug reaction,
* giving the wrong medication or the wrong dosage,
* amputating the wrong limb,
* surgery on the wrong patient,
* leaving sponges or implements in a patient after surgery and so on.

Most of these medical mistakes would not have happened if the proper controls and checks were in place, and a culture of safety and learning from mistakes had existed. To add insult to injury patients are typically billed for the cost of the additional care they need to recover from hospital mistakes.

A double error

CNN reported in 2003 on an unnecessary double mastectomy. It was nightmare news every woman dreads to hear. Linda McDougal was told she had breast cancer, so she underwent a double mastectomy. However, the news got worse. Doctors admitted it was all an error, that she never had cancer, and that it was all a big mistake.

An unfortunate mix-up

In 2006, RTE reported that a 26 year old man whose entire stomach was removed by mistake was awarded €450,000 in damages. Mr Alan O'Gorman (23) was rushed to hospital in 2002, with severe stomach cramps. Doctors removed his appendix, diagnosed a perforated ulcer, and took a biopsy of stomach tissue as a precaution. His biopsy indicated he had stomach cancer. Most of his stomach was removed but when he was examined there was no cancer.

His biopsy had been mixed up with another patient, a 70 year old man who actually had stomach cancer. The medical mistake left him seriously and permanently injured. A simple exploratory procedure called an endoscopy (a long slender medical instrument used for examining the internal organs), would have prevented the error from happening. The fact that the patient was so young should have also alerted the medical staff that something was amiss. Sometimes a little common sense goes a long way.

In 2009 a landmark compensation award of £5.2 million, was made to a boy born with cerebral palsy after a series of errors at a Scottish hospital. In a similar case in Ireland (Leo Conroy v Rotunda Hospital) in 2009, an infant who suffered oxygen deficiency at birth, due to medical negligence, was awarded €5.25 million plus legal costs. The infant suffered catastrophic mental and physical injuries, and will remain permanently and physically disabled. The hospital, in typical fashion, defended its case right up to the end, even though it was obvious that they had made an unfortunate mistake.

In Tallaght Hospital in Ireland more than 57,000 X-rays, taken at the hospital between 2005 and the end of 2009, were not reviewed by a consultant radiologist. The X-rays were for various tests including cancer, heart checks and orthopaedics. A review into the scandal found that the backlog of unreported X-rays was caused by the hospital having too few radiologists. This was compounded by an increased and more complex workload, problems with IT and systems and secretarial services, and deficiencies in governance and administration. This happened despite the warnings of a cancer specialist in 2006. He raised concerns about a 17 day delay in reporting an X-ray on a major lung condition, and maintained that such delays were commonplace. As we know a late diagnosis can mean the difference between life and death, or reduced life expectancy.

Lack of basic knowledge
Sometimes a lack of basic knowledge can have fatal consequences. For example, in a community teaching hospital, a 58 year old man struggles for his life. His heart does not seem to be pumping sufficient blood to his organs. To solve the problem a doctor in training decides to place a catheter (tube) in the patient's neck vein, advancing it through the heart, and lodging it in the pulmonary artery. He tears the pulmonary artery, and within seconds the patient bleeds to death. The doctor had advanced the catheter 75 cm. This was done despite the fact that it was well-known, in medical circles, that inserting the catheter more than 60 cm risked puncturing the patient's pulmonary artery.

The doctor either does not know or forgets this detail. Unfortunately this tragic error is not rare, and could have been prevented if the doctor knew what he was doing. However, these types of errors are still happening in our hospitals. Because one error in a hospital equates to one death, unlike aviation where one error may equate to hundreds of deaths, there is not the same sense of urgency to get their act right like there is in aviation.

Own up to your mistakes
The best course of action is to do the decent and ethical thing and admit your mistakes. In February 2003, doctors at Duke University Hospital in North Carolina USA committed one of the worst mistakes in modern medical history. They transplanted the wrong heart and lungs into a 17 year old girl who died as a result.

Despite the natural tendency to suppress, cover up and stonewall, three weeks later the hospital admitted their mistake and offered a sincere apology on the CBS 60 minutes programme. The hospital came across as hu-

Inspiration

"To err is human, to cover up is unforgivable but to refuse to learn is inexcusable."
Sir Donaldson

man, honest, sincere and contrite and vowed to change its procedures and restore its reputation. It is a lesson that other hospitals might learn from. After all physicians have an ethical responsibility to report mistakes to their patients and to the hospital authorities.

How Can We Prevent Mistakes?

The redundancy principle helps to protect us from mistakes. Reducing the level of workplace stress will prevent mistakes. We should learn from our mistakes so that we do not repeat them in the future. The more knowledge and expertise we have the less likely we are to make mistakes. Checklists have reduced the number of mistakes in aviation and medical care. Trial runs, and knowledge management systems, will help organisations reduce errors. Techniques for reducing mistakes include root cause analysis and simulation training.

The Redundancy Principle
In humans, nature uses redundancy as a fall back mechanism to keep us alive if some of our major organs fail. For example, we have two kidneys and two lungs, so that if one fails we have one to survive with. Similarly, in aviation they have instituted a number of engineering solutions to keep us safe, such as the duplication of safety devices like back-up engines. Hydraulic pumps are designed with failure in mind. Aircraft are given three hydraulic systems to ensure that loss of one, or even two systems, will not result in disaster. Organisations have emergency generators to fall back on in case of national grid outages.

High-reliability-organisations (HRO) expect to make errors and train their employees to recognise and deal with them. They are almost error free despite operating in very dangerous fields. They achieve this through their ability to react to unexpected situations through constant training, and "redundancy," where there is more staff and equipment than appear to be necessary. They continually rehearse scenarios of failure, and strive hard to imagine novel ones. They generalise their failure and build suitable safeguards into their systems. Electricite de France which operates 58 nuclear power plants, meticulously tracks each plant for anything even slightly out of the ordinary, immediately investigates whatever turns up, and informs all its other plants of any problems.

Reduce the Level of Workplace Stress

Most organisations could reduce the number of mistakes if they reduced the level of stress in the working environment. Research consistently shows that people working under stress make more mistakes than others who work in less stressful situations. Mistakes tend to happen at times of pressure, hurry, interruptions, distraction or working excessive hours.

Learn from Your Mistakes

Ask questions and get feedback on what happened. Reflect on what happened. Find out what works and what doesn't work. If it doesn't work do something about it by taking corrective action, so that the mistake does not happen again. David Packard and Bill Hewlett, the founders of Hewlett Packard, were known for telling stories about failures and successes as they wandered around HP's labs. They realised that storytelling was a great and compelling way of learning and creating a culture that shares, forgives, and acknowledges failure.

If we brief ourselves mentally, before and after events, it will help us learn from them and reduce the possibility of error. Before an event, we should set out our expectations of what is likely to happen. After the event, we should consider what went right, what went wrong, and what could have been done better. During the event, we should carry out checks to make sure everything is working smoothly and that interim goals are being achieved. Some people find it useful to keep a diary to record, review and reflect on their mistakes so that lessons will be learnt for the future. We can thus learn from our own mistakes, and indeed from the mistakes of others.

Employees must feel safe admitting to and reporting mistakes. They should be confident that the emphasis will be on learning from mistakes, and preventing them from happening in the future rather than blaming and shaming individuals. Being accountable and accepting responsibility in a no blame culture is a vital aspect of the process of learning from our mistakes. In addition, junior staff should not be afraid to question decisions made by more senior staff, a strategy which has greatly improved the safety of air travel. For example, the culture and power in medical teams, which tends to be competitive rather than cooperative, often leads to junior doctors and nurses not questioning, or seeking clarification, of the decisions of senior doctors and consultants. In fact, consultants are often put up on pedestals, and treated like demi-gods.

Preventing Mistakes Through Training

Experts now believe that it is human error rather than mechanical failure which is the chief cause of air accidents. Although in recent times it is thought that systemic problems are also a major contributor. These include management decision-making, deficient safety culture, policies, recruitment and selection, training or system design.

Many mistakes are caused by a lack of knowledge and expertise. In selecting personnel we can hire those with the best education, aptitude, competence and experience. For example, in aircraft maintenance those with a mechanical aptitude and a keen eye for detail will be less prone to making mistakes. In addition, we can improve our knowledge and skills through training, education, experience and reflection, and thus reduce the possibility of error.

When we do something, we should reflect on it, observe the consequences and consider how we could do it better next time. The Royal Air Force defines the following competencies for their trainees, all of which are also relevant for other professions:
- Confidence and resilience;
- Oral communication;
- Problem solving ability;
- Team working.

We can also model our behaviour on the skills of experts by examining their techniques and studying how they make decisions and solve problems. In aviation pilots undergo proficiency tests every six months in order to keep their flying licence. A similar situation operates in medicine. Continuous professional development is now a requirement of most professions if they want to continue to practise. Indeed it is acknowledged generally that we need to upgrade our skills continuously if we want to remain proficient and competitive. The skills and wisdom of our more experienced colleagues can be passed on through mentoring and coaching.

One form of mentoring growing in popularity is peer mentoring. During peer mentoring, peers provide feedback on performance, point out mistakes and inconsistencies, make suggestions for improvement, and provide support to their co-workers. Mentoring is more likely to be successful when organisations encourage employees to take an active role in learning from and teaching others, and provides opportunities for this to occur.

Preventing Medical Mistakes

It's all about teamwork, leadership and getting along with others. Pilots in the cockpit, and medical staff in the emergency room, act as part of a team. So it is important that they get training in team building skills.

Lecturing is ineffective for teambuilding, with simulation training better to impart the practical skills of teamwork. The failure of a flight crew or a healthcare team may result in serious injury or loss of life. The importance of effective team work is critical to safety. Breakdowns in communication, interpersonal relationships, leadership and teamwork within the cockpit, or emergency room, can have dire consequences.

A simple and straightforward way of preventing mistakes is through improved communications and interpersonal relationships. Many medical errors would have been avoided if physicians just listened to their patients and their families, and to their colleagues.

The culture in the health care sector strives for perfection, which means a non-acceptance of mistakes. Their training instils the same attitude. This attitude contributes to feelings of guilt and shame when mistakes are made. In addition, to the fear of making mistakes, there is also the anxiety of being reported and reprimanded, if one makes a mistake. Furthermore, there is the added fear of litigation and the adverse publicity if a story about medical mistakes appears in the media. All of these factors are a disincentive to be transparent about medical errors. When we do make mistakes we should avoid blaming and scapegoating others, and accept responsibility for our own mistakes.

Doctors are known for their bad handwriting. Medication errors, when filling prescriptions, caused by illegible handwriting, can be eliminated by installing a computer medication ordering system. Surgery on the wrong body part can be avoided by a well-proven technique of using marks on the parts of the body to be operated on.

In the course of their training medical students should be told about mistakes and how to prevent them. Misdiagnosis can be reduced if physicians keep up to date with new literature and new procedures.

Learning from Mistakes
In the last ten years a new profession has emerged called a patient safety officer. Their job is to report on any medical error, or near-miss. As a consequence, a culture of safety, active questioning, sharing of insights and concerns, reporting and transparency has emerged in hospitals, where a patient safety officer is employed.

Twice a month medical professionals in teaching hospitals throughout the world meet to discuss successes and failures. These meetings are called Morbidity and Mortality conferences and it is where the medical profession learns from their mistakes. Behind closed doors they review unforeseen patient outcomes, and deaths that happened on their watch, determine what went wrong, and figure out what to do differently next time. At these conferences they can talk frankly about their mistakes without the fear of blame or litigation. Similarly post-mortems are carried out on dead bodies to determine the cause of death, and to prevent any mistakes from occurring again.

Importance of Checklists

Health care staff should standardise work processes, use checklists so that patients receive evidence based interventions consistently, improve communications to reduce errors, and use scientific methods to identify and reduce risks. Nurses should run through a checklist of steps before an operation begins. During the operation if the doctor misses a step or fails to follow the checklist procedure, then the nurse shouldn't be afraid to ask the doctor to stop the procedure and correct the error.

Atul Gawande, the patient safety advocate and author of several books on the topic, is a surgeon at Boston's Brigham and Women's Hospital. His work has led to the World Health Organisation adopting a checklist approach to safety in the operating theatre. It is the team rather than the individual that is the root cause of most accidents and incidents in both aviation and medical care, and so everything should be done to improve teamwork and eliminate errors.

Think Before You Speak and Tell The Truth

Sometimes we should keep our thoughts to ourselves rather than express them out loud. If we think before we speak we would eliminate the source of many mistakes. Take the case of Gordon Brown the ex-Prime Minister of England who passed an inappropriate remark about a constituent while on air, causing a major adverse publicity incident, which subsequent efforts to calm the waters, proved to be unsuccessful. Since the damage had been done, it was too late and a waste of time, to visit and show empathy to the constituent after the event.

One of the justifications for the Iraqi war was a lie. The pretext for invading Iraq was that it had weapons of mass destruction. It was subsequently discovered by the media that this was false. President Clinton when interviewed on television about Monica Lewinsky maintained that he did not have sexual relations with her. Apparently, he did not accept that oral sex should be classified as sex. Of course when you lie on television it can be replayed years after to highlight your inability to tell the truth.

Preventing Corporate Mistakes

In a corporate context systems can be designed to highlight and prevent mistakes from taking place. Quality control, maintenance checks, and internal audit, can highlight mistakes before they escalate into serious problems. Safety laws and regulations can prevent mistakes from happening and record those that happen so that preventative measures can be taken in the future. However, simple cross-checking by an independent third party is a traditional but cost effective way of preventing mistakes from happening, despite the advances in information technology.

Company policies, procedures, protocols, guidelines and standard operating procedures, are put in place to help eliminate mistakes. The nuclear disaster at Chernobyl was caused by the operators not following procedures. They wrongly switched off successive safety systems, thus creating the immediate trigger for the catastrophic explosion in the core.

In the aviation industry, the flight recorder, or black box, can measure about 1000 variables, which provide valuable information about how the flight went. This can be analysed after each flight. There is also a voice recorder, which is analysed only after accidents. This is akin to a post mortem in medicine.

High staff and management turnover can contribute to the incidence of mistakes as inexperienced staff are more prone to making errors. Generally the more experienced staff and management are the fewer mistakes that are likely to happen.

Risk management, and risk assessment, can be used to anticipate catastrophic situations, and put contingency plans in place to deal with them if and when they arise. There are a host of tools and services to manage risk including disaster recovery plans, anti-virus software and firewall technologies. You are always better equipped to deal with unlikely situations, if you have rehearsed contingency plans in place to deal with them. Your employees should be trained in advance and know what to do, when the server crashes, the phones goes down or the office floods.

Trial Runs

Pilot schemes and parallel running, can be used to test out sophisticated information technology systems before the actual systems are finally put in place. Problems can be ironed out in advance, without the inconvenience of major problems arising, if the system was finally up and running.

Prototype products, market research, and test marketing can be used to try out products, with a representative sample of customers in the market place before an actual launch. It is always better to try something out on a limited scale before committing huge capital and revenue expenditure resources. Ironically, the hunger to be successful may hinder the success of the official launch. Managers in charge of test marketing may design ideal conditions, rather than representative ones. Thus the test marketing doesn't provide knowledge about what won't work in a practical situation.

Knowledge Management Systems

Knowledge management systems can be put in place so that companies learn from their experience. A system should be put in place to capture mistakes, and even near misses. Aviation has used this as its principal method to increased safety. Near misses have the advantage of carrying less emotional baggage, and so defences against addressing them are likely to be lower. The cumulative effect of small errors can have major consequences.

Knowledge management is about creating a corporate culture that learns from experience, so if mistakes happen, they won't be repeated. It is important that information and knowledge is available to the right people at the right time, so that they can work more efficiently and effectively. Learning organisations engage in lifelong learning and continuous improvement, and strive for zero defects in their systems and procedures. Information technology systems can be used to create a database of errors and incidents, so that companies can be aware of and learn from their past mistakes.

Techniques for Preventing Mistakes

Well-known techniques for preventing mistakes include root cause analysis, scenario-based training, quality assurance, preventative maintenance, total quality management, simulators and due diligence.

Root cause analysis (RCA) is a technique which seeks to identify the origin of a problem. It is a widely used technique to learn from mistakes and mitigate hazards, and has been used in medicine and in high reliability organisations, such as aviation and nuclear power. It tries to find out what happened, why it happened, and how to reduce the likelihood that it will happen again. Generally, mistakes do not just happen, but can be attributed to three basic causes. RCA looks at the three basic types of causes: physical, human and organisational to determine why the mistake took place and what the organisation can do to prevent a recurrence.

Scenario-based training is a training method involving making decisions within a 'real world' context, similar to those we would come across in an operational setting. This means that when we are confronted by similar situations in real life we will know what to do.

Preventive maintenance makes sure that equipment and aircraft are safe to operate and fly. The quality of the maintenance is controlled internally through quality assurance, and externally through regulation. As we have seen some workplace accidents and aircraft disasters have been caused by shoddy maintenance.

Total Quality Management (TQM) and soliciting feedback from customers are well-known techniques for discovering errors in routine operations. It is commitment to the production of a zero defect product.

Simulators are used in aviation and medicine to help train pilots and surgeons in life threatening or emergency situations, without the risk of operating in the real situation. It provides opportunities to become familiar with equipment, and test 'what if' scenarios, and to make mistakes in a

Inspiration

"An engineer's life is 99 per cent failure. You don't learn much from success and your successes are few and far between. An innovative engineer goes to work each day excited because you know there are hundreds of problems that you have not solved. Failure is actually like a drug that keeps you living on the edge and trying to come up with the right solution."
James Dyson

safe environment. This means people can become proficient without en-dangering lives.

Due diligence is an investigation into anything to ensure that everything is as it should be. It helps a buyer or investor make sure that there are no unexpected problems with the asset or investment. Due diligence can be a complex formal process in the case of a company acquisition. When buy-ing a house due diligence is getting a chartered surveyor and solicitor to check out the house before purchase, to ensure that there are no structural faults, or legal impediments to ownership and that everything is in order. When hiring an employee you should conduct a due diligence on the em-ployee's background, including checking out references and ringing for-mer employers to make sure that you don't finish up hiring an unsuitable person, or someone who is not what they claim to be.

What Are the Consequences of Mistakes?

If we fail to learn from our mistakes we will go on making them. Ideally, we should not repeat the mistakes of history. No one progresses in their career without making mistakes, and learning from them. If people fail to acknowledge their mistakes they will not take responsibility for them, and will try to hide them and blame others. If you keep on doing the same old thing you will keep on getting the same old results. If you want to suc-ceed in life you must learn from your mistakes and do things differently.

People who suffer from the mistakes of others may take legal action to compensate for the wrong done and the pain suffered. People may have to pay high insurance premiums to protect them against the potential loss, if people take claims for compensation against them. Even giving poor advice can land professional people in trouble, hence the need for public liability insurance.

Physicians may become risk averse because of the possibility of legal ac-tions against them for medical mistakes. To protect themselves against being sued they may call for unnecessary tests and procedures.

Physicians who admit their mistakes to their patients are less likely to have legal claims made against them. One study revealed that most pa-tients desire a sincere apology, and an acknowledgement of even minor errors. It suggested that such honesty could actually reduce the risk of legal action. Moreover, patients who were not told about the mistake by their physician, but who learned about it by some other means were sig-nificantly more likely to sue.

During the good years people who took out loans and mortgages be-yond their means and who misread the market, are now paying the price through bankruptcies, repossessions and foreclosures. Hopefully, the next generation will learn from our mistakes.

People who make mistakes will lose credibility, and the confidence and trust of others. When trust is lost it is very difficult to get back. In addition, they may lose their self-belief and self-confidence. It is important that people acknowledge their mistakes, and deal as effectively as possible with them when they occur, so that their general sense of competence is strengthened rather than weakened. We learn best from our own mistakes because of the personal, emotional and immediate impact involved.

People who make major controversial mistakes may attract unwarranted media attention and prying into their private lives. In a worst case scenario if they break the law, they may find themselves facing judicial proceedings, or even jail.

Mistakes may result in lost business, lost customers, lost time and lost productivity. Customers are unwilling to do business with companies who continually make mistakes. It is much more difficult and expensive to get new customers than to retain your existing customers.

Inspiration

"The successful man will profit from his mistakes and try again in a different way."
Dale Carnegie

Automobile, aviation, and medical mistakes may result in serious injury and even death. In particular medical mistakes contribute to higher societal costs, in the form of additional treatment, prolonged hospital stay, sick leave, and the loss of income. In addition, to the emotional distress and psychological pain suffered by the patient and their relatives, the medical staff responsible may also suffer mental strain, loss of face and trauma, because of the mistakes made. Despite 12 years or more of heightened awareness, that medical errors result in hundreds of thousands of deaths throughout the world each year, hospitals have still not become safer.

What Lessons Can We Learn From Mistakes?

We need checks and balances to counteract the possibility of abuse and error. The death of innocence has been caused by the frequent occurrence of scandals in all aspects of life. Companies have installed knowledge management systems to track and learn from their mistakes. Royal watchers are hoping that Prince William and Kate Middleton will learn the lessons of his parent's unsuccessful marriage. There can be unexpected upsides of making mistakes.

Checks
We need controls in the form of laws, rules, regulation and checks. One of the reasons for the collapse of the banking system was a failure to regulate. We should trust, but at the same time verify, to make sure that what people say is going to happen actually happens

The Death of Innocence
Scandals in all areas of business and public life have seen the death of innocence. People have no longer the same blind faith and trust in authority figures, such as doctors, accountants, solicitors, bankers, religious

authorities and so on. Because of the reckless behaviour of bankers in the past people no longer trust them. Similarly, blind trust in doctors and other medical professionals has been eroded due to the high number of medical malpractice cases reported in the media. Accountants and solicitors come out no better because of the reckless misappropriation of client funds. Consequently people no longer have any hesitation in questioning authority figures.

People now realise the importance of values such as honesty, integrity and fairness in their personal and business dealings with others. These values have been found to be sorely lacking in the banking, legal and accounting professions.

People need to work in a psychologically safe environment, if they are to admit, discuss and learn from their mistakes. People need to be able to discuss their mistakes, without fear of ridicule or punishment. Managers should encourage others to admit their mistakes, and model fallibility by admitting their own errors, in order to demonstrate its okay to make mistakes provided you learn from them. The emphasis should be on clearly understanding what happened, rather than 'who did it' when things go wrong. Avoid judging and fault finding. People don't have to make the mistakes themselves to learn. They can also learn from the failures and mistakes of others.

Need for Knowledge Management Systems
Companies are determined to learn from their mistakes, and many have installed knowledge management systems. The learning organisation has become fashionable with its emphasis on lifelong learning and continuous improvement. Learning from mistakes is a powerful way to accelerate learning and increase productivity and competitiveness.

Small mistakes are early warning signs that people or systems are not functioning properly, which if detected and addressed, may be the key to avoiding serious mistakes in the future. If we have access to a centralised databanks of mistakes, it will help us reduce and eliminate mistakes and learn from them.

Need for Personal Change
People who want to lose weight meet their goals by learning from past mistakes. They realise that permanent weight control is a difficult learning process. As part of this process they must change their behaviour, eating habits, and lifestyle. They try out diets until they find one that works for them. They may cut down on the amount of bread that they eat, choose fish, fruit and salads for a meal, eliminate biscuits and sweets, from their diet, walk to work, use the stairs, instead of the lift, and go to the gym at lunchtime. They find new ways to reduce calories, and cram in a few extra minutes of exercise into their busy lifestyles. Cumulative small changes can result in major weight loss.

Royal watchers maintain that Prince William is determined to learn the lessons from his parents' nasty divorce and make his marriage to Kate Middleton last. The body language between them suggests that the relationship is harmonious and that they are very much in love, unlike that of his parents.

Ted Huston, a professor of human ecology at the University of Texas found that a long courtship does not guarantee a more stable union, but a harmonious one does. Couples very quick or very slow to wed, are more likely to divorce, but harmonious courtships tend to be a sign of a happy marriage whereas turbulent ones suggest problems.

Unexpected Benefits

Sometimes mistakes have a huge and unexpected upside. Consider Columbus who set out for India, but made the fortuitous mistake of discovering America instead and consequently became very famous indeed because of this error!

Thomas Edison doggedly pursued the development of the phonograph even though he believed the idea would have no commercial value. His invention paid off in one of the most commercially successful products of all time.

Edison is attributed with inventing the light bulb after more than 1,000 attempts. What is not widely known is that the first light bulb was invented by Sir Joseph Wilson Swan. He demonstrated the theory, but gave up trying to develop a practical application after only three attempts. In contrast, Edison developed the first working light bulb through sheer self-belief, persistence, determination and dedication.

Edison saw mistakes as learning opportunities. Similarly we should reframe our perception of mistakes from sources of frustration to sources of learning, and continue our quest for lifelong learning and continuous improvement.

Information Technology consultants made a fortune out of the Millennium Bug mistake, when they predicted that computer systems would go awry on the 1st January 2000. When the date finally arrived nothing happened. Wild predictions were made that planes would fall from the sky, corporate information technology systems would fail, and that major disruptions would occur in society when computers malfunctioned.

When Citibank proposed giving credit cards to students in the 1980s, experts said it was a big mistake, but instead went on to be a huge success story for the bank and has been adopted by other banks since.

An oil company deliberately makes mistakes when exploring for oil because it knows that the potential gain exceeds the cost of the mistake. It knows that it is likely to get nothing from nine out of ten wells, but realises that if it succeeds on the tenth exploration attempt it will make a lot of money.

Summary

Humans are prone to error with fallible memories. We tend to be forgetful and are easily distracted with limited powers of concentration. Many of us have the wrong attitude, and thus we fail to see mistakes as learning opportunities. Ignorance of the law is no defence when you make a mistake with legal ramifications. Bureaucracies in particular tend to have a shame and blame culture rather than a learning culture.

The sunk cost fallacy prevents managers from withdrawing from their pet projects until it is too late. Poorly designed systems, equipment, products and structures may facilitate mistakes. The efficient market hypothesis is thought to be one of the reasons for the unwise investment decisions made by financial institutions, which plunged the world into the current economic recession.

In the business world mistakes are made in all areas of corporate life. Similarly, in our personal lives many of us made poor financial decisions and personal choices. We can prevent mistakes by asking questions and reflecting on what worked and what didn't work. In companies quality control and internal audit can highlight mistakes, before they escalate into serious business problems. Generally, the more experienced staff and management are the less likelihood of mistakes happening.

Prototype products, market research and test marketing, can be used to prevent inappropriate product launches. Learning organisations engage in lifelong learning and continuous improvement, and zero defects, hoping to reduce or eliminate the incidence of mistakes.

People may have to pay high insurance premiums to protect them from the cost of adverse legal decisions in the event of compensation claims being taken against them for inappropriate professional advice. People who make mistakes may lose the confidence and trust of others.

Because of the reckless and unethical behaviour of bankers in the past people no longer revere and trust them. Similarly, blind trust in doctors, consultants and other medical professionals has been eroded due to the high number of medical malpractice cases reported in the media.

Inspiration

"Success seems to be connected with action. Successful people keep moving. They make mistakes, but they don't quit."
Conrad Hilton

Five Activities to Improve Learning From Mistakes

1. Reframe your attitude by looking on mistakes as learning opportunities rather than sources of frustration.
2. Prevent mistakes by critically reflecting on what worked and what didn't work. If you want to succeed in life you must learn from your mistakes, and be determined not to repeat them in the future.
3. In addition to learning from your own mistakes you can learn from the mistakes and failures of others.
4. Adopting high moral and ethical standards will keep you on the straight and narrow and prevent you from making stupid mistakes.
5. Take the example of the aviation industry and introduce checklists into your life to help you eliminate errors and get things right first time.

Chapter 6
Lifelong Learning Skills

Learning is the most basic of all human drives. It starts before and lasts longer than the sexual drive to procreate. Lifelong learning is continuous education and training throughout life, involving formal, non-formal, and informal methods of learning. It aims to provide the best possible development in personal, social and professional life.

There are many benefits of lifelong learning such as reaching your potential, and keeping up to date. We should take every opportunity during our lives to undertake lifelong learning by continually pursuing learning objectives. To become a lifelong learner you must be totally committed and be enthusiastic about the pursuit of learning, and believe that learning is a journey and not an end in itself.

Successful learners must realise that learning is a lengthy process of four stages that must be gone through before you become competent in your chosen area. You become a competent learner by exploiting your strengths. These strengths are considerable, as it is now believed that you have seven or more potential abilities waiting to be developed, so that you are cleverer than you think. Adult learners have unique needs that must be met. There are social and personal barriers to learning that should be addressed.

Lifelong learning takes place in the workplace, in colleges, libraries, clubs and professional bodies, in the community, and at home. We are all lifelong learners, but some of us are more motivated, organised and purposeful than others. We can be inspired by, and model ourselves on, current and past famous lifelong learners, or closer to home we can be inspired by people we just know and admire.

What is Lifelong Learning?

Lifelong learning is continuous education and training throughout life, using formal, non-formal, and informal methods of learning, with the objective of improving knowledge, skills and competence for personal

WHAT YOU'LL LEARN IN THIS CHAPTER:
- What is lifelong learning?
- Why undertake lifelong learning?
- When should you undertake lifelong learning?
- How do you become a lifelong learner?
- Where should you undertake lifelong learning?
- Who are the lifelong learners?

development or employment. Lifelong learning leads to change, development and a desire to learn more.

Formal learning takes place in education and training institutions, leading to official certificates, diplomas, degrees and post graduate qualifications right up to doctorate level. It also includes the awards of professional bodies, such as accountants, human resource practitioners and engineers.

Non-formal takes place alongside mainstream systems of education and training, but does not lead to formal qualifications. It may be provided in the workplace, or outside work, in voluntary organisations, such as trade unions, charities, community groups, sports clubs, art and literary societies and political parties.

Informal learning is unstructured, unintentional, and unconscious learning that occurs during work, or in collaboration with others. The three most important forms of informal learning are: learning on-the-job, learning from more experienced work colleagues, and working as a team member. Learning from professional journals, networking with others, and through self-analysis and reflection, are other forms of informal learning.

Learning from cradle to grave

Lifelong learning is learning from cradle to grave. It is a way of fulfilling your interests, abilities, ambitions and dreams, throughout a lifetime. It may include work, hobbies, volunteering activities, cultural activities, sports, health and fitness, and formal study. It includes learning about life, rather than just work, and should be more about personal development and satisfaction rather than mere competency in work related skills.

It is continuous improvement brought about through the acquisition of relevant skills, knowledge, and experience. It is concerned with those who finish their education without adequate knowledge and skills for a self-sufficient and successful life, and for those who missed education the first time around. In addition, it is concerned with those who need to update and acquire further education, training and skills for career advancement, personal development, or job changes, throughout their lives.

Lifelong learning is synonymous with self-regulated learning. Self-regulated learners develop the ability to teach themselves, and are self-motivated by the inherent curiosity, excitement, challenge, and enjoyment that learning provides. They accept responsibility for the planning, organisation, time management, and monitoring of their own learning. They proactively seek out learning opportunities and creative solutions to solve everyday problems. They realise that there is always a better, cheaper, faster and smarter way of doing anything, and their aim is to find it. They are passionate in their pursuit of learning.

To survive successfully, in a rapidly changing world, we must keep up to

Inspiration

"We now accept the fact that learning is a lifelong process of keeping abreast of change. And the most pressing task is to teach people how to learn."
Peter F. Drucker

date; otherwise we will mentally stagnate and die. During our life cycle, we will need new knowledge and skills, to deal with the unique challenges and opportunities that each stage brings us. Some of these stages include, leaving full-time education, becoming economically self-sufficient, getting married, becoming a parent, and an active citizen. Each of these stages introduces a continuous sequence of new responsibilities and tasks presenting their own unique learning challenges.

Learning to learn skills include learning maps, speed reading, memory, research, and thinking skills which are dealt with elsewhere in this book. We need to acquire these skills to learn and study effectively and efficiently. The ability to learn, and to go on learning, is now seen as core competency life skills by many firms. We also need to engage in deep rather than surface learning.

Deep versus surface learning

Deep learning is where you learn with comprehension, knowing the what, why and where of things. Deep learning becomes part of who you are. Deep learners are able to view the subject matter as a whole, and see how it relates to other areas. They are able to analyse, synthesise and evaluate information, to make it understandable and pertinent to their needs. Knowledge acquired meaningfully is usually retained longer, facilitates future learning and can be applied in practical situations, and be used in novel problem solving and creative thinking. Surface learning is rote memorisation without any real understanding and so is quickly forgotten.

Why Undertake Lifelong Learning?

There are many benefits of lifelong learning including the challenge of learning, the recognition it brings and the sheer joy of discovery while learning new things. The acronym SARCASM will help you recall some of the more important benefits.

The benefits of lifelong learning
- **S**tructure. If you continually pursue learning objectives you will have a purpose and structure to your life as you undertake new challenges. Some people pursue learning as a leisure pursuit. You will always have something to do as you pursue and acquire your latest skills or knowledge, or as you learn new experiences.
- **A**ctualisation. We all have an innate desire to reach our full potential – to become what we are capable of becoming. We will never know what latent and hidden abilities we have, unless we purposefully go about developing them. We need education, training and practise to bring forth our talents, improve our job satisfaction, increase our self-esteem, and make a worthwhile contribution to a democratic society.
- **R**eputation. Acquiring a formal academic qualification, such as a degree or professional qualification, in addition to fulfilling personal

ambitions, will bring us self-esteem, status and prestige, as well as increased earning power. Acquiring a new skill brings us personal satisfaction, and increased self-worth and confidence. On a broader plane it also enhances social capital because we are equipped to make a greater contribution to society.

- **C**ompetitive. In a rapidly changing world we must keep up to date in order to survive. We must constantly learn, constantly upgrade our skills and knowledge, and constantly adapt to change. A new skill or qualification helps our personal development, increases our added value, flexibility and employability, and may help us progress in our career. The opposite is stagnation and getting stuck in a rut. Remember, learning is an appreciating rather than a depreciating asset, and it will always stand to you no matter where you go in life.
- **A**lzheimer's. This is a disease of mental decline which is associated with old age, but can be acquired even when relatively young. Lifelong learning is said to delay or even permanently defer the onset of Alzheimer's. Generally, lifelong learners enjoy better health, because their high incomes enable them to adopt a more nutritious and healthy lifestyle. In addition, they tend to live more prosperous and longer lives.
- **S**ocial contact. Most of us prefer to learn in groups. Groups provide opportunities for networking and learning from others. We learn from others by sharing knowledge, ideas and expertise. In fact, some lifelong learning is undertaken purely for recreational purposes where the learner learns for 'learning sake,' rather than for career advancement or a financial return. Incidentally sometimes recreational learning can open up career opportunities.
- **M**ain goals. Humans keep committed, motivated, purposeful and mentally alive, by pursuing learning goals throughout their lives. A purpose keeps us interested and engaged with the world around us.

Useful skills for living and working

Most people with a degree, find when they enter the work market they need to top it up with a professional qualification in say law, accountancy, human resource management or marketing. A first degree is no longer sufficient to guarantee a career in the labour market. Postgraduate education is now seen as essential as a means of differentiation, and securing an advantage over other graduates. Thus, if you have a degree in finance, it is probably worthwhile to top it up with a chartered qualification in accountancy or an MBA. In addition, many people change careers a few times during their lifetime, which may create the necessity to obtain a professional qualification in a different field.

Personal development skills you can improve through lifelong learning include interpersonal relationships, communication, influencing, negotiating, writing, decision making and problem solving. Self-improvement should be a continuous process throughout life. Personal development skills are called soft skills, and are just as important to your success in work and in life generally, as hard or technical skills such as computer literacy.

In the home, we need practical everyday survival skills such as money management and budgeting skills, cooking, computer literacy, house-keeping, gardening, painting and DIY skills. We can also develop hobbies such as drawing, crafts, woodworking and photography.

In addition, for a fulfilling and interesting life outside of work, we need to be able to discuss current affairs, and appreciate music, art, literature and architecture. People who are able to discourse on a wide range of topics are seen as attractive for other people to be with, and therefore, make lasting friendships, and are never lonely.

When Should You Do Lifelong Learning?

There are critical stages during our lives when we will need to undertake lifelong learning. These stages include transition from education to work, during periods of unemployment, or when there is a need to update knowledge and skill. Changing jobs, promotions, career breaks and retirement, as well as continuing professional education, also presents opportunities for lifelong learning. Furthermore, during recessionary times it may be a good time to top up with additional qualifications, so that you may be equipped to exploit the opportunities presented when the recession inevitably ends.

Inspiration

"Those people who develop the ability to continuously acquire new and better forms of knowledge that they can apply to their work and to their lives will be the movers and shakers in our society for the indeterminate future."
Brian Tracy

We should undertake lifelong learning every day of our lives for as long as we live. We should use waiting time and commuting time productively, by acquiring new knowledge in subjects that we are interested in. We can anticipate these events and bring a good book along with us for reading and reflection. People studying formal qualifications can use their time productively by bringing stationery cards, with relevant principles and facts, with them for perusal and study, during spare moments of the day. They can also listen to compact discs in their cars, while they are driving to and from destinations.

The dark nights bring opportunities for lifelong learning
Most people think about self-improvement and further study when autumn comes in and the dark nights arrive. This is the time of year when part-time evening degree and professional qualification course are offered in third level colleges. If this doesn't suit, you can do a range of qualifications in your own home through distance learning, and on the internet. People who are very interested in a subject may decide to spend an hour in the morning studying before they go to work. Alternatively, you may be able to fit in an hour at night before you go to bed, or spend some time at the week-ends at your studies.

You need to develop good time management and organisation skills in order to exploit learning opportunities. The greatest enemy to lifelong learning is procrastination, where we have great plans and intentions, but never seem to do something to make them happen. We need discipline, and action plans and schedules to get started.

How To Become A Lifelong Learner

In your quest to become a lifelong learner don't neglect your reading. Reading is one of the best and most flexible and accessible tools of lifelong learning. Reading is a key to expanding your knowledge. Maintain a list of books, articles and papers that you want to read for self-development or to update your technical knowledge. Update this list frequently, and add new material as you discover them. Apply the reading skills covered in chapter 3 to scan the material quickly to determine its value, and to find the material you want. A properly organised and catalogued system of filing can be a great source of reference, when you want to do some research.

Inspiration

"Be a student so long as you still have something to learn, and this will mean all your life."
Henry L Doherty

The journey to lifelong learning
The acronym PRACTICED will help you remember how you can become a lifelong learner.
- **Priority.** Make the practice of lifelong learning a priority in your life. Set aside at least half an hour a day, to build up that knowledge or skill, in the area of expertise that you need to acquire. Nothing will happen unless you make it happen and put in the effort.
- **Reflect.** Reflection is a most important aspect of learning. Think deeply about what you have learnt. Build in review periods into your learning so that you do not forget. Information is quickly forgotten unless reviewed, and skills fall into decay unless practised. Observe how others learn, and model the behaviour of the best learners. Listen to what people have to say, and look for feedback on your performance and behaviour. Don't take criticism personally as it may be a pointer to your shortcomings. Continuous improvement should be your aim as a trigger of self-improvement.
- **Action learning.** We learn best by doing things, and we acquire skill by doing things over and over again. Most skills take a considerable amount of time to acquire and perfect. World-class musicians hone their skills up to eight hours a day. Athletes and footballers constantly practise and have sports psychologists to advise and motivate them. Professional golfers finish 18 holes, and then head to the driving range to practise. Tiger Woods has a coach. So has Rory McIlroy, the current world champion golfer (2012).
- **Curiosity.** A curious mind is a receptacle for learning. The secret of genius is to carry the wonderment of childhood into adulthood. We should be inquisitive and ask questions like how, what, and why, all the time. It is through questions seeking answers that we learn. Develop your powers of creativity by looking for alternative ways to

do things or solve problems. Einstein wisely maintained that asking questions and imagination was more important than intelligence.

- **Teach.** A great way of learning is to teach others as it consolidates and reinforces our knowledge. We can do this by showing other people how to do things, and by demonstrating, coaching and mentoring. Channels used for mentoring usually include a combination of Email, telephone and face-to-face meetings. Mentoring can be a great source of informal and non-threatening support.

- **Insight.** Discovery consists at looking at the same things as everybody else, but seeing something different. Many people saw the apple fall, but it was only Newton through insight and reflection, who discovered the laws of gravity. Similarly, many scientific discoveries have happened through unique insight.

- **Concentration.** We must develop powers of concentration if we want to learn and excel. Concentration is comprehensively dealt with in chapter 2.

- **Exercise.** Build in programmes of exercise into your lifelong learning habits so that you will keep mentally and physically fit. The brain as well as the body thrives on oxygen and proper nutrition.

- **Different learning styles.** There are different learning styles but most of us use a combination of these. Academics have classified learning styles in different ways. One popular method can be recalled by the acronym VAT which stands for visual, audial and tactile. Put simply, we learn by seeing, hearing and doing. Another classification is Activist, Reflector, Theorist and Pragmatist. In other words we do something, think about it, understand it, and then based on our understanding we may do it differently. This is how we learn.

Total passionate commitment

To become a lifelong learner you must be totally committed to, and be enthusiastic about, the pursuit of learning, and believe that learning is a journey and not a destination. As a self-directed learner you must be responsible for your own learning. Only by knowing your shortcomings can you take steps to address them. Plato's ancient advice "Know Thyself" is still relevant today.

You must identify your learning needs, set your own goals, identify human, money and material resources needed for learning, monitor your progress, evaluate learning outcomes at each stage and modify your learning strategies as necessary.

Compare your current skills, knowledge and experience, with your desired level of skills, knowledge and experience. Identify the gap and draw up a learning plan to meet it. For example, if you are weak at public speaking you should avail of every opportunity to improve it by making presentations, getting feedback, addressing your weaknesses, and making improvements for your next event. Learning is a continual process of improvement.

To become a successful lifelong learner you must be self-motivated. You must develop a passion and interest in your chosen subject. This passion is often expressed through a hobby or volunteering work.

The Four Stages Of Learning

Successful learners are aware of the four stages of learning. They realise that learning is a lengthy process that they must go through to become competent performers. It would be foolish to get discouraged, and give up too early on the way to your learning goals. Just like Rome, learners are not built overnight. The four stages of learning are:

1. Unconscious incompetence. You don't know what you don't know. For example, the novice driver, who has never driven, has no idea of the amount of skill involved in driving a car.
2. Conscious incompetence. You know what you don't know. When you start to drive you realise how awkward you are, and this undermines your confidence until you acquire some skill. Driving is slow, but thoughtful and subject to error.
3. Conscious competence. You know how to drive, but you are very conscious of your movements, which are awkward, as you are not proficient yet.
4. Unconscious competence. At this stage you are proficient in driving and can do so without any conscious effort. The driving has become automatic, which means it is more efficient and more effective, consuming less energy. You can drive, converse, and listen to the radio at the same time.

The multi-talented you

You become a competent learner by exploiting your strengths. Previously our intelligence was mainly measured in relation to verbal and mathematical skills. However, Howard Gardner, has discovered that we have many potential abilities. It is now believed that we have at least seven abilities that can be developed, so in fact we are cleverer than we think! People can become lifelong learners, and be very successful in life by developing a single ability, or a combination of abilities.

These seven abilities can be recalled by the acronym SIMILAR:

*   Spatial. People with spatial intelligence are good at identifying and drawing objects, shapes, charts, diagrams, pictures and maps. They can visualise maps in their heads, and have a well-developed sense of direction. To enhance this ability, use learning maps, diagrams, graphs, flow charts, and powers of visualisation. For example, when studying you can summarise your work in the form of learning maps, flow charts and diagrams.
*   Interpersonal. These people are good at interpersonal relationships and understanding the motives of others. They have a good sense of empathy, and get along well with others. They are good at interpreting the nuances of body language, and picking up hidden agendas.

They are good practitioners of office politics. To enhance this ability, get involved in teams, debating societies, teach, coach and mentor others, engage in small talk with shop assistants, and socialise as much as possible.

- **M**usical. Professional musicians have this ability to a high degree. However, most of us with lesser musical ability can exercise this talent by listening to music, developing a sense of rhythm, and singing along to a tune. To enhance this ability, relax to music and study or read to Baroque music playing softly in the background. Inventing jingles and rhymes for critical information will help you remember it better.

- **I**ntrapersonal. People with this intelligence have self-knowledge and understand their own feelings, strengths and weaknesses. Without self-knowledge people often make poor decisions in their personal lives with serious consequences. Pay particular attention to your mistakes, and determine to learn from your experience, so that you do not repeat them in the future. To enhance this ability, reflect on your life's experiences on a daily basis, and record them in a diary. Better still get involved in a learning set that systematically goes through the learning cycle. This includes reviewing and reflecting on actions taken, sharing experiences, drawing conclusions, and trying out new ideas. Meditation and visualisation would strengthen this ability.

- **L**inguistic. These are people who are good at reading, writing, talking, making analogies, debating, and languages. They tend to have a good vocabulary, be fluent speakers and good all-round communicators. Your ability in this area can be developed throughout your life, and into ripe old age. To enhance this ability, learn from books, compact discs, lectures and seminars. Do crosswords and debate issues with friends. Take up part-time lecturing, volunteer to coach or mentor others, and join Toastmasters.

- **A**nalytical. This intelligence is associated with deductive reasoning. It involves the ability to recognise patterns and to work with abstract symbols and geometric shapes. People with this ability are good at logic, problem solving and decision making, and doing maths. To enhance this ability, do mental arithmetic, prepare a cash budget for your personal expenditure, and balance your cheque book. To improve your analytical reading skills, follow the **PEACE** approach which stands for looking for key **P**oints, **E**vidence, **A**ssumptions, **C**onclusions and **E**xamples. This will help you separate facts from fiction, and arrive at sound conclusions based on factual evidence, rather than hearsay and assumptions.

- **R**eflex (physical). This is the physical or tactile intelligence we need to develop proficiency in our skills. Athletes, racing drivers, dancers, mime artists and gymnasts all have this intelligence. Surgeons, and the skilled trades such as carpenters and plumbers, also need this ability. To enhance this ability, take notes, make models, undertake DIY jobs at home, learn on the job and practise your skills in order to become highly proficient. The hands-on approach to work, such as developing PC skills and developing a wide range of skills through job rotation, job enrichment and job enlargement will develop your practical skills. In your social life, playing sport, keeping fit and doing voluntary work of any kind will enhance this ability.

The theory of multiple intelligences highlights the need to recognise and value the diversity of abilities that we have. By developing a variety of approaches to lifelong learning, and by recognising our strengths and weaknesses, our potential for learning and understanding can be enhanced. Some of us may have poor linguistic skills. We may be unable to express something in writing, but may be well able to illustrate it by a drawing or a diagram. Play to your strengths while at the same time addressing your weaknesses.

The Unique Needs Of Adult Lifelong Learners

Research shows that the ability to learn improves throughout adult life. However, to become a successful lifelong learner you must acknowledge that as an adult learner you have unique needs. These include the need for respect, the need for objectives, the need for autonomy and the need that their learning experience is relevant.

The acronym ROAR will remind you of them:
- **R**espect. In a formal learning situation, adults expect that they will be able to express their opinions freely, and that their experience should be acknowledged, respected, celebrated and shared with others. They like to be encouraged to ask questions, exchange views and argue freely. Adults like to be treated like adults and share their life experiences, and learn from others in a supportive and non-threatening learning environment.
- **O**bjectives. The learning experience should be in line with and address their learning needs. Adults are motivated by the desire to fulfil their dreams and achieve learning goals. You should use a wide range of learning methods to support your learning goals, including the internet, reading, observing others, working with challenging and interesting teams, carrying out stretching projects, attending part-time educational programmes and so on.
- **A**utonomous and self-directed. Adult learners like to have control of their own learning, and to participate actively in the learning process. Learners should be able to choose when and how they wish to learn, and at what pace learning takes place. Adults learn by doing, with built in periods for practice, revision and reflection. In a formal learning situation, they prefer to be facilitated and treated like adults, rather than be taught like children.
- **R**elevance. Adults like to use their experience and existing knowledge in the learning process. They like to see the relevance of the learning concepts to their immediate lives. They like to know the reasoning behind the concepts, and how they can apply them to improve their

lives or work. They expect the learning to raise their self-esteem and self-confidence.

Social Barriers To Lifelong Learning

Some people work for companies that lack a culture of learning. They are not encouraged to use their initiative, introduce change, or to train and develop themselves further. In such circumstances, workers may feel alienated from their work, and thus don't view it as a learning and developmental opportunity. Similarly, some people come from families lacking a tradition or culture of learning. This means that they are disadvantaged from the start of their lives, as they haven't been inculcated with a love of learning.

People with third level education and from professional backgrounds, are more likely to become lifelong learners than others without this advantage. It seems the more learning you have the more you want, and the more that you get. This has become known as the "Matthew Effect," named after a biblical verse in the Gospel of Matthew: "For unto everyone that hath shall be given, and he shall have abundance. But from him that hath not shall be taken away even that which he hath." So it seems the rich get richer and the poor get poorer!

People from disadvantaged backgrounds often drop out of education at an early age, and are less likely to involve themselves in lifelong learning. On the other hand, children with well-educated parents, with professional and managerial backgrounds, tend to have better literacy because they are helped and encouraged to learn from an early age. This gives them a head start in education, and motivates them to engage in lifelong learning.

A virtuous circle
Participation in lifelong learning tends to follow closely early success in education. The more education you have the more likely you are to avail of lifelong learning opportunities. However, undertaking one episode of lifelong learning increases the probability of undertaking further episodes in the future. It becomes a self-fulfilling prophecy.

In addition, managers and professional staff in companies are more likely to get further training and development than operatives. One survey found, that skilled workers are six to eight times more likely to receive company training than the low-skilled. For example, in the British National Health Service (NHS), administrative and clerical staff, maintenance and ancillary staff, ambulance support staff, and part-time staff have the least access to training. This means that low-skilled workers are particularly vulnerable if they become redundant, as they lack the flexibility, confidence and resilience that come naturally with higher education and further training.

Inspiration

"You cannot teach a man anything – you can only help him to find it within himself."
Galileo Galilei

133

The size of the company that employs you affects the training opportunities provided. Large companies tend to offer more and better training opportunities than small firms. While small firms generally offer employees fewer workplace learning opportunities, the informal training provided is often just relevant to the company, as it just concentrates on improving job performance. This type of training provides job-specific skills, rather than portable skills and qualifications, which would facilitate the employees' career and job prospects elsewhere.

Barriers of age and disability

Modern information and communications technology (ICT) has created a so called "digital divide." Many people in our society still do not have access to personal computers, nor do they have the skills to use them. Some haven't the financial means to afford technology and broadband access. This means they are excluded from a whole world of e-learning opportunities, social networking, and access to services that the internet provides. Wider access to ICT is needed in libraries, community centres and schools and colleges.

In particular, some older people find it difficult to adapt to the demands of personal computers and the internet. With the trend towards internet shopping and banking, this has put them at a significant disadvantage. There are also age related barriers to lifelong learning with older workers being less likely to be nominated for further training by a company.

People with disabilities may find it difficult to access learning, as our educational and training opportunities are organised around able bodied people without regard to the needs of the disabled. Refugees and asylum seekers may encounter physical, language and cultural barriers when trying to access learning opportunities.

Personal Barriers To Lifelong Learning

Personal barriers include:
- Lack of ambition. Some people lack the ambition or drive to become lifelong learners. They have 'a know enough already attitude,' and don't feel any need to continue with either formal or informal learning. They feel competent at doing their existing job, and have no desire to progress any further. The trouble and challenge involved in learning anything new makes them feel threatened, inadequate, and inferior.
- Responsibility. Some people may not want the responsibility, inconvenience, disruption, and change of lifestyle that comes with promotion, and therefore, see no point in undertaking further learning. Managers who have reached a career plateau may not have the support or incentive to undertake further learning.
- Poor experiences at school. People, who had negative experiences of school and examinations, may not be willing to get involved in fur-

Inspiration

"New information and communications technologies can improve the quality of life for people with disabilities, but only if such technologies are designed from the beginning so that everyone can use them. Given the explosive growth in the use of the World Wide Web for publishing, electronic commerce, lifelong learning and the delivery of government services; it is vital that the Web be accessible to everyone."
President Bill Clinton

ther formal education and training. The teacher may have made them feel stupid and thus demotivated to engage in further education and learning. On the other hand, others when they become adults may view this as a way of compensating for poor earlier school performance, providing them with the incentive to continue learning.

- Poor literacy skills such as an inability to locate, read, comprehend and evaluate information. Acquiring and maintaining literacy and research skills at the highest level, is of prime importance to becoming a successful lifelong learner.

- Life balance. Many people find it difficult to balance family commitment with the demands of their work and formal learning. As they are pressurised for time they feel they don't have the space in their lives for further learning and personal development.

- Fear. Fear of moving out of your comfort zone. We all like the familiar and often feel threatened by change. As one famous writer said: "feel the fear and do it anyway."

- Failure to learn from our mistakes. We learn by correcting inappropriate actions, assumptions, and behaviours. Building on prior learning, and learning from mistakes, will help you grow and develop. Chapter 5 dealt comprehensively with learning from mistakes.

- Inappropriate learning style. Play to your strengths by using your favourite learning style, while at the same time developing the others by combining visual, audial and tactile styles as appropriate. Combining all the styles will make your learning more effective and memorable.

- Negative attitude for learning. You need a growth mindset, rather than a fixed mindset for learning. A growth mindset as explained in chapter 1, means you believe you can grow and develop intellectually, and that you have unlimited potential, provided you are prepared to study and work hard. On the other hand, a person with a fixed mindset believes that their potential is predetermined by their innate intelligence, and that there is nothing they can do about it. These types of people give up before they start because they don't see the point.

Where Does Lifelong Learning Happen?

Lifelong learning happens in the workplace, in colleges, libraries and clubs, in leisure activities and in the community, and at home. In the home we can read self-help books, listen and watch educational compact discs and DVDs, specialist magazines, and watch TV documentaries. Most professional bodies have now mandatory continuing professional education, to update and upgrade our skills.

At work we can learn formally, off-the-job through seminars, courses, workshops and attending colleges. Seminars and conferences provide learning opportunities and the ability to network with colleagues. If time constraints and budgets limit this approach, go on the internet instead and check out available e-learning and webinars. We can learn informally, on-the-job through apprenticeship schemes, induction, shadowing, job

Inspiration

"I am enough of an artist to draw freely upon my imagination. Imagination is more important than knowledge. Knowledge is limited. Imagination encircles the world."
Albert Einstein

rotation, job enlargement, and job enrichment. We can be coached and mentored by more experienced people. Mentors offer personal instruction, guidance and encouragement, and real time immediate feedback.

We can learn through secondments, projects and teams. Secondment to another organisation will broaden your range of skills and experience. Working on challenging projects will stretch you and provide great learning opportunities. Success on a leading edge project will ensure that you are ready for the next big challenge. Travel is a great educator, and working on projects overseas will broaden your horizons, and offer you more challenges than working at home.

Learning in teams is a great way of collaborative learning and developing critical thinking skills. We learn from other team members, by observation, debating, asking questions, and by sharing ideas, knowledge, and expertise.

Learning through information technology

Some companies have provided their own corporate learning centres, providing different types of media to facilitate learning, including access to internet resources, compact discs, DVDs, books and magazines. Other companies show their commitment to lifelong learning by creating lifelong learning accounts for their employees. They fund these accounts with a certain amount of money each year, so that employees can undertake educational or training courses of their choice. These courses need not necessarily be job related, and will follow them if they leave and go elsewhere.

The development of information and communications technology (ICT), now facilitates M-Learning or mobile learning. The availability of smartphones, e-book readers, netbooks, tablets and user friendly applications, is facilitating the rapid adoption of mobile learning for personal development, and in the workplace. People can get short nuggets of learning on a just-in-time basis, by accessing the internet from their hand-held devices, or can download personal development books on their e-book readers for study, as they commute to and from work. Mobile learning now complements the more traditional learning and development options.

Most colleges now provide a vast range of full-time and part-time certificate, diploma, degree, and post graduate courses. These may cater for your personal development needs, or be vocational in nature. They are aimed at novice and mature learners. Some provide distance learning programmes, which can be done over the internet in the privacy of your home, with the minimum amount of travel.

Public and corporate libraries provide great resources for the lifelong learner, and they do so at little or no cost. In addition to books, they may have compact discs, DVDs, newspapers and magazines, and access to internet resources. They also will have a friendly librarian to cater for your lifelong learning needs, and answer your learning queries. If you are researching material, to write an article or book, they are wonderful sources of information and guidance.

A great way to learn new skills and make new contacts is to volunteer for work in local clubs, and community organisation. They are always looking for people to help them and they provide a wide range of sources of learning. They will help you to acquire administration and interpersonal relationship skills, while learning on-the-job.

You can build up resources for lifelong learning at home. Over the years you could build up a personal library of books and other resources in the subject areas that interest you. In addition, if you are connected up to the internet you have access to a wide variety of resources for learning, including Wikipedia, Google Scholar, Onelook (a comprehensive on-line dictionary with pronunciation facilities) and other educational websites.

Continuing professional development

Professional bodies realise the importance of keeping up to date, and have continuing professional development (CPD) for their members. CPD is about providing opportunities for individuals to obtain the knowledge and skills needed to ensure that they remain competent in their role. CPD activities include approved courses, seminars, lectures, conferences, workshops, web-based seminars, and e-learning.

Most professions have now made such training compulsory, if you want to renew your licence to practice such as medical doctors, airline pilots, engineers and accountants. For example, the Institute of Chartered Accountants in Ireland (ICAI) has had mandatory CPD since the 1990s. Chartered Accountants are required to maintain their competence throughout their careers. Participation in CPD programmes run by the ICAI, or other providers, is an important part of expanding knowledge and maintaining competence.

In the case of engineers, half of what they know will become obsolete within five years. In the case of software engineers, it is about half of that time. This emphasises the importance of continuing professional development in keeping current. Lifelong learning and keeping up to date is now a formal part of most professional and occupational training.

Factors Influencing Lifelong Learning In A Corporate Setting

We spend a significant part of lives at work. It is therefore important, that the environment in which employees work is conducive to and supportive of learning. Some multi-national companies, such as General Electric and Motorola, have even considered it worthwhile to set up their own corporate universities.

The following are some of the factors that influence lifelong learning in an organisation:

- Openness. Employees are more likely to engage in lifelong learning where new ideas are encouraged and valued by management. People are encouraged to question why things are done in a certain way and employees are incentivised to develop better, quicker, cheaper and smarter ways of doing work.
- Learning opportunities. Employees are assigned work that stretches and challenges them so that they are continually learning. Jobs are re-designed and enriched to make them more stretching and interesting. Career opportunities are provided for those willing to study further and work hard to achieve them.
- Peer support. There is a culture of collaborative learning rather than competition in the organisation, with co-workers encouraged to share knowledge and expertise, so that people can learn from the experience and encouragement of others.
- High performance expectation. Individuals are held responsible for their own learning, so that learning is seen as an essential ingredient to personal and corporate success.
- Managerial support. Managers act as role models of learning, and make sure that employees who go on training programmes are encouraged to apply the learning to their jobs. New technologies and developments are continually being exploited to improve, methods, systems and procedures.
- Tolerates mistakes. Mistakes should be seen as learning opportunities, and the lessons learnt should be applied on the job. A risk-averse organisation can create fear of failure, encourage conformity and inhibit learning, initiative and innovation.
- Resources. The resources to enable learning such as tools, equipment and on-the-job training, should be provided to ensure that continuous learning and improvement takes place.
- The helicopter viewpoint. Individuals who understand how their jobs relate to other jobs within the organisation, are in a better position to align their personal goals with corporate goals, and therefore, more likely to be better informed and more productive.

Who Are The Lifelong Learners?

We are all lifelong learners whether we realise it or not, but some of us are more organised and more purposeful than others. We should strive for certification, engage in action learning, draw up a personal development plan, evaluate our learning, network, develop a wide range of interests and keep up to date.

The key ingredients for lifelong learning programmes

On a personal level the acronym CAPTURE will help you remember the key ingredients for a personal lifelong learning programme:

- **C**ertification. Most of us like to have official recognition for our learning especially if we want to include it on our curriculum vitae (CV). However, much of our learning is informal, such as learning from work colleagues, but just as useful to our personal development. In addition, skills developed outside of work, such as DIY skills and housekeeping skills such as cooking and budgeting, help us become all rounded people.

- **A**ction Learning. We learn best by doing. This is also called experiential learning, or learning acquired through experience. Unless we are in a deep coma, we cannot but learn as we go through life, giving us an opportunity to apply our skills and learn from others. We are in fact learning biological machines reacting to and continually absorbing information from our environment.

- **P**lan. Although learning takes place unconsciously as well as consciously, nevertheless, we should take every opportunity to formalise and plan our learning. A self-audit, and strengths and weaknesses analysis will identify your learning needs. This can be formally translated into a written learning plan. For the long-term, you can draw up a career plan and personal development plan, setting down your learning objectives for the future. As part of their appraisal system, during which the educational and training needs of employees are discussed, some companies help employees draw up personal development plans to meet those needs. The company facilitates the process of lifelong learning, and may provide the opportunities, but the employee retains responsibility for their own training and development. In this context, it is a good idea for the employee to keep a personal development portfolio, as a record of their learning and development activities including training courses attended.

- **T**raining bodies. Training bodies run courses on a variety of vocational and personal development topics, which will help you to meet your training and development needs. Many employers run courses internally, or send their employees to outside trainers. These are usually funded by the employer. Courses are a great way to keep up to date, meet people, make friends and create networks.

- **U**p-to-date. Keeping up to date in your speciality is a must for any lifelong learner. Skills and knowledge can go quickly out of date, so it is vitally important that you continually keep current in your field, as otherwise you will find yourself passed out by events, and passed over for promotion. Stay in touch with your speciality by reading your professional journal or specialist magazines in your subject each month.

- **R**ange of interests. Lifelong learners keep themselves informed on a wide range of topics, so that they can quickly adapt to different things if the need arises. They do this through reading, reflection and self-education. Being a specialist is fine, but you must also broaden your interests so that you have the flexibility to identify and exploit opportunities if they arise. Most people will have many careers during their lifetime, demanding different knowledge, skills and abilities. Make sure that you don't put all your eggs in the one basket, so that you have a portfolio of skills to exploit opportunities as they arise.

- Evaluation. This should include a needs analysis, to identify your learning and training needs. The needs analysis should be used to help you formulate your learning and training objectives. You should then draw up a learning plan to meet your needs. Finally, evaluation tries to determine if the intended learning or training has worked and produced the desired results. Has your behaviour, performance, knowledge and skill level, efficiency and productivity been enhanced? Lifelong learners are persistent in their learning, and modify their strategies as necessary, to reach their goals and improve their learning.

Facilitators Of Lifelong Learning

We all stand on the shoulders of giants and thus have been helped by those in the past who have made the process of lifelong learning easy for us. It started with oral language and storytelling as a way of passing on culture to future generations. Before printing books were handwritten and unavailable to the masses. Printing then came along and helped anyone with reading skills to be self-taught. Today, information and communications technology have opened up vast stores of knowledge and made it accessible to millions.

Johannes Gutenberg (1398-1468), was probably the original and greatest facilitator for lifelong learning. He is reputed to be the inventor of printing, which enabled education and learning, and the spread of knowledge. He brought learning to the masses by making books cheap and widely available, and so transformed the world, and changed the course of history. He therefore, made possible the spread of information and lifelong learning, which up to that time was confined to those in seats of power, universities, monasteries and the very rich. People with the ability to read could now independently self-educate themselves, and pursue interests throughout their lives.

Charles Babbage (1791-1871), invented the analytical engine which was the precursor of the modern computer. The personal computer, which brought computers into the home, was invented by Dr Henry Edward Roberts (1941-2010), who was an engineer, entrepreneur and medical doctor. He is known as "the father of the personal computer." This was followed by the internet, invented by Timothy John Berners-Lee, which opened up a world of information and learning at a click of a mouse to the masses.

Practitioners Of Lifelong Learning

Teachers, lecturers, writers, scientists, and research academics are examples of modern lifelong learners. Research academics spend their lives formulating novel questions in their area of interest, and seeking solutions through research. Their academic status and worth is determined by the number of research papers they get published, and peer reviewed, in academic journals. They work in a profession where "publish or perish" is the motto. Many continue to learn and research even past retirement, when all external motivators have been removed.

Those who get to the top of their organisations, and become chief executives, usually spend many years learning about the various aspects of the business, such as finance, operations, marketing, human relations, and management. They usually amass experience in these areas on their journey to the top. The basics may be learned in college, but there is no substitute for hands on experience, and the challenge involved in operating at a senior managerial level in a business, making decisions, and learning from feedback on their successes and failures. Their key to development is to acquire broad experience, and to take on more complex responsibilities and challenges, as they progress through their careers. Many chief executives praise the role that mentors played in their development and success.

Famous Lifelong Learners

Famous lifelong learners can act as inspirational role models. Many people have spent all their lives learning, and in the process have made major contributions to knowledge, invention, engineering, medicine, science and business.

Science
Leonardo da Vinci (1452-1519), was the original Renaissance man, and spent his whole life learning and developing his wide range of skills and interests. He was an artist, sculpture, scientist, engineer, and inventor, and is thought to be the greatest genius that ever lived.

Charles Darwin (1809-1882), was a naturalist, geologist, biologist and author, and one of the most influential figures in history. He is famous for his theory of evolution which he expounded in his 1859 book, On the Origin of Species. He was a lifelong learner, and spent his whole life proving his theory of evolution through natural selection. He learned through reading, research, reflection, observation, experimentation, questioning and experience. He came from a wealthy background, which financed his quest for knowledge, in the field of natural science that excited and fascinated him from an early age. Despite poor health during the last 22 years of his life, Darwin continued with his experiments, research and writing, right up to his death.

Gregor Mendel (1822-1884), a monk and contemporary of Darwin, had a lifelong interest in botany and discovered the basic principles of genetics now known as "Mendel's Laws of Inheritance," after experimentation, research, and dedicated hard work. He is an example of a lifelong learner with a passion and enthusiasm for his subject, who showed perseverance in the pursuit of his ground-breaking ideas. His discoveries have revolutionised the cultivation of plants, and the selective breeding of domestic animals for desirable traits. He published his findings in 1865, but they aroused little interest. His ground-breaking research and findings were not understood or appreciated during his lifetime, much to his frustration and disappointment. Like many other great people his work was not recognised until after his death in 1900, when it was rediscovered and acknowledged by other biologists.

Business

Thomas J Watson (1874-1956) was chairman and CEO of IBM. He was a firm believer in lifelong learning, corporate training and leadership development, and set up a formal training organisation in IBM. Engraved on the granite of the training department's lobby were the words: "think," "observe," "discuss," "listen," and "read" which demonstrates how passionate he was about learning. He died in 1956, one of the richest men of his time and was known as the world's greatest salesman.

Richard Branson (born 1950), is an example of a lifelong learner who showed great entrepreneurial flair from an early age, and learned from experience rather than formal schooling. He successfully set up a magazine called Student when only 16. In 1970 he founded a record mail-order business, and in 1972 he opened a chain of record stores. Branson's Virgin brand grew rapidly in the 1980's with Virgin Atlantic Airways, and expansion of his music label. Branson had ideas, worked hard, studied the competition, kept up to date, took action, and learned from his successes and failures. Branson is now a billionaire despite the fact that he has dyslexia, did poorly at his academic studies and left school at 16.

Summary of Chapter Six

Lifelong learning is learning from cradle to grave. Learning should not stop when you leave school or college, but should continue as long as you live. There are many benefits of lifelong learning, including providing opportunities for social contact, and giving a structure to our lives. We should organise our time productively so that we are continually involved in lifelong learning projects, becoming more knowledgeable, improving our learning skills and continually renewing our learning objectives.

To become a lifelong learner you must identify your learning needs, set your learning goals, monitor your progress, and modify your learning strategies as necessary. Lifelong learners should be aware of the four

Inspiration

"Develop a passion for learning. If you do you will never cease to grow."
Anthony J. D'Angelo

stages of learning, so that they anticipate the difficulties involved. They should realise that they are multi-talented, and that during their lives they should try to develop some of their talents. Research shows that the ability to learn improves throughout our lives, and that adults have unique learning needs. There are social and personal barriers to learning which you should identify and overcome.

We all aspire to be lifelong learners, and we should be aware of the key ingredients of a successful lifelong learning programme. We all stand on the shoulders of giants: people in the past who have facilitated the process of lifelong learning and made it easier to do. Teachers, lecturers, writers, scientists, research academics and business people are examples of modern lifelong learners. Famous lifelong learners can act as inspirational role models and motivate us to realise our dreams.

Five Activities to Improve Lifelong Learning Skills

1. Set yourself the goal of continually improving your interpersonal relationships skills, communication, writing, influencing, negotiating, decision making and problem solving. These are the soft skills that will put you on the road to success and keep you there.

2. Identify your learning needs, set your learning goals, plan your learning, monitor your progress, and modify your learning strategies as necessary. A strengths and weakness analysis will help you identify your learning needs.

3. Take responsibility for your own learning. Plan, organise and pursue your own learning goals. If you work for a company with a corporate learning centre make sure you avail of its services.

4. Draw up a personal development plan (PDP), and take the appropriate steps such as undertaking formal and informal learning programmes to meet your objectives. Use your PDP to evaluate and plan your learning.

5. Build up resources for lifelong learning at home. These would include a library of books and audio visual aids such as compact discs and DVDs. Collect and study in particular books, cds and dvds on learning skills such as learning maps, speed reading, memory, concentration and thinking as these will help you become a more efficient and effective learner.

Chapter 7
Memory and Learning

There are four types of memory which can be recalled by the mnemonic WISE: **W**orking, **I**mplicit, **S**emantic and **E**pisodic. To remember something you must register it on your imagination, and transfer it from your short-term to your long-term memory. Memory skills, and in particular mnemonic devices, will help you accelerate the rate at which you absorb new information. There are little tricks you can learn to solve everyday memory problems.

A basic way to improve your memory is through impression, repetition and association. First get a vivid impression of what you want to remember. Repetition will get the information into your long-term memory, and association will link the information to something that is already familiar to you. The law of reversed effort suggests that the harder you try to remember something the less you succeed.

The **PLAN** system of memory is a comprehensive system covering the **P**lace, **L**ink, **A**lphabet and **N**umber rhyme/shape systems. These systems are widely used by memory experts and public speakers. Mnemonic devices, like acronyms, acrostics and rhymes, have been used by students over many years, to help them recall vital information to pass their exams.

You can improve your memory for recalling names by practising the system recommended. Generally, you can improve your memory by practising mnemonic devices, by studying memory books, or by attending memory improvement courses. A wide variety of people can benefit from using memory skills, including actors, lecturers, public speakers, politicians and students. Mnemonists make a career out of using and demonstrating their memory skills.

What is Memory?

Memory is the power to remember and recall events. It is the store of memories that we carry in our heads, and is a critical part of our iden-

WHAT YOU'LL LEARN IN THIS CHAPTER:
- What is memory?
- Why are memory skills important?
- When can I use memory skills?
- How can I improve my memory?
- Where can I improve my memory?
- Who can use memory skills?

tity and life story. Without memory we are nothing. Alzheimer's robs us of our sense of who we are, and transforms us into a near vegetative state. Mnemonic devices are strategies used to enhance memory. The term mnemonic is derived from the name of the ancient Greek goddess of memory called Mnemosyne. Mnemonic literally means to aid the memory. The types of memory we have can be classified and easily recalled by the mnemonic **WISE**, which stands for **W**orking, **I**mplicit, **S**emantic and **E**pisodic.

Working memory

Working memory is our short-term memory (STM). STM is the amount of information you can recognise and recall after a single presentation without practise. It enables you to link new ideas with existing knowledge or experience, and generate completely novel ideas. Like long-term memory (LTM), interference or lack of attention, seems to be the prime cause of forgetting in STM. The classic example of STM is when you phone a new number. You look up the number and hold it in your memory for just as long as it takes to dial the number. In the meantime, if you are distracted, it is very likely that you will have to look up the number again and recommence dialling.

Inspiration

"The one who thinks over his experiences most, and weaves them into systematic relations with each other, will be the one with the best memory."
William James

Some people refer to STM as the 'blackboard of the mind.' Others compare it to random access memory (RAM), the working memory in a personal computer. If you turn the computer off the data in RAM is lost. Similarly, if you are involved in an accident, and you are knocked unconscious, you will have no recollection of what happened to you immediately before the accident. The importance you place on something, your level of concentration, and the amount of rehearsal, organisation and elaboration you do, determines whether or not it eventually gets into your LTM. The hippocampus is the part of the brain involved in turning short-term memories into long-term memories.

STM decays rapidly without rehearsal. Miller's law of memory maintains that the capacity of STM is between 5 and 9 items of information, and lasts for no more than 30 seconds, unless it is rehearsed. When designing a memory cue it is important to keep this fact in mind, as if this range is not adhered to it could make the memory cue ineffective. However, the capacity of memory can be extended if you are astute enough to group or chunk the information. For example, a memory span of 7 letters can be increased to 35, if the letters form seven five-letter words.

Therefore 'chunk' the learning points into related groups of between 5 and 9 items. The isolated words can be easily remembered, if you organise them into a meaningful sentence, or a little story. Whole areas of a topic can therefore be recalled quite easily. In memorising, say a definition, the central part requires more attention than the two extremes. So make the central part unique and outstanding, and you will remember it better. Better still, if you emotionalise the content you will engrave the content on your memory. The amygdala is the part of the brain involved in the processing of emotional events.

Implicit memory

Implicit memory is called procedural memory and is part of our LTM. This is the memory for skills, abilities, competencies, routines or procedures – things that you do unconsciously without really remembering how. As I'm typing this into my personal computer, I'm using procedural memory. I remember where the key strokes are, without consciously looking, from years of practise. Implicit memory is thus our memory for automatic responses, such as walking, driving, cycling, typing, tying our shoelaces, and brushing our teeth. Much of our knowledge started off as explicit learning, such as language, but over time, through practise and use, it became implicit. Barring some major physical or psychological disability, until we die we will remember how to walk, pick up a glass and drink, or sign our name.

Semantic memory

Semantic memory is our memory for languages, information, rules, principles, facts, concepts and general knowledge. It is like a vast encyclopaedia stored inside our brain, and helps us navigate around and make sense of the world. It is part of LTM. It helps us to remember the countries of the world, and the capital cities of those countries. For example we know that London is the capital of England, that Dublin is the capital of the Republic of Ireland, that Washington is the capital of the USA, and that Paris is the capital of France.

Vocabulary is a type of semantic memory, as it helps us read, write, talk and think effectively, and to identify everyday objects and actions. It helps us categories things as plants or animals, and the meaning of the red and green signals on traffic lights. The deeper the mental processing used when learning a word, the more likely it is that we'll remember it. For example, creating a mental image of a word and linking it to other words that are familiar to you, are more likely to enhance memory and learning than just rote repetition.

Episodic memory

Episodic memory is our memory for autobiographical details, and specific personal historical events such as our first day at school. It is part of LTM, can be recalled quickly, and gives us our sense of identity, and self-awareness. Books have been written, and films have been made, about people who lose their autobiographical memory, raising fascinating questions about identity and personality. When we reminisce about our childhood we are using episodic memory. This is the memory evoked by photos from the family album about treasured memories, and old sentimental possessions which act like mnemonic devices, recalling milestone events of personal significance, and meaningful stories in our lives.

When I recall the first time my father took me to see my favourite soccer

Inspiration

"Intellectual growth should commence at birth and cease only at death."
Albert Einstein

team, Manchester United, playing at Old Trafford, I am using episodic memory. In addition, personal recollections of your first day at work, your wedding day, and the birth of your first child are calling upon episodic memory. In many societies, storytelling and the oral tradition as passed on through the elders, is an example of cultural episodic memory. Storytellers over aeons have used tricks like rhythm and rhyme to help them remember vast quantities of information to pass on their traditions and culture.

All of the types of memory discussed above are retrospective memory, because they recall already acquired knowledge. On the other hand, prospective memory helps us remember things that we plan to do in the future, for example, a meeting we have to attend to-morrow, a purchase we intend to make or a friend we intend to see.

Figure 12
Types of Human Memory

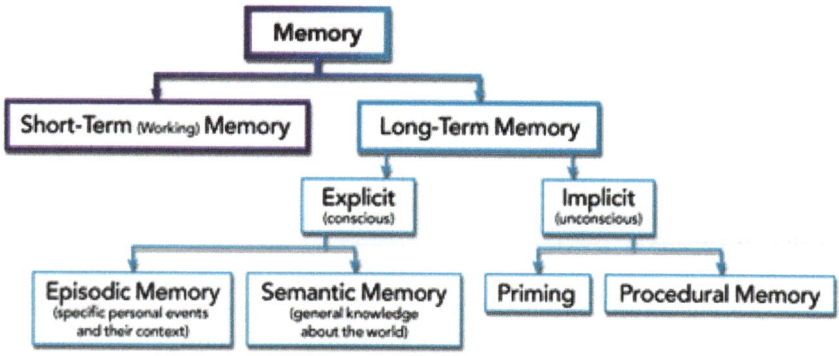

Short-Term To Long-Term Memory

The three Rs of memory are Reception, Retention and Recall. GIGO is a well-known acronym used in computer circles – 'garbage in, garbage out.' The same idea can be used in learning and memory. Obviously, to remember something you must register it on your imagination, and transfer it from your STM to your LTM. Sometimes we fail to register information because we are preoccupied with our thoughts, or get distracted by other issues.

Constantly reflecting and thinking about your subject will help the process of registration take place in memory. It will ensure that the information is retained in your LTM. What you are doing, of course, is overlearning the information. Recall is the ability to retrieve information when needed. When you read, use your vivid imagination to make the written information memorable. Written words are just symbols and in themselves are dead. The author had pictures in his head before writing the words, and so you must transform these words back into active pictures when you read. This process will imprint the information on your imagination, and make it easier to recall what you have read.

Why Are Memory Skills Important?

Memory skills, and in particular mnemonic devices, will help you acceler-ate the rate at which you link and absorb new information. They will help you to solve problems more logically and effectively, by linking new ideas to existing information and experience. This is in contrast to rote learning, which emphasises memorisation of specific information through sheer repetition without examining relationships within the material. Creating mental images of new material, making inferences, and drawing networks of relationships and associations all increase learning. Using mnemonics will improve our LTM.

Without memory you could not function as a normal human being. With-out an autobiographical memory, you would have no history of who you were, who your family were, where you came from, and how you lived in the past. Without this information it would be impossible to socialise and relate to other people. It is your ability to remember names and faces, and put them in context, that facilitates the social process.

Mnemonic Devices Help Learning

Without memory you could not learn and remember information, laws, formulas, facts, concepts, and lines in a poem or play. You would lack the span of attention to follow directions or follow a storyline. It would be im-possible to get a basic education, and study for degree and post-graduate qualifications. Mnemonic devices are now used extensively, when learn-ing law, social science, economics, literature, management, engineering, science, foreign languages and dramatics.

Actors usually develop their own memory systems for remembering lines, which usually make use of memory cues or mnemonic devices. Pub-lic speakers, debaters and politicians also use mnemonic devices, to help them remember their speeches, without relying too much on notes. Some college lecturers use learning maps to research and prepare their lectures. Many use memory aids to help them make their lecturers more natural and free flowing, without constant reference to notes.

Without memory you would not be able to engage in personal develop-ment opportunities. In a career you need to learn and remember new knowledge and skills if you are to progress. You need a good memory to expand your vocabulary by committing new words to memory, and by integrating these words in your everyday writing and conversation. An improved memory saves time, lowers stress and enriches your speaking skills, when making everyday conversation or formal presentations.

Inspiration

"Memory is the moth-er of wisdom."
Aeschylus

Memory Skills And Work

In the work context you need different types of memory to be successful including procedural, semantic and conceptual memory. Companies are run through rules, regulations, policies, systems, and procedures. Systems are supported and implemented through detailed procedures. Procedures are step-by-step instructions to perform a particular task. They must be done in a specific sequence in order to achieve a particular outcome. Organisations have numerous systems, and thousands of procedures that employees must learn, remember and follow habitually on a daily basis.

These procedures range from issuing invoices, making payment, and handling customer queries, to answering the phone. Most procedures are now computerised, so that employees must be familiar with the software that operates the systems, as well as being able to use a computer. Procedures in an average business include stock control and purchasing, debtors control and sales, and creditors control and payments. The more quickly and effectively employees can learn, memorise and operate the procedures, the better run and more efficient the organisation.

You need semantic memory to be successful at work. This is the memory you need for facts, jargon, terminology and acronyms, which you need to learn and memorise, to work effectively and efficiently in your daily conversations with work colleagues. You often need to memorise frequently used phone numbers, product names, codes and ranges. You need to memorise organisation charts and the names of the people who occupy the positions in the company. In everyday business you need to be able to remember the names of suppliers and customers.

You need conceptual memory for strategic thinking and problem solving. Problem solving is any activity that involves original thinking to develop solutions for unique problems, or develop new products or services. Employees need to engage conceptual knowledge when they are confronted by a unique situation needing prior knowledge, concepts, principles, theories or original thinking to solve.

Original thinking and successful problem solving creates the greatest added value to an organisation, and the greatest satisfaction for the employee who solves it. The creation of new approaches to doing business, brainstorming novel ideas, or the development of new engaging methods of advertising, are just some of the ways that drawing on conceptual memory can pay dividends.

Solving Everyday Memory Problems

Did you ever forget where you put your keys, forget a friend's name, or have no idea why you're standing in front of the refrigerator? Then read on! The following are everyday memory problems and suggestions on how to solve them:

Keep appointments

Remembering intentions is much more difficult than remembering things that have happened because we lack retrieval cues about future events. We all forget to keep appointments or do things from time to time. Jog your memory with visual cues. If you want to remember your appointment with the doctor, put your pill bottle near your cereal bowl. Better still, put the appointment in your diary, and adopt a routine of reviewing it every morning. If you want to remember to take your brief case to work in the morning, place it just inside the front door before you go to bed at night.

 If you are going away for an overnight stay, and you want to make sure that you don't forget your suitcase, pack it the night before, and place it near the hall door. To remember to bring all you need for your overnight stay, have a list of things to take with you stuck prominently on the inside of the case. Visual cues may be just 'post-it-notes,' stuck in strategic places around the house, in the bathroom or office that you are certain to see. The more eccentric the cues the better, as their uniqueness will remind you exactly what you want to remember.

Make lists

Lists can be prioritised, ordered and categorised to suit your purpose. The act of writing will engage your visual and tactile memory, so that you will remember better. So start each day with a list of things to be done. Strike off the items from your list as you complete them, as this will give you a sense of achievement and motivate you to continue. Keep the list in the same place, such as attached to your calendar or diary, or on your desk. Also make lists for long-term projects for self-improvement, such as countries, cities and famous sights you want to visit, books you want to read, subjects you want to study, documentaries and films you want to see, or educational audios you want to listen to.

Mislaid things

Consider all the time and effort you waste, just looking for things that you have mislaid, and can't find. Be organised! It's worth keeping the old adage in mind 'A place for everything and everything in its place!' So have a designated location for everything, and put things back in their designated place. You won't mislay your keys, if you keep them hanging up or located in the same place. Similarly, you won't mislay your spectacles, if you always keep them in the same spot when you are not using them.

You can always use a customised string or chain, available from your optician, so that your spectacles are permanently tied around your neck. This will prevent you putting them down at a checkout payment point, or coffee table, and walking off without them. Another option is to keep a spare set of spectacles in a specific location, like in your car or desk at work, as a backup.

If despite everything you mislay something, think back and retrace your steps to where you last had the item. Try to visualise what you were doing the last time you used the item. Look in the usual places you might have left it. If the last thing you were doing was washing dishes, then this might remind you that the thing you're looking for is next to the sink.

A desk bureau with designated drawers and pigeonholes will help you keep organised for paying your household bills. For example, one drawer could be reserved for your chequebook and bank statements, while another might be for insurance policies. One pigeonhole could be for invoices awaiting payment, while another could be for invoices recently paid.

Most stationery stores stock all kinds of organisers, including cardboard boxes, plastic bins, folders and files that will help keep you organised. Hardware stores stock little plastic bins that will keep your nails, screws and bits and pieces organised, if you like to do some home improvements. A tool box will help keep your tools organised so that you can find them when you need them. Some people are very organised at work, but fail to apply the same principles to their home life.

Forgetting where you parked your car

This can happen quite easily in a large shopping centre car park. People are often distracted and preoccupied with other thoughts when they park their car, and hence the problem. To counteract this tendency, be very conscious and attentive of your surroundings when parking your car. Some car parks have numbered colour coded isles, and you should mentally note these, and where the car is located within the isle. Take notice where you have parked the car, in relation to landmarks, such as prominent buildings, or the entrance to the shopping centre.

Similarly, if you park in a multi-storey car park, make sure you note the floor number your car is parked on. Within that floor you should note which row it is parked on, and relate this to the shopping centre entrance point. If you park your car in an airport car park, write down the number of the section you're parked at on a piece of paper, and also take a mental note of it in case you lose the piece of paper.

You might like to use the peg rhyme system, discussed later on, to convert the level numbers into words that you can then relate to the location of your car. For example, if you parked your car on floor five, this could be converted into 'hive.' You could then imagine returning to your car which is surrounded by bees, emanating from a hive above your car. You could use a similar method to remember where you parked your car at the airport.

Establish a routine

Habits and routines are difficult to forget. Establish a routine for the more mundane and regular things that you do, until they become habits. A routine allows you to do things automatically without thinking. Routines should follow the same sequence, and be done in the most logical and efficient order. Before you go to bed at night, you may have a routine to shut the front gate, lock the front and back doors, set the house and smoke alarm, check that the television and other electrical appliances are switched off, that all internal doors are closed, and that all the lights are turned off. Similarly, when you get up in the morning you may follow the routine of putting on the radio, showering, brushing your teeth, dressing, combing your hair and so on.

Routines minimise effort, while at the same time ensuring that everything gets done in an efficient manner, and nothing is overlooked. Forgetting to pack everything before you leave a hotel room is a very common experience. Some common items left behind include shoes, mobile phone chargers, and electric shavers. To avoid this operate a routine before you depart. Check the bathroom, bed, wardrobe, tables, drawers, and the areas not in your line of sight, before you leave. This simple routine may save you a lot of potential hassle later on.

Leaving briefcases or shopping bags behind
This may happen in a coffee shop or pub after a day's work or shopping. It is more likely to happen when the contents are out of your line of sight, and not of great significance. If you keep your briefcase or shopping bag near you, or in your line of sight all the time, rather than under a table or seat, you are less likely to leave it behind. It's often a case of out of sight, out of mind! Paying more attention when putting your briefcase or shopping bag down, and mentally noting what you have done will help you remember. If you're desperate you could tie the briefcase to your wrist!

Forgetting to send birthday or Christmas cards
The easiest way not to forget is to keep a list, make a note in your diary, or compile a database of names on your computer. You should keep a permanent record of all the people who send Christmas cards to you, so that you can return the compliment. There is nothing more embarrassing than to forget to send cards to people who have sent you cards, especially close friends and relatives. Whatever you do, don't forget to send your partner, husband or wife a birthday card!

Locking your key inside your car
Unfortunately this is a very common memory problem. Some people may absentmindedly put the car keys on the seat, while they are attending to something else, and then forgetfully lock the door. Other people leave their keys in the ignition and close the car door. I have known people who put their car keys in the boot, while they were unpacking, and then locked the booth with the car keys inside.

People have been known to exit from their car and lock it, and then put their car keys in their jacket or overcoat pocket. Because it is a warm day they decide to return to their car to take their coat off. They open the car boot and then absentmindedly put the car key back into the jacket or overcoat pocket, before taking it off and depositing the coat in the boot. They then shut the boot and their problem begins.

There are a few solutions to this problem. Keep a spare key with you at all times in case the worst comes to the worst. Establish a routine that you always take the keys out of the ignition before you exit the car. Never put your key on a seat or anywhere else. Never put your keys in your jacket pocket, and never deposit your jacket or overcoat in the car or boot. Always put your car keys in your trouser pocket or purse. In a worst case scenario, maybe the police or Automobile Association may be able to help you gain access to your car.

Forgetting what you went into a room for

This is a common memory problem. To counteract this problem, concentrate, stay relaxed and don't be distracted by other thoughts. Think back to where you started out from, and mentally rehearse the steps you took to get there. If this doesn't work, physically revisit the room where you began, and retrace your steps. As a routine you should get into the habit of forming strong visual associations between your goal and your destination. So if you went into the kitchen, with the intention of getting some paper, visualise the contents of the kitchen wrapped in paper. When you go into the kitchen this should trigger the link, and remind you that you are there to get some paper.

When Can I Use Memory Skills?

Memory skills can be used at any time in the home, at study or at work. In the home, you can use memory skills to help you remember the list of chores, or do-it-yourself jobs, you plan to do around the house. Draw up a list and cross off the items as you attend to them. Put the list in a prominent place, so that you are constantly reminded about what you need to do.

At school, and during their everyday activities, students should be introduced to the many memory devices available, such as mnemonics and learning maps, so that they are aware of them from an early age. They are then likely to use them when they go to college. Research consistently shows that students who use these memory aids do better in examinations than students who don't use them.

Many students at college now use learning maps as a matter of course for note taking and review purposes. Mnemonic devices are used extensively by medical students when studying, and they are also popular with psychology, education, business and even accountancy students.

At work many managers use mnemonic devices such as learning maps

Inspiration

"The secret of a good memory is attention, and attention to a subject depends upon our interest in it. We rarely forget that which has made a deep impression on our minds."
Tryon Edwards

for taking minutes of meetings and for planning their presentations. Others use acronyms, acrostics and rhymes to help them remember appointments and phone numbers. Obviously, the range of applications during the work day depends on the creativity of the manager and the need to remember.

Training officers use learning maps for researching and planning their presentations. During the presentations they can use mnemonic devices to help them recall the names of course participants. Many use acronyms to organise key points so that course participants can readily recall them, and apply them to their work situations when they return to the job.

How Can I Improve My Memory?

This section recommends practical approaches to help you remember things better, especially in the areas that concern you most – work, study, socialising, and personal development. It will show you how to use mnemonic devices, such as acronyms, acrostics and rhymes, for organising key points that you want to memorise, and recall instantly. Mnemonic devices are widely used by students and lecturers, in the fields of medicine, psychology and education. People remember better with mnemonics they create themselves, rather than ones provided by others for them.

Inspiration

"Memory is the diary that we all carry about with us."
Oscar Wilde

Knowledge of the laws and principles of a good memory will help you use your memory more efficiently and effectively. The three basic laws of memory, from which all other principles are derived, are impression, repetition and association (IRA). This is my first easily remembered acronym, which you should now commit to memory through rehearsal, organisation and elaboration.

Impression
Form a deep vivid impression of what you want to remember. To do this you must concentrate and focus your attention on the material you are trying to remember. A camera won't take good pictures in poor or foggy lighting conditions. Similarly, your mind will not register and remember impressions, when there is vagueness and inconsistencies in your mental ideas of a subject. Impression is, therefore, the ability to imagine or picture what you want to remember in your mind's eye. Reading is a left-brain function – the side of the brain specialising in logic, words, numbers and language. To make your reading more memorable, you must also engage the right side of the brain, specialising in creativity, imagination, colour and daydreams.

The more senses you engage when learning, such as visual, hearing and touch, the greater the impact on memory. Visual for pages, diagrams, cartoons and pictures. Use the sense of hearing for paraphrasing, recitation, reading aloud, and listening to recordings. Touch for note taking and compiling learning maps. Forming mental images, or drawing diagrams, flow charts and learning maps of topic key points, will help you deeply understand them, and imprint them on your brain for future recall. Note taking uses the left or language side of your brain, while imagination uses the right or visual side of your brain. Consciously using both more than doubles your ability to recall information.

Repetition

The second law of memory is repetition. Muslim students memorise the Koran – a book as long as the New Testament – by repetition. Repetition is how we learn the multiplication tables at school, and also how we learnt the alphabet. Psychologists call this overlearning. The learning is embedded in our LTM. This is the approach to adopt when learning key points and important definitions, say for that critical presentation at work, or when preparing for that vital college or professional exam. Build up your database of key points and concepts in your topic, and you can expand on this yourself.

When using the repetition technique keep the following points in mind:
- Rote learning is not recommended on its own, but should always be combined with understanding the material you are committing to memory.
- Space out your repetition for better recall. Go over it a few times, then drop it; come back later and go over it again. Reviewing at intervals in this way, will help you memorise in about half the time it takes at one sitting.
- Review is particularly important within 24 hours, and less frequently thereafter for information that you want to remember.

The MUD principle

Repetition may get information into your LTM, but for deep learning you need more than repetition. You also need reflection and elaboration such as suggested below. The MUD principle will help you remember the ingredients for deep learning. **MUD** stands for **M**emory, **U**nderstanding and **D**oing.
- Memorising through repetition is but one of the ingredients of effective memory, but you need more if you want deep and lasting learning to occur. The others are attention, association, review, paraphrasing and self-testing.
- Understanding involves questioning, comparing, contrasting, analysis, synthesis, problem solving and reflection. All of these assist deep rather than shallow learning.
- Doing involves some sort of physical activity, with practice sessions to achieve perfection. So organise your material, be thorough, and make sure that you understand what you are committing to memory. Without practise your memory for events will quickly decay.

Association

The third law of memory is association – linking new information with knowledge and experience that you already have. Wide and extensive reading will provide a sound foundation on which additional knowledge can be built. It will increase your fund of knowledge; give you greater insight and understanding, and ability to make meaningful associations. If you are studying for professional or post-graduate examinations, relate them to your work, and try to integrate them with your everyday experience.

Apply the questioning technique to build up the necessary links, and to engrave the subject matter on your memory. Why is this so? How is this so? When is it so? Where is it so? Who said it? What else could be deduced? The brain is the only organ that expands through use. The more it is used, the more memory associations are formed. The more associations are formed, the easier it is to remember previously acquired information, and also to form new links.

According to Dominic O'Brien, a former 8 times world memory champion, visualisation and association are at the heart of a perfect memory. Lists of words can be easily remembered if they are linked together in the form of a story. It seems our minds are naturally receptive to the imagery suggested by stories.

The four laws of association

There are four laws of association that you may find useful in your quest for a good memory:

1. The first is the law of similarity, which states that two ideas may be associated if they resemble each other. For example, people with the same name or with similar features or characteristics. This law suggests that comparing information is an effective way of learning. You may remember a number, if it is similar to your address, telephone number, date of your birthday, or the date of a well-known historical event.

2. The second law of association is the law of contrast, which states that two ideas may be associated if they contrast with each other. For example, fat and thin, tall and short, black and white, good and evil, day and night. This law suggests that contrasting information is an effective way of learning.

3. The third law of association is the law of contiguity, which states that two ideas may be associated if they have occurred together. For example, if two important events happened on the same day, or near enough dates, one may be recalled by reference to the other. We all probably know that the First World War started in 1914. Frederick Winslow Taylor, known as the Father of Scientific Management, died the following year in 1915. Connect the two events and you can easily recall the date of Taylor's death. Similarly, Woodrow Wilson was the

US President in 1918. The First World War ended in 1918, and Wilson helped to draw up the peace treaty that determined the shape of the post-war-world. It is easy to remember significant historical events that coincide with your date of birth.

4. The fourth law of association is the law of cause and effect. If you can identify a cause it will help you recall the effect and vice versa. A cause is something that makes something else happen. An effect is what happens as a result of the cause. To find the cause, ask the question 'why did it happen?' In science, Isaac Newton's third Law of Motion, states for every action, there is an equal and opposite reaction. For example, if you were to hold your hand over a candle flame (the cause), the effect would be that your hand would get burnt and cause pain (the effect). In sentences, connecting words like because and therefore are used to show the link between cause and effect. In everyday life the law of cause and effect is succinctly stated in the sayings: 'you reap what you sow,' and 'what goes around comes around.'

Laws Of Memory – FIBRES

Brain cells, when viewed under a microscope, look like tiny octopuses with tentacles or fibres emanating from them. These in turn connect to other fibres, creating an elaborate network of neurons, dendrites and synapses. This should help you link the acronym **FIBRES** with memory. FIBRES is an elaboration of the three basic laws of memory discussed above, and stands for **F**requency, **I**ntensity, **B**elonging, **R**ecency, **E**xpectation or effect (Pygmalion) and **S**tand out (unique and outstanding).

Frequency
Frequency means exactly the same as repetition. The more often you learn something the better you understand and recall it. One of the most startling discoveries is that we forget 80 per cent of what we read within 24 hours, unless we review. This natural process of memory decay happens to us all. To prevent this, review critical information within 24 hours, and thereafter working to a systematic review plan of your choice, if retaining information is important to personal development, or your career.

The best way to commit a verse to memory is by the progressive part method. The learner adds a new line while continuing to rehearse the other lines. This is the standard way of learning poetry at school. For example, learn line one, and then learn lines one and two. When you have memorised lines one and two, you tackle lines one, two and three, and so on. Such a procedure ensures:
• That your STM is not overloaded.
• The practise and retention of earlier lines, otherwise forgotten through interference.

The progressive part method should be preceded by the whole method for best results. Belonging or the 'whole method,' is the mind's preference for dealing in the larger natural systems. So get an overview of the material first before using the progressive part method. Rote memorisation should always be combined with understanding for deep learning. Rote is shallow encoding, and focuses on the superficial aspects of words, such as the number of vowels and the sound or structure of words. Deep encoding focuses on drawing connections between words, and other information already in memory. Deep encoding takes more effort but memory lasts longer and recall is better.

Intensity

Intensity, motivation, interest and confidence are all interlinked. Each re-inforces the other. The more success you have with memory tasks, the more confident, self-assured and motivated you become. Similarly, the more interest and enthusiasm you have about a topic the better your recall. For example, a teacher may think a pupil is stupid and indifferent at studies, and yet the schoolboy may have an encyclopaedic capacity to recall the names all the players in his favourite football team, the positions they play in, what matches they won, who they played against and who scored the vital goals. He has no problem recalling all the teams in the league and the names of the more prominent players. The reason for this amazing feat of memory is that soccer has fired his imagination, enthusiasm and interest.

Mediocre performers at work are often people whose interest has not been emotionally engaged by the job. In their private lives they are often extremely passionate about their hobbies, such as philately, coin collecting, and photography, bird-watching, fishing or motor sports. In these specific areas they often display high levels of knowledge and expertise, combined with an encyclopaedic memory.

However, for whatever reason, their jobs have failed to excite their interest, and capture their imagination, to the same degree. In reality it is hard to have an intense interest in all aspects of your job, nevertheless be aware of the intensity factor, and try and build up enthusiasm and interest for the company you work for, its history, products or service and the different functional areas. Keep up to date about current business issues, particularly those related to your own company. It will pay dividends in the end!

Belonging

Belonging is sometimes called the 'holistic' method. In business we have the helicopter factor and this is a similar concept. The mind likes to have an overview of a topic before it starts filling in the details - just as we tackle a jigsaw puzzle. We study the illustration, and then start from the outer edges and work our way inwards. We are using an overview approach; going from less detail to more detail, until an unstoppable momentum, and a critical mass is built up. Psychologists call this the 'Gestalt' approach. Learning maps discussed in a previous chapter are an application of this idea.

Recency/primacy

Recency means we remember better what we did last, that is, most recently. We forget 50 per cent immediately of what we read, and 80 per cent within 24 hours, unless we review. Primacy means we remember better what we did first, rather than what come subsequently. We remember our first day at school, our first day at work, and our first love affair and so on. This is the novelty concept, and the reason why as a child you learnt so well, as most things were new to you.

When you go to a new country for the first time, your senses are aroused by the novelty of your surroundings. Similarly, when you are reading a non-fiction book for the first time, consciously make as much use of the novelty concept as possible. The recency/primacy principle suggests the more starts and finishes in a reading or study period the better. Of course, after each reading period of approximately one hour, take a five minute break. This will consolidate and improve your recall of the material read. Psychologists have found that immediately after taking a break is the time when your memory is best. This is called the reminiscence effect. Frequent breaks allow you to take advantage of this phenomenon.

Expectation or effect

The Pygmalion effect suggests that you live up to the expectations of significant others, and your own expectations. Educationalists and management consultants have found that praise produces greater effort than criticism. A little praise now and again will enthuse and energise your performance and reinforce your will to succeed. By the way, don't wait around for other people to praise you. Self-stroking or praising yourself is a type of autosuggestion, and is almost as effective as praise from others. It builds up your self-esteem and powers of positive thinking.

Positive self-belief in the power of memory will also help you. Affirm to yourself each day that you have a strong active reliable memory. If you have a motivational manager at work, who treats you as an intelligent, mature and able person, and sets you high standards of performance, you are likely to live up to that manager's expectations. Similarly, if you have high expectations for yourself you are more likely to live up to them. This is a type of 'self-fulfilling prophecy,' and McGregor's management 'Theory Y' philosophy, in action

Stand out (outstanding)

In psychology this is called the Von Restorff effect. If you want to recall something, make it unique and outstanding. If you dramatize, personalise and emotionalise something you are more likely to remember it. Pop stars often dress in an outrageous fashion or do outrageous things to attract attention and publicity. Likewise you can make things novel and unusual to make them more memorable.

Think of the acronym MUSE, previously mentioned, so that you put Movement, Unusualness, Slapstick and Exaggeration into your mental images. In other words, if you want to remember something, visualise it moving in an unusual context, using vivid imagination, colour, exaggeration and humour. This will make the information more memorable. In Greek mythology a Muse was one of the nine goddesses inspiring learning and the arts.

Law of Reversed Effort

This is another law which is worth knowing about. The law of reversed effort is a slightly tongue-in-cheek description of how, sometimes when you are trying very hard to remember something, the more you try to remember it the less you succeed. Try to become relaxed, as anxiety blocks memory. If you worry about an elusive name, word or tune, it will only make it more difficult for you to remember. However, if you dismiss it from your mind, and start to do other things, the chances are that what you are trying to remember, such as a name, will unexpectedly jump into your mind. Another approach is to go through the alphabet, trying each letter in turn. The answer will often pop into your mind when you least expect it.

In an exam situation a memory block can be quite costly, in the form of precious and critical marks lost. I have experienced the phenomenon myself. Soon after coming out of the exam hall, when the stress of doing the exam had gone, the information I needed popped into my head. Alas too late as far as earning vital marks is concerned! Blocking can be one of the most frustrating memory glitches. Memory devices, such as mnemonics, will help you overcome memory blocks, and help you remember the order of information which is sometimes necessary for exams.

Ironic effects of mental control

On a similar vein, sometimes when you try to control your thoughts the opposite happens. For instance, when you try to fall asleep quickly, you actually stay awake longer. When you try to relax, you often get more anxious, when you try too hard to be happy you become sad, and when you try to suppress a thought, it becomes more intrusive. Psychologists refer to the phenomena as the ironic effects of mental control.

In sport overthinking may cause the brain to freeze, especially during pressure moments such as taking a penalty kick. Even though a rugby player may have practised the same penalty kick successfully hundreds of times, if they begin to consciously think about the magnitude of the moment, their autopilot breaks down, worry takes over, and they miss the kick. This is not a problem with Ireland's international rugby player, fly-half Ronan O'Gara. He is the highest point's scorer for both Munster and Ireland, and rarely misses a penalty kick, and can be relied upon to deliver even in the most pressurised moments and awkward positions.

Inspiration

"What we learn with pleasure we never forget."
Alfred Mercer

161

PLAN system of memory

The PLAN system of memory is a short insightful acronym which will give you an easy, practical and comprehensive overview of everything you need to know to improve your memory.

PLAN stands for:
* **P**lace system
* **L**ink system
* **A**lphabet system
* **N**umber rhyme, number shape and number phonetic systems

I'm not suggesting that you learn all of these systems of memory. But it is an advantage to be aware that these systems exist, and have the opportunity to use some or all of them if you wish to do so. However, if one of these systems happens to suit your learning style, you should use it to improve the effectiveness of your memory. It is the way these systems work, and the principles on which they are based, that are important to understand.

Place system

The Place system is also called the method of loci, or room systems, and was used by the Greeks and Romans in ancient times. Legend says that Simonides, a 5th century BC. Greek poet gave a speech at a banquet. After the speech he went outside just in time to witness the roof of the banquet hall collapse. By mentally visualising where the guests were sitting when he gave his speech, he was able to locate and identify every victim. In those days oratory was a highly prized skill, and the ability to address an audience for hours, without the use of notes, was highly valued and respected.

In more recent times, a Russian man known as 'S' who started his career in the 1920s as a journalist, but eventually became a professional mnemonist, and earned his living using his memory to entertain. He could memorise lengthy lists of random words, and recall them perfectly decades later using the method of loci memory technique. He is mentioned by A.R. Luria in his book *The Mind of A Mnemonist*.

He used three basic processes, usually together, for remembering verbal information:
1. The first was to use rich visual images to represent information.
2. The second was to use well-known locations, such as stops on a familiar street, to place the images mentally for later retrieval and
3. Third was to create a story with appropriate interactive images to retrieve the information.

The basic idea of the method of loci or Place system is to use the rooms and items of furniture in each room in your home, as hooks to associate or link things to. The hooks in a room might be door, lamp, window, clock, chair, table, bookshelf, TV, and fireplace. Associate the items you want to remember with these links. Then when you want to remember your list, or the key points of your speech, take a mental stroll around your house, visiting each room, and picking off the items, or key points, as you go. It is important that you follow the same sequence each time, and use the same memory hooks. As Andi Bell, the 2002 world memory champion says: "Once you learn a technique like the location technique it takes everything beyond what you can do naturally."

It is easier to associate items with familiar pegs, hence the advantage of using your home for the room system. It is also expandable in relation to the number of rooms, and items in each room in your home and indeed the objects in your garden. The pegs used can also be items you encounter on a familiar walk or car route. For better retention use concrete words for abstract items – for example, justice, liberty, equality and fraternity. To remember these think of a judge, the Statue of Liberty, the women's liberation movement, and a group of relatives who have turned up unexpectedly at your home.

Visualise the judge sitting on your favourite fireside chair, the Statue of Liberty on top of the TV, a group of women debating equality issues, and your relatives sitting and conversing vigorously on the sofa. Use the MUSE principle to imprint the items on your memory – Movement, Unusualness, Slapstick and Exaggeration. When next making a presentation, why not use this approach to mentally structure your material, or the following methods, to commit information to memory?

Link system

The Link system uses your powers of vivid imagination to associate items together in sequence. Again apply the MUSE principle. In other words, see things in an action-related interactive context; larger than life; millions of them; in a humorous situation and in colour. For example, say you want to remember a list, such as dog, television, pencil, and apple. Picture the dog devouring the TV, the TV with pencils stuck out of the screen and screaming apples being knifed with pencils. The more vivid, action oriented, and unusual the association, the better you'll recall it. In addition, the more unusual the story line the more memorable it is.

Alphabet system

In your early school days you committed to memory the 26 letters of the alphabet. This means that you already have 26 memory hooks for associating things to. The idea here is to invent words to represent each letter of the alphabet and commit them to LTM. Where possible I have used words that sound like the letters. You should make up your own list if these don't suit but here is mine:

1. A. An Ace motor cyclist's in bright colourful attire triumphantly winning first prize.

2. B. Two Bees buzzing around your head causing alarm and consternation.
3. C. As in Sea. Imagine you are happy at the seaside frolicking with three friends.
4. D. Deed as in the deed for your house that just happens to be numbered a fluorescent 4.
5. E. Easel. You put the vibrating number 5 on your easel's flipchart.
6. F. Effigy. Think of discovering 6 unusual fearsome effigies such as those on Easter Island.
7. G. Gifts. You are surprised and happy to have received 7 gifts for your birthday.
8. H. H-bomb. Visualise the H bomb explosion in Hiroshima. H is shaped like an 8.
9. I. Eye. Visualise tears shaped like a nine falling down your cheek.
10. J. Jay. Visualise a packet of 10 dancing 'J' clothes.
11. K. Cage. Visualise a lion trying to aggressively rip two bars of a cage to get out.
12. L. Elastic. Visualise the number 12 as two pieces of elastic dancing and romancing with each other.
13. M. Ember. You are scared out of your wits sitting by your fireside on Friday the 13.
14. N. Enamel. Imagine you have 14 bright sparkling white enamel teeth in your upper mouth.
15. O. Oboe. Visualise a musician playing the oboe in an orchestra of 15 lively musicians.
16. P. Pea. There are 16 anxious frightened peas in a peapod waiting to be devoured.
17. Q. Queue. There are 17 impatient people in a queue outside a house which is no.17.
18. R. Artist. Visual an artist painting a two-dimensional figure 18 in bright red on their canvas.
19. S. Eskimo. The Eskimo lives in a luminous igloo in 19 Eskimo drive.
20. T. Tea. Think of 20 excited tea bags left in a box waiting to be scalded.
21. U. U-boat. The U-boat has surfaced with a no. 21 painted brightly on it.
22. V. Victory sign. Think of the no.2 precariously balanced on each finger.
23. W. WC. The number outside the door for the WC is a huge two-dimensional 23.
24. X. X-ray. The X-ray department is in room no. 24 (the numbers are radioactive).
25. Y. Wife. Your beautiful wife or girlfriend is wearing a colourful tea shirt with a luminescent no. 25 written on it.
26. Z. Zebra. Visualise a herd of 26 zebras galloping along the street.

If you want to remember 26 items you link or associate them with these ready-made hooks. You can also convert numbers to words to help you remember pin codes and so on. If you have difficulty remembering pin

Inspiration

"Develop a passion for learning. If you do you will never cease to grow."
Anthony J. D'Angelo

codes, you could use this system to solve the problem. For example, say your pin number is 2514. This converts to the word BEAD (B = 2, E = 5, A = 1 and D = 4). Picture yourself withdrawing money and instead of money, beads come out of the ATM.

Number systems

There are three basic systems, called number rhyme, number shape and number phonetic:

1. Number rhyme. The number rhyme is a well-known memory system used in scores of memory books: 1 is gun, 2 is shoe, 3 is tree, 4 is door, 5 is hive, 6 is sticks, 7 is heaven, 8 is gate, 9 is wine, 10 is hen, 11 is a soccer team and 12 is a shelve. The same principle of memory is used. You associate or link items you want to remember with these easily recallable hooks. The next time you go to the shop for groceries try this system and see if it works for you. You can always bring a list with you for backup, in case you forget, or until you feel comfortable with the system.

2. Number shape. The number shape is based on the idea of animated digits: 1 could be a pole, 2 a swan, 3 a butterfly, 4 a sailing boat, 5 a hook, 6 a snake, 7 a ship's bow, 8 an hourglass, 9 a walking stick, and 10 a bat and ball. These could be used as hooks, or could be substituted for numbers. To recall 26, visualise a swan devouring a snake. To remember 47, visualise a sailing boat crashing into the bow of a ship.

3. Number phonetic system. This is a fairly complex system, a favourite with memory experts, and takes considerable time and patience to master. It involves linking the numbers 1 to 0, with groups of consonants whose shape resembles the numbers:

    1 = t or d (t has one down stroke)
    2 = n (n has two down strokes)
    3 = m (m has three down strokes)
    4 = r (r is the last letter of the word four)
    5 = l (the Roman numeral for 50 is L)
    6 = j, sh, ch, soft g (j is almost a mirror image of 6)
    7 = k, hard c, hard g (k can be formed from a pair of 7s)
    8 = f, v, ph (hand-written f is somewhat like an 8)
    9 = p, b (p is a mirror image of 9)
    0 = s, z, soft c (zero is 0, and s and z, have similar sounds)

How to use number systems

You can use the number phonetic system in two ways. You can invent a series of hooks based on the consonants, and use them as permanent memory hooks to link items to. For example: 1 is tie, 2 is Noah, 3 is ma, 4 is rye, 5 is law, 6 is shoe, and 7 is cow. 8 is ivy, 9 is pea, 10 is toes (you have 10 toes). In this system you ignore the vowels. Of course, you can expand this system ad infinitum and hence the popularity of this system with mnemonists, who make their living performing memory feats. They usually spend several hours a day, over many years, perfecting their art. Most amateurs find this system too cumbersome, although some people may find it intriguing.

The second way of using this method is to recall numbers. Modern everyday living entails memorising numerous codes and pin numbers. We are frequently required to remember numbers, such as social security numbers, pin numbers, access codes, car registration numbers, mobile phone numbers, and the address of friends' houses. Suppose the number of your friend's house is 74 and you want to commit this to LTM. You think of the word 'car' to represent 74 (c is 7 and r is 4, and you ignore the vowel under the phonetic system). So you visualise your friend's car on the roof of his house.

To remember that Columbus discovered America in 1492, code the number 1 as t, 4 as r, 9 as b, and 2 as n. This converts to TRBN. Add the appropriate vowels and this becomes TURBAN. Now imaginatively link 'turban' to Columbus (picture him wearing a turban), and you have a mnemonic device for remembering the date. A better way to remember this is through the well-known rhyme: 'in fourteen hundred and ninety-two, Columbus sailed the ocean blue.' Rhymes will be discussed in more detail further on in this chapter.

Acronyms, Acrostics and Rhymes

Acronyms are popular mnemonic devices used to enhance learning and improve recall. Their genesis goes back thousands of years to Greek and Roman times. Acro is a Greek word meaning 'end' or 'tip,' and an acronym is a word formed from the first letters of other words. Mnemonics such as acronyms have been used throughout this book, and particularly in this chapter, as they are very useful for jogging memory.

A well-known acronym for remembering the chemical constituents of coal is NO CASH: where N stands for Nitrogen, O for Oxygen, C for Carbon, A for Ash, S for Sulphur and H for Hydrogen. To remember the six counties of Northern Ireland, just think of FAT DAD, which stands for Fermanagh, Antrim, Tyrone, Derry, Armagh and Down. To remember the five Great Lakes of North America, think of HOMES: this stands for Huron, Ontario, Michigan, Erie and Superior. You can also use personal acronyms to remember everyday items. Say you want to remember to get oranges, tomatoes, apples and broccoli at the grocery store. With a little reorganisation you invent the acronym BOAT (broccoli, oranges, apples and tomatoes) to help you recall the items when you get to the shop.

Business acronyms

In a business and lecturing career spanning over 40 years I found the following acronyms very useful. Many I've invented myself, but others I've picked up on the way.

Accounting acronyms
- ALORE – Assets, liabilities, owner's equity, revenue and expenses – for remembering the elements of the accounting equation.
- FIFO – First in, First out – used in stock valuation and also used in HR.
- LIFO – Last in, First out – used in stock valuation.
- PAIN – Payback, accounting rate of return, internal rate of return and net present value – for investment appraisal methods.

Business management
- ADDIE – Analysis, design, development, implementation and evaluation - for system design.
- ARSES – Ad hoc, representative, standing, executive and sub-committees – for types of management committees.
- GIGO – Garbage In, Garbage Out – used in computing.
- KPI – Key Performance Indicator.
- PERT – Programme evaluation and review technique – used in project management.
- PLOCS – Planning, leading, organising, controlling and staffing – for the main functions of management.
- MBWA – Managing By Wandering About.
- TEAM – Together Everyone Achieves More – the synergy effect of teams.
- WIIFM – What's In It For Me?
- WYSIWYG – What you see is what you get – for typing and word-processing.

Strategic planning
- SMARTS – Specific, measurable, attainable, rewarded, timely and supported – the characteristics of good objectives.
- SPEWSIC – Strategic objectives, Position audit, Environmental analysis, WOTS up analysis, Strategies to fill the gap, Implementation and Control – for the strategic planning process.
- APES – Annual plan, profitability, efficiency and strategic – the major controls in a business.

Problem solving and creativity
- CAP – Cover all possibilities – for creative thinking.
- CAMPERS – Combine, Adapt, Modify, Put to other uses, Eliminate, Rearrange, Simplify – for generating ideas to improve things.
- IDEAL – Identify, Define, Explore, Action, Look back – a problem solving approach.
- SREDIM – Select, record, examine, develop, install and maintain – the work study approach to solving problems. It can also be adapted and used to recall the key steps in the problem-solving or decision-making process.
- STAR – Stop! Think! Act! And Review! – used in the nuclear industry to help operators remember a solving problem process.

Marketing
- AIDA – Attention, interest, desire and action – an aspect of sales promotion.
- BOGOFF – Buy One Get One For Free – used in advertising.
- DAGMAR – Defining advertising goals for measuring advertising results – highlights the importance of goals for measuring advertising effectiveness.
- FAB – Features, Advantages, Benefits – used in selling.
- PEST – Political, economic, social and technological – for environmental analysis.
- USP – Unique selling point – for selling and marketing.

Training
- ABC – Accurate, brief and clear – for communications.
- APEL – Accreditation of prior learning – used in education and training.
- ASPIRE – Assess your current position, SWOT analysis, plan, implement, review and evaluate – used for self-development.
- BID – Break it down – to make it easier to follow.
- CAP – Cognitive, affective, psychomotor – three main types of learning.
- KASH – Knowledge, attitudes, skills, habits.
- KISS – Keep It Simple Stupid.
- NLP – Neuro-Linguistic Programming.
- NOTES – Needs analysis, objectives, training design, evaluation, and styles of learning – the elements of successful training.

Initial –letter alliteration
This involves a repetition of the same sounds which can improve memory.
- 5 C's of communication – Concise, clear, courteous, complete and correct.
- 5 C's of planning – Proper planning prevents poor performance.
- 4 Ps of Marketing – Product, price, promotion and place.
- 7 Ps of Marketing – Product, price, promotion, place, people, process, physical evidence.
- 4 Ps of Presentations – Planning, preparation, presentation and post mortem.

As you can see acronyms can be used in accounting, business management, marketing and strategic planning. Instruction of elementary accounting principles, at university level, has been shown to be strengthened by the use of mnemonic devices.

Acrostics
An acrostic is a mnemonic device, where the first letter of words in a sentence helps you recall items, as the letters correspond to the words you want to remember. To remember the names of the planets in the solar system, use the sentence, 'My Very Educated Mother Just Showed Us Nine

Planets' – Mercury, Venus, Earth, Jupiter, Saturn, Uranus, Neptune and Pluto. The colours of the rainbow can easily be remembered by the sentence, 'Richard Of York Gave Battle In Vain:' Red, Orange, Yellow, Green, Blue, Indigo and Violet.

<u>Memory spelling strategies</u>
Acrostics can also be used to spell out a word that people find difficult to spell. An acrostic for spelling 'rhythm' is: Rhythm Helps Your Two Hips Move. An acrostic for spelling 'because' is: 'Big Elephants Can Always Understand Small Elephants.'

Some people have difficulty differentiating the meaning and spelling of the word 'affect,' from the word 'effect.' Affect means to influence or change, while effect is a noun meaning the result of an action. The acrostic RAVEN will help you distinguish the one from the other:
Remember Affect Verb - Effect Noun.

A handy way to remember when to use an 's' or a 'c' as in Practise or Practice is covered in the following little ditty:
S is the verb and C is the noun,
That's the rule to stop you frown.

Similarly, the word desert and dessert are often confused. A desert is sandy while dessert has two s's in it like Strawberry Shakes. To spell 'necessary' use the first letter of each word in the following sentence: Never Eat Crisps, Eat Salad Sandwiches And Remain Young.

To distinguish 'stationery' from 'stationary,' visualise a large Envelope for stationery and remember your car (Automobile) is stationAry when parked. To remember how to spell the commonly misspelt 'Separate,' whether it has an E or an A, after the letter P, just think of 'SEPARATE A RAT.' If you want to spell 'ACROSS,' just remember that there is only ONE SEA ACROSS to America. Similar and familiar are often confused. Think of LIAR, if you want to spell FAMILIAR.

Some words can be learned phonetically (by the sound of the word). If you pronounce the word correctly, it may sometimes help you spell it correctly. However, the spelling of some words has to be memorised. In other cases mnemonic devices will help you spell the word correctly. Principle and principal are two words often misspelt and confused. To remember them for all time learn 'Principle is a rule while principal is a pal.' If you have problems remembering how to spell 'believe' just remember to 'Never believe a lie.'

Some people spell 'argument' incorrectly as 'arguement.' I lost an 'e' in an argument, will help you how to spell it correctly. To spell the word 'cemetery' just remember that all the vowels are 'e's' just like screech! Personally I find it difficult to remember where to put quotation marks when

I quote something. The rule is: put Q after P. In other words put the quotation mark after the period or full stop (Q comes after P in the alphabet).

Rhymes

As advertisers and educationalists know, rhymes, ditties, songs and poems are effective ways of remembering things. Rhymes and songs engage memory for words and sounds. They may be particularly useful for those who can memorise tunes, songs or poems easily. If you have difficulty remembering which way to turn a screwdriver, the following little ditty may help: 'Righty tighty, lefty loosey.' To remember when to put the clock forward and back, think of 'Spring forward and Fall back.'

The following well known rhyme will help you remember the days in each month of the year:
30 days hath September, April, June and November
All the rest have 31
Except February my dear son
It has 28 and that is fine
But in a Leap year it has 29.

Some people use sentences to remember numbers. If you want to remember the value of pi to 20 places (as a party trick to amaze your friends) learn the following ditty:
'I wish I could determine pie
 Eureka! Cried the great inventor
 Christmas pudding Christmas pie
 Is the problem's very centre.

You can get the value of pi to 20 places by counting the letters in each word. The value is
3.14159265358979323846

Schoolchildren learn the spelling rule 'I before E except after C.' There are exceptions to the rule which are covered if you add:
'Or when sounded like ay
As in freight, weigh and sleigh.'
This covers most of the exceptions, although still leaves out 'foreign,' 'forfeit,' etc. There are some words where you just must memorise the spelling through repetition!

The following are some popular rhymes purporting to forecast the weather.
'Red sky at night: shepherd's delight.
 Red sky in the morning: shepherd's warning'.

'Rainbows in the morning: travellers take warning.
 Rainbows at night: traveller's delight.'
Rainbows indicate humid air. A morning rainbow is seen in the West. This

is the direction storms come from, and so indicates bad weather. Evening rainbows appear in the East, and usually indicate the passing of stormy weather.

Medics learn the following to deal with people who faint:
'If the face is Red raise the head.
If the face is Pale raise the tale.'

How to remember parts of speech

The parts of speech can be learnt and memorised from the following poem (if I knew this when a child at school, it would have saved me a lot of grief).

"Every name is called a NOUN,
As field and fountain, street and town;
In place of noun the PRONOUN stands,
As he and she can clap their hands;
The ADJECTIVE describes a thing,
 As magic wand and bridal ring;
The VERB means action, something done –
To read and write, to jump and run;
How things are done, the ADVERB tell,
 As quickly, slowly, badly, well;
The PREPOSITION shows relation,
As in the street, or at the station;
CONJUNCTIONS join, in many ways,
Sentences, words or phrase and phrase;
The INTERJECTION cries out, 'Hark!
I need an exclamation mark!'
Through Poetry, we learn how each
Of these make up the PARTS OF SPEECH."

Conclusion

The strength of memory depends on how deeply information is processed, not how long it is processed. This means reflecting, rehearsal, organisation and elaboration, to make information meaningful. You can do this by linking it with something you know already. You will learn a telephone number quicker, if you notice that the numbers include (for example your home address, the number of your car's registration number plate, the date of a historical event, or the date of your own or your partner's birthday).

To summarise you won't learn the technical and typographical skills involved in driving a car by reading a book. Similarly, it takes considerable time, effort, persistence and practise to become proficient in the PLAN system of memory. One way to learn some of these systems fairly effortlessly, is using down time, such as walking along the street, waiting in a queue for a bus, or commuting on a bus or train. You could occupy and challenge your mind, to see how fast you are able to convert numbers into letters and words, and vice versa. Practise this until you can instantly do it. Such mental gymnastics and games will sharpen your mental powers, productively entertain you in spare moments of the day, when you have nothing else to do, while at the same time acquiring a useful memory system that you can use to benefit you socially and career wise.

Why not invent your own acronyms, acrostics, rhymes and mnemonics for important areas of your work, personal life or studies, or for vital information that you want to commit to memory? Research shows that people, who consciously use memory devices, when they are studying a list, learn two or three times better than those who use traditional methods.

Remembering Names

Most people find it difficult to remember peoples' names. Where remembering names is an essential feature of your job, then economic loss can be added to the embarrassment. However, with attention, concentration, and practise you can improve your capacity to remember names. Use the acronym MEMORY system as follows:

Minutes not seconds.
When we meet someone for the first time, we are often shy and self-conscious, and so are preoccupied with our own thoughts, rather than concentrating on the other person. In any event, most people find that introductions do not register, and inevitably go straight over their heads. We are so anxious thinking about what we are going to say next, that we fail to hear the other person's name. In addition, our attention is distracted by focussing on the person's appearance, rather than on the name.

Instead, consciously concentrate on the other person, and take the time to imprint their name on your memory. Your STM is only of 30 seconds duration, and then is lost unless you frequently review. If you're conscious of this fact, you will realise how important it is to focus on the name, and repeat it as often as possible without making it too obvious. So if you fail to pick up their name at the start, ask them to repeat it. Say their name immediately after being introduced. If the name is unusual, ask them to spell it and then spell it back. The distinctive sound of their voice will also help you remember them. Say the name during the conversation, and when departing repeat the name again. By the way it is common courtesy, when talking to someone you do not know, to introduce yourself. This prevents the other person getting embarrassed, and may help you make friends.

Evaluate.
Ask questions about the name. Inquire about the name's history and background. Names usually have a story behind them. Where did the name originally come from? What does it mean? What familiar words does it sound like? All these questions will help give the name context, and im-

print it on your mind. The other person will only be delighted that you are taking such a keen interest in them.

You can break a name into syllables, and turn these syllables into images. For example, you might consider Mr Hutton sounds like 'hat on,' and so imagine Mr Hutton with a hat on to remind you of the name. Punning associations may also help you remember names. For example, if you meet someone at a party named Frank, you may have found him to be very forthcoming, and frank in his views.

Make an effort.
Use the name frequently during the conversation, but not so frequently that you irritate the other person. Make sure you address the person by name when saying your goodbyes. Link the face to the name in a memorable cartoonish fashion, such as an exaggerated feature of the face, or personality trait. For one person it may be a prominent nose, or a high forehead, for the next it may be prominent protruding ears, and for another it may be thick lips, or a sharp pointed chin. Others may have a distinctive speaking voice, heavy eyebrows, attractive eyes, or unusual mannerisms that make them stand out.

Steve might have a muscular build like a stevedore, and Angela might have an angelic look. In addition, use your powers of visualisation. Link the name to a famous person, or to a friend or person you know already with the same name, and imagine the pair shaking hands with each other. If introduced to a Mr White, you could imagine him standing on white snow. You might remember Barbara, by visualising barbed wire protecting her. Another way of remembering someone is to put them into a humorous context. Associate the person with something funny, ridiculous or bizarre. When the mind is relaxed it functions more efficiently in learning and remembering situations.

Organise.
Do this by exchanging business cards if these are available. At the first opportunity, and while the information is still fresh in your mind, write the name and a few key points about the individual into your name and address book, to help you place them in context in the future. This might include the person's occupation, family or where they come from. The place they come from is often a good cue to remember names. Who are their friends, what leisure time pursuits do they like and so on? If you are attending an event, course or seminar you could study the list of participants before you go. Preparation will ease the process and stress of remembering names at the course.

Repeat and review.
Unless you refresh your memory from time to time you are going to forget. If you are likely to meet these people again in the future, even though on an irregular basis, it pays to review and recall their names, so that you

are prepared and relaxed, rather than embarrassed and anxious, when you meet them. At the end of the day review the names of all the new people you met and repeat their names aloud as you visualise their faces. Use your powers of imagination to picture their facial characteristics, demeanour and general appearance.

Find images that rhyme with the sound of the name. Mr Jones might be recalled by 'Mr Bones,' particularly if the person has a thin face. Mr Barrett might be linked to 'carrot,' particularly if Mr Barrett is a vegetarian. If you meet people on a regular basis their names will go into your LTM, and so you won't have much difficulty remembering their names. Affirm your memory for names every day. If you want affirmations to work they should be personal, positive and be in the present tense. An effective affirmation might be: 'Every day in every way my memory for names is getting better and better.'

Your curiosity.
Exercise your curiosity about the person you are likely to meet frequently, and build up a dossier by inquiring with others who may know something about them. You are more likely to remember people if you know something unusual about them. They may have unusual hobbies or recreational activities. Look up the telephone number in the directory and see if they are listed. If they are members of a professional body you are linked to, looking up the membership directory will reinforce the name, and will give you their qualifications and occupation.

Where Can I Improve My Memory?

People can improve their memory in any context and in at any place. Some may get self-help memory books or memory courses off the shelf, and study them at their own pace. They can practise the mnemonic techniques during spare moments of the day as when commuting to and from work. Others may prefer to attend a formal training course which covers the general principles of memory, how to use mnemonic devices, where to use them, and how to compile and use learning maps.

In a work context, learning maps have been used during meetings to take down key points discussed and decisions made. Acronyms are used in everyday business to recall important dates, concepts and processes. People use mnemonic devices to help them better to recall names in social situations, and to recall their PIN numbers when they need to do so.

What is learnt in one environment is best recalled in the same environment. Students should try to study in the same place each time. You will then mentally associate a particular place with study. In fact, research suggests that students who sit for their exams in the room where they study do better academically than those without this facility. Divers who learn things underwater may have difficulty recalling the same items on dry land, but little difficulty remembering them when they are underwater again. It seems context has a major impact on our ability to remember.

People, who acquire a foreign language when they live abroad, and then return home, often feel that they will lose the language through lack of practise after a few years. Fortunately, when they return to the foreign country, the language comes rapidly back, suggesting that it was inaccessible, rather than permanently forgotten.

Socially, you can improve your memory for names by using the MEMO-RY mnemonic discussed in the previous section. You can improve your memory generally by learning the PLAN system of memory.

As previously mentioned, the context in which events take place is very important for memory. For example, if you want to recall historical events it is vital to place them in the context in which they occurred. This is the reason why when you meet people out of context (their normal surroundings) you often have difficulty remembering their names.

The internet is a great source of information on all aspects of memory, and the Google site will provide you with endless hours of entertainment on the topic of memory.

Who Uses Memory Skills?

We all use memory skills to a lessor or greater degree during every moment of our lives. Some people with special training use their memory more efficiently and effectively than the rest of us.

Professional memory people, such as memory consultants and mnemonists, make a good living out of using their memory skills. Many of them turn up on TV shows, from time to time, demonstrating their astounding talents to appreciative audiences.

Memory experts

Harry Lorayne has written numerous books on memory, and has also made a living from performing as a mnemonist. Similarly, Dominic O'Brien, who is an 8 times world memory champion, has written books on the topic, and made a good living out of his memory. He has demonstrated his amazing abilities on TV shows, and his memory for playing cards is so good that he is banned from many casinos around the world. Dominic claims he was an average student at school and that he had a bad memory. He was not born a genius but has spent years diligently training his memory. He claims anyone can do likewise, if they are interested, committed and motivated enough to spend the considerable time and practise needed to learn the mnemonic devices.

Jerry Lucas, who won the Basketball Player of the Year Award three times,

Inspiration

"A man's real possession is his memory. In nothing else is he rich, in nothing else is he poor."
Alexander Smith

developed a lucrative career as a memory expert after retiring from sport. He is the author of more than sixty books on the subject of memory, and has developed memory training and learning systems.

Joshua Foer, a sceptical journalist, took up memory training as a challenge, and went on to win the USA memory championship in 2006, proving it is possible to acquire and practise the memory skills of an expert, provided you have the interest, commitment and time to do so. He subsequently wrote a best-selling book called 'Moonwalking with Einstein' about his experiences. It takes about 10 years of study and practise to become proficient in any subject area, and you can be sure it takes just as long to become a world class memory expert. Most people with amazing memory abilities, including those who win the World Memory Championship, use mnemonic techniques the most popular one being the method of loci.

Memory consultants offer memory training courses for executives in large multi-national companies. They teach employees mnemonic devices to help them, remember names and faces, telephone numbers, computer passes, overhead and job codes, figures from financial statements, and to make presentations without notes. The ability to make a speech without reference to notes is widely admired in politics and in the business world. Salespeople who know their products and who can readily remember their customers' names create and retain business, and so are quickly promoted up the hierarchy.

Experts tend to have a superior memory within their area of expertise, but outside of that their recall is no better than novices. Experiments with chess players have proved this. When chess experts were presented with arrangement of chess pieces that could never occur in a game, their recall was no better than novices. This suggested that they had developed an ability to organise certain types of information, rather than possessing eidetic ability. On the other hand, famous chess player Harry Pilsbury (1872-1906) once played 32 games simultaneously, blindfolded at the Franklin Chess Club in Philadelphia in 1900. In 1902 he played 21 games while blindfolded (winning 13, drawing 2, losing 1). He was as well known for his memory as he was for his chess expertise.

Autistic people
Some autistic people have a remarkable memory, and use mnemonic devices naturally to help them achieve astounding feats of memory. In the world of autism, Temple Grandin is very famous and popular. She is a college professor, consultant to the livestock industry on animal behaviour, and captivating speaker at autism conferences, and has written many books on her life and experiences. She is a high profile advocate and role model for autistic people. She is the subject of an award-winning 2010 biographical film, Temple Grandin, and was listed in Time magazine as one of the most influential 100 people in the world. She has a strong visual memory which enables her to notice small details. This has helped

her to design humane animal-handling equipment. She was the subject of the Horizon documentary 'The Woman Who Thinks Like a Cow,' first broadcast by the BBC on 8 June, 2006.

Some people diagnosed with a disorder called savant syndrome have phenomenal memory but most of such cases are incapable of abstract thought. The 1988 film Rain Man starring Dustin Hoffman covered the topic in a very sensitive way. The character in the film was inspired by the true story of Kim Peek. Although Kim was born with severe brain damage and was unable to look after himself, he went on to become world famous because of his amazing memory. He was said to have read 12,000 books, and could remember everything about them. He could recall facts and trivia from 15 subject areas including history, geography and sport. After the film he became famous, and spent time travelling around the USA with his father, demonstrating his astounding memory to captivated audiences.

People with a special talent for remembering have always existed throughout human history and are said to have an eidetic or photographic memory. Many are just ordinary people who have developed an extraordinary interest in memory, and a talent for remembering what they want to remember. In ancient Rome, Lucius Scipio, a Roman senator, was able to remember the names and faces of all the people living in the city. Whether or not he had an eidetic memory, or used a method of loci, is not known.

Bill Clinton, 42nd President of the United States is said to have a near photographic memory. John von Neumann, one of the greatest mathematicians of modern history, had powers of total recall. He could quote a book or article verbatim after one reading, and could do it again years later without hesitation. Stephen Wiltshire, MBE, a prodigious savant, is capable of drawing the entire skyline of a city after a helicopter ride.

Superior autobiographical memory
ScienceDaily (14 March 2006) reports that researchers at University of California, Irvine spent more than five years studying the case of Jill Price, a 40 year-old woman with incredibly strong memories of her personal past. They are studying the phenomenon hoping it will give them new insights into memory and conditions such as Alzheimer's. Perhaps they will discover how hidden underdeveloped talents within each person can be tapped. Given a date, Jill can recall a vivid depiction of that date in her head, what she was doing on that date, and what day of the week it fell on.

Amongst her friends and acquaintances she is known as the human calendar. She laments it is not easy having a phenomenal memory, as it is 'nonstop, uncontrollable and totally exhausting.' Nevertheless, as a religious education coordinator, her memory does help her remember everything she needs to know about the students. Because her case is the first of its kind, they have named her condition as 'hyperthymesic syndrome,' based on the Greek word 'thymesis' for remembering, and' hyper' for more than normal. These people are neither autistic savants nor mnemonists, yet they can remember key events from almost every day of their lives.

In more recent years other people with hyperthymesic syndrome have been found. The Wall Street Journal reports (22 December 2010), that the actress and author Marilu Henner, is apparently one of only six Americans diagnosed with this condition. Marilu is best known for her role in the 1980s US TV series Taxi. She claims to have the ability to recall detailed moment-to-moment memories, news headlines, and weather conditions from decades past. She claims this has helped her in her acting career, because she can easily recall all kinds of feelings and emotions which help her empathise with and get inside her role.

New York-based violist, Louise Owen, who appeared on the US news show 60 Minutes, claims she can remember every day since she was 11 years old. Ms Owens demonstrated her extraordinary memory talent on the show. It is important to make a distinction between hyperthymesia and other forms of exceptional memory that generally use mnemonic strategies to recall information. The memories recalled by hyperthymesic individuals tend to be autobiographical accounts of significant and mundane events in their lives.

In September 2012, UK's Channel 4 screened the documentary The Boy Who Can't Forget. This profiled the memory of a 20 year-old named Aurelien Hayman from Cardiff, a student at Durham University, who remembers practically every day of his life since the age of 10. Hayman is the first Briton to be identified with hyperthymesia. When his brain was scanned during a test, a series of visual areas of the brain lit up quicker than would be expected in a normal brain.

People with synaesthesia
Scientists have known about synaesthesia since 1880, when Francis Galton, a cousin of Charles Darwin, published a paper on the phenomenon. Synaesthesia is derived from Greek and means 'union of the senses.' It is thought that cross wiring of neurons in the brain leads to mixed sensory perceptions. Science is aware of about 50 different types of synaesthesia with one person in 200 with the condition. The condition runs in families and may be more common in women.

People with synaesthesia (known as synesthetes), have heightened senses which they use to remember things more effectively. Not only do they have great powers of visualisation, but they can also incorporate into the image other sensations such as smells, tastes, sounds, textures and colours. They see the ordinary world in extraordinary ways because their senses are mixed up instead of being separate.

A person with synaesthesia may 'hear' colours, feel the emotion in words, see numbers, words, and dates in colours, or see and feel musical tones. Many musicians claim they see sounds in colour, and artists claim they can taste colours. In fact, the condition is more prevalent in creative people, such as painters, poets and novelists, than in the general population. It seems that we have different memory systems, in different parts of the brain, for sights, sounds, smells, tastes, emotions, words, numbers and colour, so that the more memory systems we engage the stronger our memory.

There is a strong link between synaesthesia and an enhanced memory. A.R.Luria, the late Russian neurologist, described a mnemonist called 'S,' who had remarkable recall because all five of his senses were linked. Synesthetes have used their special gift memorising names and telephone numbers, mental arithmetic, and also in artistic endeavours like art, music and theatre. Most are happy with their condition and consider it a gift rather than a handicap. Unfortunately, 'S' spent his final days in a mental institution having been overwhelmed by his amazing memory.

People who use memory devices

Most of us haven't the time to pursue memory to the same extent as memory experts, but there is no reason why you can't adopt some of the strategies and mnemonic devices that memory experts use to improve everyday memory. I have a very average memory but have found mnemonics very useful during my personal and professional life for learning and remembering. I found them particularly useful as a mature student when studying for my professional accountancy qualifications, and a master's degree in training and development. I found them particularly useful as a third level college lecturer and as a training consultant. Students were intrigued with my learning maps and mnemonic devices which I used to summarise key points.

Actors, lecturers, lawyers, public speakers, politicians and students all rely on a good memory for their work, and many of them use mnemonic devices to help them. In the case of actors, the dialogue back and forth provides a constant series of prompts and cues to help them remember their scripts. Lecturers win the admiration and respect of their students, if they are seen to be able to talk knowledgeable about their subject without constant reference to notes. Barristers need a good memory to get to grips quickly with a brief, remember details of the most complicated law cases, and remember the various statutes, the names of jury members, and the testimony of witnesses. Public speakers and parliamentarians impress when they can speak without the need of notes. As previously mentioned students who use mnemonic devices are more successful in exams than those who don't use such aid.

Summary of Chapter Seven

Memory is the power to remember and recall events, and is a central part of our identity and life story. We have four types of memory – working, implicit, semantic and episodic. All of these types of memory are retrospective, unlike prospective memory which helps us remember things that we plan to do in the future. There are simple strategies that you can adopt to overcome everyday memory problems.

Memory skills can be used in the home, study, personal development or at work. You can improve your memory by adopting the three basic laws of memory: - Impression, Repetition and Association (IRA). The PLAN system of memory is a comprehensive system covering the Place, Link, Alphabet and Number rhyme/shape systems. These systems are used by professional mnemonists, orators and public speakers.

Acronyms, acrostics and rhymes are used by students to memorise vital information needed to pass exams. They are also used extensively in medical, legal and business training, as well as in a variety of other occupations, such as memory consultants, barristers and managers. An effective system for remembering names is recommended.

Most of the systems covered in this chapter require a considerable amount of time to master. Pick the ones that suit your learning style. The effort and time involved will be more than rewarded, by your improved memory and overall ability to learn more effectively. Improving memory is a lifelong and continuous process and not a once off operation. You should aim to make it an on-going enjoyable part of your life.

Five Activities to Improve Memory Skills

1. You can improve your memory through simple changes in your lifestyle such as learning mnemonic devices, healthy eating, physical exercise and stress reduction.

2. Memorise the three basic laws of memory: - Impression, Repetition and Association (IRA), and use this approach in your everyday approach to remembering things you want to remember. This means you should get a vivid impression of what you want to remember, repeat it a few times, using spaced repetition, and link it with something you know already.

3. Use the MEMORY approach recommended for memorising names of people you want to remember and improve your social skills.

4. Use acronyms, acrostics and rhymes, as appropriate, to commit what you want to remember to memory. Make up your own as these will be more effective as memory cues than ones made up by somebody else.

5. For your next presentation use the place system, just like the Greek and Roman orators used to do, to recall the key points of your speech. Your colleagues will be amazed by your astounding memory, and ability to recall information without reference to notes.

Chapter 8
Creativity

Creativity is creating something that wasn't there before, seeing novel relationships between things, ideas and people. Creativity is important because companies need to survive and thrive, in a time of global competition, rapidly changing technology, and the shortening of the product life cycle. Sometimes bright ideas unexpectedly occur when people are doing other things, working on other problems, researching other issues, thinking about other matters, or engaged in recreational pursuits.

Most people now believe that creativity is not only the province of artists and inventors, but is a learnable skill that can be enhanced through practise, training, imitation, and knowledge of techniques. There are five stages of creativity; namely preparation, effort, incubation, insight and evaluation. Practical creativity can be encouraged by combining, adapting and modifying, eliminating, simplifying and rearranging things.

Creativity techniques can be neatly classified under three headings: paradigm preserving, paradigm stretching, and paradigm breaking techniques. The more original ideas can be generated by using paradigm stretching and paradigm breaking techniques. Brainstorming is probably one of the best known and popular techniques for generating ideas. Other techniques include fantasy, attribute listing, reverse brainstorming, metaphor and SWOT analysis. Creative problem solving is a systematic approach to creativity and problem solving.

The barriers to creativity include conformity, the one right answer, and evaluating too quickly. Negativity, criticism, short-sightedness, and lack of perspective are some of the ways to stifle creativity. Creativity can happen in the home and at work. Most people are creative, but certain people are seen as creative such as designers, writers and artists. Famous creative people are remembered for the unique contribution they made to the welfare and lives of people.

WHAT YOU'LL LEARN
IN THIS CHAPTER:
- What is creativity?
- Why is creativity important?
- When does creativity happen?
- How does creativity happen?
- Where does creativity happen?
- Who is creative?

What is Creativity?

Creativity is creating something that wasn't there before; seeing novel relationships between things, ideas, artefacts, products, places and people. Creativity is often about seeing something unusual in the usual. Apart from making something new, creativity can also be improving, refining, changing or combining things in new or novel ways. It is about building on existing ideas and finding inspiration in unlikely places.

Think of the word creative and other words like imagination, originality, innovative, unpredictable, divergent and lateral come to mind. These words convey the message of generating ideas, and looking at problems from different and new perspectives. It involves the flexibility of being able to switch from one perspective to another, and to make unusual links or associations between things.

Inspiration

_____

"Every child is an artist; the problem is staying an artist when you grow up."
Pablo Picasso

Creative thinking is not much use if we can't tell the difference between a good idea and a bad one. Our imagination should be rooted in reality. Ideas must be useful, practicable, actionable and marketable. Business people produce a prototype of their ideas to test their commercial viability. This is where the analytical thinking process comes in.

Creativity turns problems and challenges into opportunities and solutions. Creative people go outside the conventional way of seeing and doing things. Picasso was a creative genius who threw convention to the winds, but nevertheless his work was built on solid art principles. The art he produced challenged people to look at things in new, unfamiliar, unconventional and thought provoking ways.

Creativity and Innovation

Creativity and innovation are often confused but they mean different things. Creativity is the production of novel and useful ideas in any field, whereas innovation is the sifting, refining, and most critically, the implementation of those ideas. We can see that creativity is not enough. We need innovation to turn the creative ideas into physical reality as useful and profitable products. Innovation is a far tougher proposition than creativity. It is one thing understanding the workings of the atom, but it quite another thing to apply this knowledge by building a nuclear powered electricity generation station. It is one thing to conceive a product, but it is quite another thing to bring it to fruition and market it successfully.

One of the greatest discoveries of all time was the invention of the wheel. Consider how difficult it would be to move things about without the wheel even though the Inca civilisation seemed to survive without it. The wheel in turn gave rise to countless further inventions all inspired by the wheel. All kinds of transport, machinery, instruments and equipment are based on the wheel. In fact most creative ideas are just refinements, improvements or new applications of existing things.

Take the modern omnipresent computer. Thirty years ago it was so big that it needed special purpose air conditioned rooms to accommodate it. Today it is much smaller, cheaper, better designed, and more powerful and faster than ever before. It is now as common as the radio or television was to previous generations. The technology behind it is developing so fast that it is obsolete as soon as you buy it. It comes in many incarnations such as desktop, laptop, and iPod. Computer technology has also been incorporated into other equipment such as cars, televisions, mobile phones, cameras and domestic appliances making them faster and more efficient.

Why is creativity important?

Evidence of creativity has spanned the history of human kind, from the drawings on cave walls to the modern wonders of telecommunications. Creativity has been linked to genius, in science, business, and art, and many people have attained world fame through their wonderful discoveries and inventions. Modern living has been enriched and made possible through their endeavours. Creativity is important because it creates business opportunities, fulfils design needs and presents career opportunities for employees.

Inspiration

"Originality is nothing but judicious imitation."
Voltaire

Business Needs
Global competition, rapidly changing technology, and the shortening of the product life cycle, has made creativity in business more important than ever. A business needs creative people who are prepared to take calculated risks, and challenge the conventional wisdom. Such people can identify and exploit opportunities to create new products, new markets, and new customers, to enhance profitability. To survive, a business needs to work smarter and faster, continually develop new products and services, and improve existing ones. Creativity also helps people solve the problems and challenges of everyday life, and make more informed decisions.

Creativity is needed throughout a business, from the top to the bottom, at strategic management, middle management, lower management and operational levels. The chief executive and the senior management team, should actively support creativity, and promulgate its importance throughout all levels of the organisation. Without creativity, a firm is unlikely to be innovative, and without innovation it is unlikely to be commercially viable. Creative solutions to problems can increase efficiency, productivity and profitability, and save the company substantial sums of money.

Specifically creativity is needed in areas of business, such as research and development, training and development, management services, systems analysis, product and market development, strategic planning, manufacturing processes, marketing, advertising, design and development. In a changing world, new products, services and technologies are appearing all the time. Apart from new inventions, there is continuous improvement on existing products, processes, systems and services. To keep a competitive edge you must keep up with the best and more often than not do better.

Inventiveness and creativity is becoming more important in computer programming as well. As the routine work of testing, maintaining and upgrading software is moved to low-cost countries like India, engineers with the ability to invent new software applications are in high demand. Even when the new products have been invented they need to be launched, marketed and explained, and this requires ingenuity, customer service skills and empathy to build rapport with customers.

Design Needs

Good design is now more important than ever. It's no longer sufficient to create reasonably priced, useful and user friendly products. They must also be aesthetically beautiful, unique and appeal to the senses and emotions. Even the most humble kitchen utensils must satisfy the new middle-class obsession with good design. People now want lighting, artefacts, furniture and products of good design that will enhance the home environment.

The fashion industry would not survive without constant creativity and innovation. Successful fashion companies reinvent their product line and thus their brands every season. It repeatedly brings out products that consumers didn't know they needed, often creating such high demand that the previous year's fashions are made obsolete. A fashion company that fails to innovate and please customers will surely go out of business.

Career Opportunities

The people who progress in their careers are the ones who can come up with new innovative ideas, and new and improved ways of doing things. The people who get noticed and promoted are the ones who continually challenge existing processes and methods, and are prepared to suggest better and more efficient ways of doing them, even in the face of ridicule and strong opposition. These people are confident about the feasibility and quality of their ideas, and have the determination and persistence to pursue them and push them through.

These are the people who stand out from the crowd because of their creative problem solving skills, and ability to learn on their own. Even in routine jobs, creative people will be continually questioning things in order to find better ways of doing them. The idea of continuous improvement comes naturally to such people.

Inspiration

"Problems don't get solved by the smartest or the fastest or the strongest; they get solved by the one who sees the possibilities."
Dan Roam

When Does Creativity Happen?

Sometimes problems get solved when people are working on other problems, thinking about other issues, or engaged in recreational pursuits. People have even solved problems after sleeping on them! Your subconscious is the storehouse of everything you know, even things you can't readily call into awareness.

Ideas often come to us at the most unexpected time and in the most unexpected places. It is said that Archimedes discovered the principle of buoyancy when stepping into his bath. King Hieron had posed the problem. He suspected an artisan of being deceitful by alloying or corrupting the gold in his crown, but had no way of proving it. Archimedes realised that the problem could be solved, by measuring the volumes of water displaced by the crown and an equal weight of gold. By comparing densities he could determine the gold content of the crown and thus solve the King's problem.

Your subconscious will process, recombine, adapt and consolidate ideas and suggest solutions. This is why daydreaming is so effective for producing creative ideas. Furthermore, relaxation helps creativity. It helps recharge your batteries when you feel you are tired. It is also another way to access the vast resources of the subconscious, and tap spontaneous useful insights. Mozart maintained that his best musical ideas came to him when least expected, while travelling alone, or walking after an enjoyable meal, or during periods of wakefulness at night when he could not sleep. Nolan Bushnell, the founder of the Atari Company, got the inspiration for one of his best-selling video games while playfully kicking sand on a beach.

Hypnogogic States

Thomas Edison said that most of his ideas came to him when he was dozing. He would doze off in his chair with his arms over the armrests. In each arm he held two ball bearings. He would place two plates on the floor underneath his arms. As he drifted off his hand would relax, and the ball bearings would fall and hit the plates with a loud bang. Awakened by the noise, Edison would immediately write down any ideas that had come to him in his dreamlike state. Psychologists call this dreamlike state the hypnogogic state. This drowsy creative state happens just before we go to sleep at night, and before we wake up in the morning. This is also a good time to programme our minds with positive affirmations, so that we develop a positive attitude in our lives.

Take the case of Elias Howe, who invented the lock stitch sewing machine, and claimed to have hit on the idea after a nightmare. He dreamed that while cannibals were boiling him alive he noticed that their spears had holes in the tips. This proved to be the novel solution to his problem.

Kekule, a famous German chemist discovered that many organic compounds are formed of rings, rather than open molecules. He was inspired by a dream of a snake swallowing its tail, with the realisation that the Benzene chemical compound had a circular rather than a linear structure. He thus solved a problem that had been confounding chemists for a long time. In addition, don't ignore your intuition or sixth sense, as gut feelings sometimes are inspirational, and the idea generated may have practical validity.

Otto Loewi (1873-1961), a German born physiologist, won the Nobel Prize for medicine in 1936 for his work on the chemical transmission of nerve impulses. His discovery was inspired by a dream. In 1903 Loewi had the idea that nerve impulses had a chemical rather than an electrical cause, which was the conventional wisdom at the time. However, he didn't know how to prove his idea. He left the idea incubate for 17 years, until he had an inspirational dream about how he could draw up an experiment to prove his thesis. It took Loewi another 10 years before he could carry out the tests to prove his theory to the satisfaction of his peers and critics.

Notes to Inspire

Keeping notes is a feature of people who achieve creative greatness. B.F. Skinner, the most influential behavioural scientist of the 20th century, believed that we all have good ideas, but must remember to capture them when they come, as otherwise we will forget them. He always carried a small notebook with him so that he could write down ideas as they came to him.

How does creativity happen?

The debate whether or not creative is innate or learned continues. It is obviously a combination of nature and nurture with the exact contribution of each debatable. Most people now believe that creativity is not only the province of artists, designers and inventors, but is a learnable skill that can be enhanced through practise, training and knowledge of techniques. Many companies think it worthwhile to run courses and workshops to enhance the creative skills of their employees.

We will now look at the stages of creativity and some of the better known techniques. The five stages of creativity are: preparation, effort, incubation, insight and evaluation. The stages combine divergent imaginative skills, and convergent logical skills.

Preparation

Preparation includes all of the experience, formal education and research a person has done to date on the problem. Louis Pasteur observed that fortune favours the prepared mind. Although serendipity, or the making of fortunate discoveries by chance, does happen you must be tuned into the problem to recognise the solution when you come across it serendip-

Inspiration

"Creativity is just connecting things. When you ask creative people how they did something, they feel a little guilty because they didn't really do it, they just saw something. It seemed obvious to them after a while. That's because they were able to connect experiences they've had and synthesise new things."
Steve Jobs

itiously. Preparation includes being in the right receptive mood, or studious frame of mind, to think deeply about the problem in hand.

You take ownership of the problem by thinking continuously, about it and making it part of your thinking. You become goal-oriented, obsessed, challenged, motivated and stretched, by the desire to solve the problem. You must allow your mind to roam free while playing with the problems and sleeping with it. Try and imagine looking at the problem from as many different perspectives as possible. View the problem from above, below and from the sides. Let the problem brew and gestate in your mind.

Redefine the problem using the words 'how to,' and 'in how many ways can we.' At this stage you must read widely around the problem. Has anybody solved a similar problem? If so, you may already have a ready-made, proven answer. To promote creativity, diversify your interests and reading in order to generate divergent views and analogies. Stand on the shoulders of giants by consulting experts and reading the best specialist authors on the subject pertinent to the problem. Collect all information and relevant facts about the problem, including first hand and desk research. Consult friends and colleagues to get fresh and different viewpoints. All of these preparations and approaches will help you find a solution.

Effort

You will need mental effort to generate as many ideas and alternatives as possible. Record these ideas as you go along. You may use the technique of brainstorming to generate numerous ideas. Brainstorming is a type of discussion process, in which members of a group are encouraged in a supportive and uncritical manner, to generate as many imaginative ideas and suggestions as possible, within a defined period of time, under the guidance of a facilitator.

The facilitator records these ideas for subsequent scrutiny, evaluation and criticism. The initial emphasis is on quantity rather than quality, so suspend judgement and let the creative juices flow. Seemingly unusual and crazy ideas may form the germ of perfectly practical solutions. The technique of brainstorming is covered in greater detail later on in this chapter.

Incubation

Incubation brings to mind a hen sitting on an egg waiting for it to hatch. Nothing seems to be happening for a long time, until suddenly a new life breaks through the shell. Similarly, you should reflect on the problem in your mind and let it gestate. In the meantime, do something interesting, distracting and relaxing, so that the subconscious mind takes over the hard work of problem solving for you. Once you let go of the problem, fresh perspectives will develop, and the solution will often spontaneously come to mind.

The subconscious mind is far better at coming up with creative insights than the conscious mind. In the subconscious mind ideas are free to recombine with other ideas, in novel patterns and unpredictable associations. It is also the storehouse of everything you know, including things you've forgotten and can't readily bring into conscious awareness. Further, the subconscious engages us beyond words including emotions and the deep imagery of the senses.

We are more open to insights from the subconscious mind when we are relaxed and not thinking of anything in particular. That is why daydreams are so useful for creativity. An idea that is eventually recognised by the conscious mind as a solution may have originated in a dream.

Insight

The 'Eureka' feeling of euphoria is felt when a novel solution has been arrived at, or a unique discovery has been made. Eureka means I have found it. This is a sudden flash of illumination, and a release of tension, when a difficult and seemingly insurmountable problem has eventually been solved. These insights usually occur during the most unexpected times, such as when exercising, during holidays, taking a shower or driving; or while you do something repetitive, such as housekeeping, knitting, gardening, painting, or cooking. It is now thought that the brain's right hemisphere specialises in pattern recognition and divergent thinking. This seems to offer a physiological explanation for the eureka phenomenon. After the left hemisphere has analysed a problem logically into its components, the right hemisphere may suddenly perceive a hidden pattern, just like you are able to suddenly pick out and recognise a familiar face in a crowd.

Chemist, Kary Mullis, came up with the basic principle of the polymerase chain reaction (PCR), on a spring evening, while driving up the northern California coast. PCR is the fundamental technology that makes genetic tests possible.

James Watson, the co-discover of the structure of the DNA-helix with Francis Crick, had his eureka moment in 1953 when he saw Rosalind Franklin's new X-ray diffraction picture of DNA, realising that the patterns could only arise from a double-helical structure. Nine years later they shared the Nobel Prize in Medicine with Maurice Wilkins, for solving one of the most important biological riddles; now a vital element in modern medicine and forensic science.

Evaluation

This is the verification stage and a return to logic for evaluating and criticising the solution. During the previous stages you suspended the inner critic to encourage and release the playful child within. However, at this stage you must become the devil's advocate by criticising the idea. You become a judge by evaluating the merits and demerits of an idea. Test the idea in order to see that it works. Can you implement the idea in a practical way? Unless you can it will never see the light of day.

Discard ideas that are too costly, unacceptable, unprofitable, inappropriate, or unethical. Tease out the solution against the stark realities of life – organisational politics, cost, opposition, compromise and expediency. At the end of the day unless the idea is commercially viable it is of little use to the business.

Practical Creativity

New ideas may be triggered off by means of the acronym **CAMPERS**, which stands for combine ideas, adapt a product, modify a product, put to other uses, eliminate unnecessary parts, rearrange, and simplify. This simple technique can be used to generate ideas or to prevent ideas from being forgotten.

- Combine two different ideas to create a new whole – for example, drug development requires the best ideas of biologists, chemists, geneticists and clinicians. Their insights combine and create novel solutions none of the scientists could come up with on their own. In electronics radios have been combined with CD players to create music centres, while televisions have been combined with DVD players. Mobile phones have been combined with cameras and the internet. A clock has been combined with a radio to produce the clock radio. A camper combines a car and a home. The Austrian monk Gregor Mendel, combined mathematics and biology, to create the modern science of genetics. Innovation is mostly about combining existing products and using technologies in new ways. Some companies have created links to universities to support, share and exploit research findings and ideas.

- Adapt an existing product to meet the identified customised needs of people – for example, cars can be adapted with special features to meet the personal requirements of disabled drivers. Personal computers can be built to order. Customised cars to meet the discretionary needs of wealthy clients, where expense means nothing, can be built to order. Mobile phones have enlarged key pads to meet the needs of older customers who are visually challenged. Generally, products are adapted to meet the needs of customers with diverse needs in diverse markets.

- Modify and improve an existing process or product to meet a new purpose. People can now print off their colour photographs themselves, in self-service machines designed for digital output. These machines are available in many retail outlets. Cameras have undergone many changes in line with technological developments and customer needs during the past few years. Today we have compact, disposable, Polaroid and digital cameras. Smart phones with cameras are commonplace. Even Coca-Cola has built on previous success by bringing out Lemon Coke and other varieties, with varying degrees of commercial success. Many new products and services are built on

Inspiration

"You see things; and you say, 'Why?' But I dream things that never were; and I say, 'Why not?' "
George Bernard Shaw

191

existing products or the work of others. Continuous improvement is now part of modern living. The famous golfer who said that the more he practised, the luckier he became exemplifies the principle in action.

- **Put to other uses** than the original intention – for example, memory cards are now used instead of film for storing pictures in a digital camera. Computer chips are now used in domestic appliances, televisions and cars. Viagra was originally a drug to treat high blood pressure, but is now used to help men with erectile dysfunction. G.D. Searle and Company, a pharmaceutical company, was doing research on a new anti-ulcer drug. Through chance they discovered a new substance that didn't cure ulcers, but instead tasted very sweet. Even though the company was not in the food business, they recognised the commercial potential of the product, and eventually developed and marketed the substance as an artificial sweetener with the brand name, NutraSweet.

- **Eliminate** the need for particular inputs and outputs, or for unnecessary parts or process and procedures. For example, you might redesign a form by eliminating information that is no longer required, or that duplicates information elsewhere on the same form. In a procedure you might eliminate unnecessary operations, transports and delays and consequently improve efficiency, cost and productivity. Value analysis is a technique used by engineers to reduce the number of parts in machinery and equipment. Unnecessary parts or features are eliminated after careful examination for greater efficiency and cost reduction. Reverse engineering, where a company takes a competitor's product and disassembles it to see if it could be improved in any way, is another application of this idea. World class manufacturing (WCM), and total quality management (TQM), are used in manufacturing companies to eliminate waste and improve productivity.

- **Rearrange** to create a new synthesis by re-sequencing steps, or enabling steps to be completed by different people, in new locations or at different times. For example, supermarkets many years ago introduced the self-service model, thereby delegating the task of picking groceries to customers, and reducing the number of employees they needed to operate the business. Today supermarkets are offering a wide variety of services in addition to groceries. Tesco, the supermarket chain, has combined products and services in new and unusual ways. It has introduced credit cards and insurance into its range of products, and also stocks hardware, clothing, electronic equipment, books, records and computers. It has extended opening times with some outlets even staying open 24 hours a day. It has internet shopping and delivery services to customers. Building societies are now offering current accounts while banks are offering mortgages. Amazon.com has built up a very successful retailing business by combining books and other products with the Internet. It has reframed its business to include electronic books, and has even marketed its own electronic reader. Modern information and communications technology means call centres can operate anywhere in the world, offering a wide variety of customer services and technical support.

- **S**implify an existing procedure by reducing unnecessary complexity – for example, James Dyson, the English inventor, introduced his revolutionary bag less vacuum cleaner on to the UK market in 1993. He noticed that the conventional vacuum lost suction when the bag starts to fill and get clogged, reducing its effectiveness. Rather than finding a way to improve the bag, Dyson thought more broadly about what the vacuum was trying to do. He realised that the vacuum pulls in a combination of dirt and air while needing to separate the two. He was reminded of sawmills, which use industrial cyclones to separate sawdust from air. Inspired by this and after much trial and error, Dyson developed a small version of the industrial cyclone in his portable vacuum cleaner, and in the process developed the bag less vacuum cleaner and a very successful, profitable company. Personal computers and software packages, such as Microsoft Office, are continually being updated and simplified, and are now much easier to use than previous incarnations.

Creative Perspectives

Edward De Bono, the inventor of lateral thinking, has suggested the following approach – known as the 'Six Thinking Hats' – to make people more creative and aware of other people's unique perspectives. It is a way of solving problems by adopting different insightful viewpoints. We each have a dominant thinking style followed by a preference for one or two others. The hats give you the permission and persona to adopt a particular thinking style. During the process participants can be asked to vary their different thinking styles thus helping them empathise with different perspectives.

- *White hat thinking.* This is about getting facts, figures and information, to solve a problem, or make a decision. It is a rational and logical way of thinking. A white hat thinker might say, 'Let's establish the facts before we go any further.' Accountants and engineers tend to like logic and facts and thus tend to have a preference for white hat thinking.
- *Red hat thinking.* This is concerned with hunches, feelings, intuition and emotions. The red hat allows you to express your feelings without fear and any need to justify them. It tries to engage the unconscious mind without the critical interference of the rational conscious mind. A red hat thinker might say. 'I've got a feeling this idea will work.' Creative writers and artists like to give expression to their emotions and thus tend to have a preference for red hat thinking.
- *Black hat thinking.* This is about caution, negativity, logic and critical judgement. You become the devil's advocate in action. It is useful because it helps people avoid silly costly mistakes and to see counter arguments. A black hat thinker might say, 'This proposal will never be accepted because the unions will object.' We all need to adopt black hat thinking from time to time to see the downside of our proposals.
- *Yellow hat thinking.* This is for logic, optimism, and taking up a posi-

Inspiration

"Think left and think right and think low and think high. Oh, the things you can think up if only you try."
Dr. Seuss

tive constructive point of view. The yellow hat encourages you to be creative and expansive, and see the bright side of things. The yellow hat thinker likes to make everybody feel happy and looks for the benefits and for ways of making ideas work. A yellow hat thinker might say, 'It's true that this system will take some time to work, but it will improve efficiency and effectiveness, and reduce our costs.' At the early stages of generating ideas we all need to put on our yellow hat thinking to encourage ideas.

- *Green hat thinking*. This is about creativity and progressing things forward. A green hat likes fresh innovative ideas. When stopped at traffic lights the green light gives you permission to proceed. Similarly, the green hat gives the go-ahead to generate alternatives, and explore ideas in a meaningful way. A green hat thinker might say, 'We need to develop and explore more alternatives.' Green hat thinkers will pick the best of the ideas and push them forward for further consideration
- *Blue hat thinking*. This is about managing the thinking process in a sensible way so that it becomes more productive. The blue hat thinker is very organised, and likes to manage time and take a considered thoughtful approach to problems. The chairperson or facilitator of the meeting usually wears this hat. The blue hat thinker would say, 'Let's review where we are before we proceed further.' Project managers like to follow process and thus have a preference for blue hat thinking.

The Range of Creativity Approaches

Academics classify creativity techniques under three headings: paradigm preserving, paradigm stretching and paradigm breaking. A paradigm is a new way of looking or thinking about something. It is a word used frequently in academic, scientific and business worlds. In education the talk and chalk approach is a paradigm. If you suddenly changed to a more participative approach that would be a new paradigm. In science, Darwin's theory of evolution, superseded the biblical story of man's creation, and thus created a new paradigm. In business it could mean a new way of marketing, such as using new distribution channels like the Internet to reach customers.

Paradigm preserving
Paradigm preserving techniques can be used to solve known and more structured problems. In paradigm preserving techniques the boundaries around the problem remain the same. People do not go outside their own perspectives in exploring the situation. Consequently, they develop existing ideas but do not change them significantly. Paradigm-preserving techniques can be useful as they do not require participants to move outside their comfort zones. Brainstorming and brainwriting are examples of paradigm-preserving techniques.

Paradigm stretching
Paradigm stretching techniques can be used to solve unstructured prob-

Inspiration

"One very important aspect of motivation is the willingness to stop and to look at things that no one else has bothered to look at. This simple process of focusing on things that are normally taken for granted is a powerful source of creativity."
Edward de Bono

lems. Paradigm stretching techniques encourage the participants to broaden their existing ways of thinking and looking at something. This can be done by using unrelated stimuli, metaphors and forced association. For example, you can use two unrelated words or ideas to develop new ideas. The Internet was developed by bringing together two unrelated concepts, the telephone and the computer. Similarly, smart televisions combine the television with the internet giving access to Google, radio and TV channels. It requires imagination and awareness to use this approach effectively, and consequently, they make some people feel uncomfortable as they push them outside their comfort zone.

Paradigm breaking

Like paradigm stretching techniques, paradigm breaking techniques can also be used to solve unstructured problems. Paradigm breaking techniques encourage people to look at situations from a number of different perspectives, and so come up with very unique and novel ideas. People produce creative ideas when they bring new elements into the problem situation, by developing new relationships and combinations between existing elements. This technique encourages people to change their perspectives, and break out of existing boundaries.

Paradigm-breaking techniques, like paradigm-stretching techniques, use unrelated stimuli and forced associations. In addition, these techniques also tend to rely on modes of expression other than verbal and written, such as drawing, dreaming, fantasising, visioning and role play. This can threaten peoples' sense of security, and therefore these techniques should only be used by groups who have a high degree of cohesion and trust. Galileo's discovery, published in 1632, that the Sun and not the Earth was the centre of the Universe, is a good example of a paradigm breaking discovery.

Brainstorming

Brainstorming is probably one of the best known and most popular techniques for generating ideas. It is easy to understand and use. Participants are encouraged to build on other people's ideas, and thus do not change them significantly. Just like dancing, brainstorming needs to be done standing up to generate the maximum number of ideas. This approach is therefore a paradigm preserving approach rather than a paradigm stretching, or paradigm-breaking approach.

The four stages of brainstorming
*   Suspend judgement. The emphasis is on the generation of ideas, so suspend your critical faculties. Quieten the voice of the inner critic, and put your critical faculties into neutral gear. Even though you know the idea is very silly, and all the reasons why it won't work, nevertheless, you must keep your mouth shut. In fact, the 'wildest idea' technique is sometimes used as a way of stimulating ideas by

focusing on the outlandish when they are beginning to dry up.

- Freewheel. Freewheel the ideas. Let them flow, as one idea may trigger off new ideas, combinations or novel relationships. The key thing to remember is not to get hung up on developing or assessing the worth or feasibility of ideas during this stage, as this interrupts the spontaneous flow of ideas. Group members should be allowed to communicate an idea, however strange and silly, to the rest of the group. Seemingly stupid and impractical ideas will often contain the germ of a great idea. Many of the great discoveries of history began in this way.

- Generate many ideas. At this stage you are looking for quantity of ideas rather than quality. Outrageous suggestions should be encouraged as these can often trigger off more worthwhile ideas. Some ideas can be linked, associated or combined with others to give new ideas. The most conducive environment to creativity is one in which people feel supported, non-threatened and relaxed, and where there is fun, humour, spontaneity, and playfulness. Laughter is the best medicine, as it facilitates relaxation, breaks down barriers and promotes creativity. Use irony, exaggeration, word play and absurd association to generate ideas.

- Cross-fertilise. The different people in the group will cross-fertilise by combining and improving existing ideas causing a variety of new ideas to emerge. Your group could include, inter alia, an accountant, engineer, a marketing person and a human relations manager. A mix of background, personalities and perspectives will help the group to synergise and consider the problem from many different viewpoints. Ideas will piggyback on the ideas of others in the group. On the organisational level, companies should look to joint ventures, alliances and networks, to provide alternative ways of coping creatively with competition. Whether undertaken for strategic advantage, or financial gain, these links offer opportunities for cross-fertilisation of ideas and perspectives. People from the same background will only produce sameness, while diversity facilitates cross-pollination of ideas and creativity.

Brainwriting versus brainstorming

Generally, you need to separate the creativity of idea production from the logic of idea evaluation. Both are needed together if you want worthwhile ideas to emerge. Judgement is postponed during brainstorming but not abandoned. Later on the ideas will be subjected to critical analysis, until you are left with the most promising ones. In the meantime, these ideas should be considered starting points for further exploration, rather than finished products. Considerably more time will be needed to develop these ideas into worthwhile commercial projects. This is the 99 per cent perspiration part, rather than the 1 per cent inspiration part that Edison famously referred to in the invention process. Ultimately, the value of a creative idea is determined if it can be applied successfully and profitably in a practical way.

There is some research that brainstorming may not be as useful for creativity as previously thought. It suggests that brainstorming meetings may lead people to merely mirror the thoughts of others. People may come up with more original thoughts if left to do so alone. This would suggest that brainwriting could be more productive than brainstorming. In brainwriting each participant thinks and records ideas alone. They then pass their ideas around to other participants, so that they can add to them, or use them to trigger off further ideas. After the idea gathering stage is completed, the ideas are read, discussed and evaluated with the help of a facilitator, just like traditional brainstorming.

Techniques for Stimulating Creativity

In addition to brainstorming there are a wide range of techniques like fantasy, attribute listing, reverse brainstorming, metaphors and SWOT, and creative problem solving (discussed later in this section) for stimulating creativity. These are paradigm stretching and paradigm breaking techniques. The acronym **FARMS** will help you remember them.

Fantasy.
Research has found that creative adults use fantasy for a number of purposes. Fantasy opens up other worlds of experience. In your imagination, you create your own realities unfettered by time and space. Within it you can space travel, journey to exotic places throughout the world, and shrink to the size of an atom to explore microscopic worlds. The idea of becoming miniaturised or something else, in order to understand it better, may be applied to any problem. For example, a pharmaceutical executive discovered a contaminant by visualising he was a tiny organism, and asking himself how he could get in and cause so much damage. He found the cause was miniscule cracks in the wall of a sterile room.

You can become anything the mind can think of. Albert Einstein's fantasy of himself riding a beam of sunlight played an important part in the discovery of the theory of relativity. Role-play, is a type of fantasy used in management training helping people empathise with the role they want to experience, and see things from different perspectives.

Attribute listing.
List the main characteristics of a product, object or idea. Examine each one to see if it can be improved or changed. You can make a new product by making combinations or variations on some or all of its attributes. It is a method of exploring business opportunities, rather than solving specific problems. For example, a product might have several dimensions, such as the design, the material of manufacture, the colour, the package surround, and the distribution system used to bring the product to the customer. Potential applications include, new design, exploring the use of different raw materials in its manufacture, developing different storage, promotion

and distribution strategies, determining competitive advantage, and retail location selection.

Reverse brainstorming.

This is a negative approach to brainstorming. Instead of asking 'in how many ways can we ….?' this technique asks: 'in how many ways can this idea fail?' It is a good way to tease out problems in advance, so that potential difficulties and solutions can be thought through. Play the devil's advocate with your proposals, and anticipate opposition, counter arguments, objections and obstacles, so that you are prepared and rehearsed with the appropriate answers – very useful when you are presenting proposals to your boss for discussion, as a way of anticipating and dealing with flaws in your argument.

Alfred Sloan of General Motors used the technique of problem reversal to develop ideas to save the near bankrupt company. At the time it had always been assumed that customers had to pay for their cars in advance before they took possession of them. Sloan reversed the assumption by thinking that customers could pay as they drove the car, thus opening up the idea of hire purchase and instalment payments.

Metaphor.

Metaphors and analogies are wonderful sources of creativity. The Greek philosopher Aristotle considered the use of metaphors a sign of true genius. He believed that people, who had the capacity to perceive similarities between two different things, and link them together in a meaningful way, were possessors of a special gift. Metaphorical thinking is the ability to link two different things by recognising that in some way they share a common trait or principle.

Metaphors can be drawn from science, technology, nature, industry, sport, literature and history. For example, a revolution is compared to a volcano (a build-up of pressure leading to an explosion), and electric current is compared to water flowing through pipes. Machinery has been a common metaphor used to understand the workings of modern society. We refer to the machinery of government, re-engineering corporations, and even input-output models for business and educational systems. Managing a company is sometimes compared to running a family. The structure of the human brain is often compared to a computer.

Fiona Fairhurst and her design team, at the swimwear company Speedo, were faced with a difficult challenge. They needed to design suits that would reduce drag, and thus improve the performance of competitive swimmers. For inspiration, they looked at the animal kingdom, and in particular sharks, who have no problem swimming fast despite the shape of their bodies. They analysed samples of sharkskin, and found that it had tiny structures on its surface called denticles that kept water molecules from sticking to it. The team created a fabric that mimicked the denticles, and designed full-body swimsuits with it. Soon after the new Fastskin swimsuit was introduced, world records were broken.

Metaphorical thinking can inspire people to great achievements. Alexander Graham Bell got the inspiration for the telephone from studying the human ear. The ability to play with ideas and concepts from different areas is basic to problem solving and creativity. Metaphor allows this type of play to occur. So making comparisons or analogies between, problems in business, and in nature, biology, science and so on may help to unlock problems and offer solutions.

Inspired by nature

Over the years, engineers have found that biology has been a rich source of practical parallels. Confronted with design problems, mechanical engineers might look for parallel solutions already existing in nature. They might ask: How do birds function aerodynamically? How do chameleons change their colour to match their environment? This approach has resulted in the invention of revolutionary glues and coatings, communication tools, and even equipment like carburettors.

In 1948 George de Mestral, a Swiss engineer, was out walking one day and came back with cockleburs stuck to his jacket. When he examined one under his microscope, he found that thin fins with hooks on the end were responsible for them sticking to his jacket. Over thousands of years many must have noticed the same phenomenon but nobody saw its commercial potential. George immediately recognised the potential of his discovery for a practical new fastener. It took 8 years to perfect the invention, and thus the modern Velcro was born.

The Kingfisher has the superpower to see through the glare of water to catch fish. This revelation from nature inspired a camera which is able to detect humpback wales in the sea. The same technology is now used to help find bodies in water during rescue and search and find operations. Cuttlefish change colour, shape and texture in response to changes in their environment. It has light sensitive cells all over its body. This inspired a way to camouflage army tanks by attaching panels which change the appearance of the tank in line with the environment. The tank can even be made invisible.

Scientists are studying spider silk that they produce when making their webs. It is remarkable material, very strong though thinner than hair, and its possible applications are limitless. However, its secrets still remain elusive. Crabs have extremely tough outer skeletons to protect them. This has given rise to the invention of exoskeletons which are used to help support paralysed people to walk, or provide supersonic strength to able people.

SWOT analysis.

This stands for strengths, weaknesses, opportunities and threats. Although developed for strategic planning it can equally be used for personal development. Your strengths might include your education, experience, personality, aptitudes, creativity and initiative. Your weaknesses might include a deficiency in computer skills or lack of assertiveness.

Opportunities might include training courses and possible promotional vacancies arising in the future. Threats might include possible closure of the company you work for due to competitive forces. A threat or weakness, in fact, is often a matter of attitude or perspective. A more positive approach might be to consider how to turn the threat into an opportunity. In other words, treat problems as possible opportunities. Create a mindset in which problems are examined for sources of opportunities and imaginative solutions.

Creative Problem Solving

Inspiration

"The problem is never how to get new, innovative thoughts into your mind, but how to get old ones out. Every mind is a building with archaic furniture. Clean out a corner of your mind and creativity will instantly fill it."
Dee Hock

I have adopted this from a technique used in management services called **SREDIM**, which is an acronym standing for Select, Record, Examine, Develop, Install and Maintain. It is a systematic comprehensive step-by-step approach to creative problem solving.

- **Select.** This means identifying the problems and opportunities for change or improvement. After considering alternative problems for study, you should converge on the problem that deserves further consideration, study and exploration. Question the problem thoroughly. What is the problem or problems? Where does it occur? When does it occur? How does it occur? Whose problems is it? Why does the problem occur? What are the reasons for the problem? How can the problem be overcome? They say that a problem defined is a problem half solved.

- **Record the facts.** Collect as much relevant information as possible about the selected problem. Focus on answering the following questions. What facts do I have? What facts do I not have? What facts do I need to solve the problem? How much will it cost and how difficult is it to get these facts? How urgent is the decision? Can I afford to wait for these facts? In practice, most decisions are made with incomplete information. Researching, recording and gathering facts is very time-consuming and expensive. Therefore you must devise the best and most cost effective method of collecting the facts. At a certain stage, you may make up your mind to go no further, because it is becoming too difficult, less worthwhile, and too costly to continue.

- **Examine the facts and interpret.** Adopt a critical, questioning and sceptical attitude. Apply common sense principles and make sure that your interpretation of the facts is reasonable, correct and logical. Differentiate between facts, feelings, opinions and assumptions. Disregard opinions completely and treat feelings and assumptions with extreme caution. Be aware of any preconceived biases that you may have, and discount them accordingly. If you've solved similar problems before, the same approach with slight modifications to cater for unique circumstances, might work again. There is no point in reinventing the wheel. Check out and verify the facts, and crosscheck in a rigorous objective manner. If anything proves to be incorrect it will undermine your credibility, and may rubbish your findings. Be attentive to the detail, as it may be the detail that discredits your solution in the end.

- **Develop alternative solutions.** Flexibility of mind and creativity is needed here to generate alternatives. In how many different ways could this problem be solved? Some problems may require a new perspective, or a paradigm shift to resolve them. You may need to take a new direction, or form new connections and associations, and even discover unusual patterns or relationships to unravel a solution. You may use some of the paradigm preserving, paradigm stretching, and paradigm breaking techniques, previously discussed, to come up with creative solutions.

- **Implement your chosen solution.** Having considered the alternative solutions, pick the best alternative, or combination of alternatives. Obviously there are many alternative solutions to any problem; therefore, you should rank alternatives in terms of their desirability, suitability, cost effectiveness and acceptability. Accepting and implementing change involves a big selling job to win the hearts and minds of those affected. Draw up an implementation plan. List the types of problems, constraints, obstacles that may be encountered during implementation, and have contingency plans to deal with them. When will implementation take place? How long will it take? Who will do it? Where will it happen? How much will it cost?

- **Monitor and follow up** to ensure that the solution is working satisfactorily. The review is an opportunity for feedback, leading to corrective action and improved performance in the future. Learn from your mistakes so that you do not make the same mistakes again. In the business world there is a phenomenon called 'drift.' All things are inclined to revert to their original state unless properly monitored. So it is important to do periodic reviews to see what practical difficulties have arisen, and what modifications are necessary to rectify any difficulties arising.

Inspiration

"Creativity comes from a conflict of ideas."
Donatella Versace

Barriers to Creativity

So far we have considered how to become more creative. The flipside to this is how to stifle creativity. There are many barriers to creativity but the following are the most important. If you are aware of these it will help you understand and counteract their effects.

Conformity
People do not like to be different and like to fit in socially. There are all sorts of pressures and cultural norms on us to be the same. People don't like to think for themselves, like to fit in with the crowd, and they prefer to do the accepted or conventional thing, rather than the novel or unusual.

In everyday life fashion and mores tend to standardise the way we think. Bureaucratic cultures often reward conformity and discourage difference and initiative. Standard operating procedures are the norm. There is great emphasis on creating sameness and on increasing standardisation, and reducing variability in all aspects of social and business life. This approach is the antithesis of creativity. After all conformity is comforting, while change is often threatening and traumatic.

In the work situation, if managers want to encourage creativity and innovation they must simplify bureaucracy, and reward new ideas and risk taking. Structures influence the level of creativity, or lack of creativity in an organisation. Centralised structures and control generally encourage rigidity and bureaucratic thinking, whereas decentralised structures and delegation facilitate creativity, innovative thinking, and empowerment. A blame culture should be avoided and people should be encouraged to use their initiative, and treat their mistakes as learning opportunities.

Edwin Land, the inventor of Polaroid glass, instant film and the instant camera, maintained that every significant step, in every field of endeavour, is taken by some individual who has freed himself from the shackles of conventional thinking. There are people who may be more intelligent, better educated, better disciplined, but who have not mastered the art of the fresh, clean look at old knowledge. We must be happy, playful and adventurous like children to be creative.

The One Right Answer

All our early schooling and subsequent training and education are logical rather than creative. Our education is largely concerned with language and numbers. We are taught to be rational, convergent, conventional and predictable, rather than imaginative, creative, controversial and lateral. At school and college we are taught that there is one right answer to all problems, which conveniently resides in the teacher's head, or at the back of the textbook.

However, in real life there are many different solutions to most problems, and many grey areas rather than black and white answers, and very few people have all the answers. The human mind is surprisingly adroit at supporting its deep-seated ways of viewing the world, while shifting out evidence to the contrary. Even when presented with overwhelming facts to the contrary, many people, including the well-educated ones, simply won't abandon their deeply held views.

Evaluating Too Quickly

Be the angel's advocate rather than the devil's advocate. When generating ideas write them down and suspend judgement. Let the ideas flow rather than cut them short by being critical and dismissive too early and too quickly. One person's question or comment can easily stimulate another's imagination. Let the creative juices flow – time enough to play the devil's advocate, and be critical and rational later. In the meantime, be playful and have fun.

Ask questions such as 'what if,' and 'why not.' Unless you ask lots of 'why' questions you won't generate creative insights. The objective should be to crystallise as many ideas as possible in writing, as unless you record them they are unlikely to be examined and will be forgotten. Quantity rather than quality, and encouragement rather than judgement, should be the key at this stage.

Afraid to challenge the obvious

Try to see things from different perspectives. One way of doing this is by reframing problems. For example, we don't have a health care crisis; we have a sick care crisis. By refocusing our resources from treating illness to prevention, diagnosis and early treatment, we can keep our older workers healthy and out of hospital, free up hospital beds and improve productivity.

Similarly, we do not have an obesity problem; rather we have a willpower, lifestyle, exercise, nutrition, and overeating problem. Greater willpower, more exercise, and less eating are the solution. One plus one is not always two. With a bit of creativity and playfulness it may be eleven, a cross, a T and so on. Use your imagination to generate the different possibilities and perspectives.

A questioning approach is essential to unearth issues, and see novel relationships that have not been thought of before. Sometimes we fail to see the obvious even though it is staring us in the face. The movements of the moon, and the rise and fall of the tides at sea were known since antiquity. However, it was only in the 17th century that the astronomer Keppler connected these two unrelated facts, and discovered that the moon controlled the tides.

The self-imposed barrier

Sometimes barriers are traditional and psychological rather than real. There are times when you have to go outside the box to get a new perspective, and to break away from conventional constraints. For many years it was accepted to be physiologically impossible to run a mile in less than 4 minutes. Then Roger Bannister came along in 1954 and broke the physiological and psychological barrier. In the years that followed numerous runners broke this self-imposed barrier.

Our peers and bosses can also impose barriers on us. Two research scientists had an irritating boss who was always saying 'you can't make a silk purse out of a sow's ear.' They were determined to prove him wrong, and bought 100 pairs of sow's ears in the local slaughterhouse. Treating them chemically, they extracted a silk filament, which they then made into a silk purse much to their delight, and the surprise and dismay of their boss.

In fear of looking a fool

Fear of failure, fear of ridicule, fear of not being original, and lack of self-esteem and confidence are major barriers to creativity. Some people are often inhibited to suggest ideas, because they fear a negative reaction, or that they will be laughed at. The inner critic may say to you; 'they'll think I'm foolish,' or 'that it will never work.' This may be the position in a group of staff, peers and managers at work who are extremely conscious of their status.

Employees are afraid to offer ideas in front of their managers, in case their ideas are thought to be ridiculous, and thus their chances of promotion in the future will be adversely affected. On the other hand, managers are reluctant to make suggestions, in case they look foolish in front of their peers and staff. People must trust and respect each other, to feel safe and secure enough, to express new ideas freely without fear of censure. Cynicism, negativity, and lack of trust stifle creativity and encourage conformity.

Functional fixedness

This is the term invented by psychologists to describe the condition whereby individuals from departments are constrained and stymied from thinking of novel ideas by their unique departmental culture, perspective, philosophy, knowledge, expertise and experience. We only see the obvious way of looking at a problem – the same comfortable way we have always looked at it. If the only tool you have is a hammer then you will try and fix every problem with a nail.

Individuals who want to be creative should maintain a flexible approach, and avoid relying too heavily on habitual ways of doing things, or on a particular perspective. Bureaucracy has a habit of killing off ideas before they get a chance to grow. Command and control cultures will not encourage creativity although setting goals and boundaries, like operating within budgets, and defining the problem will help.

Taboos

These are hot potatoes that companies avoid discussing, because they are politically dangerous, too sensitive, culturally unacceptable, too difficult to solve, or just too dreadful to contemplate. People often turn a blind eye to some feature of a process that is too cumbersome, to a manager whose autocratic style is driving staff demented, and even causing some to leave, or to a competitor who is gradually eroding market share.

These are the things that remain unchallenged and unsolved, and create serious barriers to creativity and business success. These problems are left to fester, when they could have been nipped in the bud, and in the long-term develop into major issues, when it is either too late or too difficult to address them. The worst thing about elephants in the room is that if you ignore them long enough, they become invisible but the problem still remains and festers away.

Anxiety

Too much and too little anxiety can inhibit creativity. An optimum amount of anxiety is needed for best results. If you're upset, your brain focuses only on what you're worried about, and can immobilise you to do anything productive. Anxiety is related to the fear of the unknown. Anxiety and creativity go hand in hand. To do something creative we run the risk of failure, rejection and being laughed at.

Actors like Al Pacino, Robert DeNiro and Jack Nicholson, instead of denying their anxiety, channel it into superior and dynamic acting performances. It is often a question of feel the fear and do it anyway! In a training session setting 'Ice-breakers,' humour, and energisers, can be used to relax people and stimulate them to be more creative.

Belief

Without self-belief and confidence in your unique talents and ability to generate worthwhile ideas for change you are unlikely to get very far. If you think you can be creative you will be, while if you think you can't you won't. So it becomes a self-fulfilling prophecy. Strong beliefs have changed the course of history.

Martin Luther King Jr. had a dream that the United States could become a society free from racial prejudice, segregation and injustice. He was inspired by Gandhi's philosophy of non-violent protest. Following the Civil Rights Act of 1964, which helped end discrimination against Blacks, King was awarded the Nobel Peace Prize for his work towards social justice. Before this, in 1963 he was named Man of the Year by Time magazine. Similarly, Mahatma Gandhi won independence for India from British rule by peaceful means. His belief in the effectiveness of non-violent protest changed the course of history and brought down the might of the British Empire.

Inspiration

"Imagination is the beginning of creation. You imagine what you desire, you will what you imagine, and at last, you create what you will."
George Bernard Shaw

How to Kill Creativity

The President of the Michigan Savings Bank advised Henry Ford's lawyer not to invest in the Ford Motor Company. His advice was: 'The horse is here to stay, but the automobile is only a fad.' In many organisations ideas are killed before they ever get off the ground. Persistence, determination, and resilience, will see ideas through in the end. Some of the well-known creativity killers include:

- 'It won't sell.' Decca Records rejected the Beetles in 1962, and instead signed Brian Poole & The Tremeloes. They said that groups with guitars were going out of fashion. Columbia and HMV, subsequently turned them down as well. They were finally offered a recording contract by Parlophone, and went on to become the most famous rock 'n' roll group in history. Jim Denny of the Grand Old Oprey, Nashville, fired Elvis Presley after his first performance, and advised him to go back to driving a truck.

- 'We tried that before and were unsuccessful.' Dr. Seuss's first book, And to Think I Saw It on Mulberry Street, was rejected by 27 publishers. Seuss was so depressed that he considered burning the manuscript. However, he went on to become the author of more than forty best-selling children's books, including The Cat in the Hat, Green Eggs and Ham, and The 500 Hats of Bartholomew Cubbins.

- 'It will upset the boss.' EMI dropped the first Sex Pistols UK single from their second label. The BBC banned their second single God Save the Queen (She ain't a human being). They believed it would upset the British Monarchy. The Sex Pistols went on to become one of the most famous punk rock bands in the world.

- 'It will cost too much.' Walt Disney's first cartoon production company, Laugh-O-Gram, went bankrupt. However, he didn't let this get him down. He subsequently went on to create Micky Mouse which became the most famous cartoon name in film animation. He produced Snow White and the Seven Dwarfs, Pinocchio, Fantasia, Bambi, and Cinderella and founded Disneyland.

- 'It won't travel.' Western Union came to the conclusion in 1876, that the telephone had too many drawbacks to be taken seriously as a means of communication, and concluded that the device was of no value to them. In 1927 HM Warner of Warner Bros, said that people would not be interested in hearing actors talk. F. Zanuck, Head of 20th Century Fox, reached similar short-sighted conclusions about TV in 1946: 'People will soon get tired of staring at a plywood box every night.' Some people thought that data processing was a fad that wouldn't last, and concluded that there was no reason for any individual to need a computer in his home. In 1943 Thomas Watson, chairman of IBM, concluded there would only be a total world market for five computers. Even Bill Gates of Microsoft in 1981, thought that 64K would be enough processing power for anybody.

- 'It's too obvious and simplistic.' Post-it-Notes, by 3M, have gone on to become one of the most lucrative products of all time. The company was looking for a new type of strong glue. One type of glue produced was too weak and this less aggressive glue was adapted for a new market, and the Post-it-Note, after many years, was eventually born. In fact, some of the simplest ideas often turn out to be the most successful and profitable.

- 'There are too many complications.' Complications didn't deter Charles Lindbergh. He became the first person to fly solo, non-stop across the Atlantic Ocean, and received the Congressional Medal of Honour from President Calvin Coolidge for his achievement.

- 'Competitors will copy our idea quickly.' Bill Gates founded Microsoft Corporation with Bill Allen. Gates designed the software to run the first microcomputer, signed agreements with computer companies to use his software solely on their machines, and became the world's richest man, and one of the world's most benevolent philanthropists.

- 'It's against company policy.' Donald Fisher, a real estate developer, was refused when he tried to change a pair of Levi's jeans for a different size in a department store in San Francisco. Frustrated by his experience he opened up his own store specialising in jeans and called it the Gap. This is now one of the most successful speciality stores in retailing history.

- 'It's impossible.' On 17 December, 1903 the Wright brothers made the first powered aeroplane flight in history. Although attended and witnessed by five people the press ignored the momentous event. At the time conventional scientific thinking assumed that such a flight was impossible. Lord Kelvin, president of the Royal Society, declared in 1895 that heavier than air flying machines could not fly. In fact, as late as 1905, Scientific American magazine still condemned the reports of the Wright brother's success as a hoax. The Wright brothers offered their invention to the US War Department, but were dismissed as cranks. It was not until their flight in Le Mans France in 1908 that their achievement was universally recognised and celebrated. History is littered with things that were once thought impossible, but which eventually became possible. Pierre Pachet, Professor of Physiology at Toulouse, declared in 1872 that Louis Pasteur's theory of germs was ridiculous fiction. People at the time thought that a wireless was an impossible and ridiculous idea, but Marconi proved them wrong.

'Yes, but' is a famous killer phrase, and denotes a negative attitude of mind. It is just one of the typical destructive statements that stultify creativity and personal initiative in a company. Why not substitute 'Yes and' which suggests positivity, expansion, and an opening up of possibilities. Why not be generous with your praise and support to encourage creativity in others?

The 'not invented here' syndrome also spells the death of many a good idea before it has time to germinate. Some people are just not prepared to entertain ideas from sources other than their own. All the marvellous products we enjoy as part of modern convenience living began with an idea.

Where Does Creativity Happen?

We can be creative at home and in the workplace.

At home
Some people think that creativity is restricted to great inventions and works of art. In fact, creativity can happen in any areas of our personal and work lives. Creativity is not about creating a masterpiece but about creating something new.

Creativity is needed in our personal lives to solve everyday problems, such as doing more with a shrinking household budget, or carrying out

Inspiration

"The creation of something new is not accomplished by the intellect but by the play instinct acting from inner necessity. The creative mind plays with the objects it loves."
Carl Jung

207

on-going repairs and maintenance to our homes. If I can better organise my day, write letters and reports in more effective ways, or make more interesting presentations, then this is being creative.

Many people find a creative outlet for interior design when they are furnishing, painting and decorating their homes. Others can develop their creative skills by designing lighting effects, rearranging the furniture in their home, landscaping the garden, or experimenting with new cooking recipes. More important is to adjust your mental attitude so that you approach life experiences with an open mind, and cultivate a belief that possibilities and solutions are always within reach, so that you are equipped to handle any challenge with confidence and flair.

In the workplace

In the workplace there are numerous opportunities for creativity to flourish. Creativity can take place in any area of an organisation, and not just in research and development (R&D), design, marketing and advertising. Innovation within companies may take the form of the development of new products, services and processes. At a more routine level, incremental innovation takes place all the time with the continuous improvement of products, services and processes.

Individually employees can become more creative by getting involved in opportunities, such as foreign assignments, cross-functional projects teams, job rotation, or being involved in a crisis situation where their abilities and skills are stretched to the limit. A static environment in the same old office with the same old desk, and working with the same old colleagues can be stifling.

Employees can also be inspired by training events such as training courses and workshops. Hallmark each year brings into its Kansas City HQ outside speakers from various artistic backgrounds. The sole purpose is to provide stimulation to the world's largest corporate creative staff of artists, designers, writers, editors and photographers who generate thousands of original designs for their cards and related products each year.

In a company there is a positive correlation between investment in R&D and sales growth. Investment in R&D is an important element in creating a culture of innovation in a company. However, it is important that R&D is focused on the needs and objectives of the company, so that products that customers actually need are created, and sales and profits grow as a result.

Companies need to be continually creative to differentiate their products from competitors in the market. They may do this through innovative pricing strategies, improved packaging and design, and better distribution channels. Creativity can even occur in accounting. I'm not referring to creative accounting here! Over the past couple of decades, there have been many innovations in accounting that are extremely profound and ethical, such as activity based costing, and zero based budgeting.

The most creative ideas often come from people working closest to the customer, because they understand the customer, and know the operational problems that they face on a daily basis. For example, in a restaurant the best ideas may come from the waitresses and waiters, rather than the management. They may have ideas about new additions to the menu, more efficient ways of paying the bill, improvements to the decor of the restaurant, and ways to attract more customers into the restaurant.

Creativity suffers greatly during a downsizing. It is even worse coming up towards the downsizing as people lose interest and disengage from the work. Communication, trust and collaboration decline significantly as does people's sense of motivation, freedom and autonomy.

Who is Creative?

Most people are creative. However, certain people like designers, entertainers, musicians, management consultants, advertisers, journalists, writers, landscapers, chefs, architects, engineers and scientists are especially so. They are often seen to be very independent minded, and because of their creativity, difficult to manage. Psychologists have identified the characteristics of creative people. These include playfulness, resilience, imagination, novel ideas, curiosity and energy. These traits are well worth developing.

Inspiration

"To live a creative life, we must lose our fear of being wrong."
Joseph Chilton Pearce

The traits of creative people
Use the acronym **PRINCE** to recall these traits of creative people:
- **P**layfulness. Creative people are extroverted and quite happy to play about with ideas that others might find childish. They enjoy the freedom to take risks, and the opportunity to explore alternatives. Being happy, rather than anxious, means that they are more likely to be creative and solve problems. During the 1930s and 1940s, laughter was a disciplinary offence at the Ford Motor Company's River Rouge plant in Michigan USA. Today, many organisations actually encourage their employees to enjoy their work with opportunities for humour and playfulness. Both Isaac Newton and Albert Einstein believed that having fun and being playful was an essential part of creativity. Laughter and humour can also be useful in providing perspectives and stimulating ideas, while creating an enjoyable and relaxing atmosphere.
- **R**esilient. They are driven by a need to create and are not put off by obstacles and setbacks. They are not too worried about ideas that do not seem to work, but just get on with the job of producing better ideas. They have an unrelenting work ethic that enables them to turn mistakes into successes and problems into opportunities. They know that creativity depends on difficulties, constraints, ambiguity

and learning from mistakes. Physicist Ernst Mach wrote that many accidental events 'were seen hundreds of times by others before they were noticed.' Most 'overnight success' stories are made after many years' hard work and struggle with a seemingly insurmountable problem. Even before this you must have acquired the appropriate expertise through study and experience in the field. It takes at least 10 years of constant study and practise to become an expert in a subject. However, you should always consider learning as a work in progress, rather than a chore.

- Imagination. It is not logic, but imagination which gives birth to new ideas. Imagination is like a muscle that strengthens with use. Expect to be creative and you are more likely to be so. Creative people have above average intelligence and are good at using imagination and fantasy. They have the ability to visualise problems and come up with new ideas. Imagination gives you the ability to explore options and see situations from different perspectives. Imagination helps you explore the past and visualise the future. We use our imagination when we give directions, describe an event, tell a story, or bake a cake. We need imagination to design a house, paint a picture, organise a party, or write a book. When executives use their imagination it is called vision. The novelist uses imagination to create characters, locations and a storyline. Chemists imagine molecules interacting to anticipate and understand how chemicals will behave when combined.

- Novel ideas. They are capable of coming up with unusual ideas. It is this facility that makes them stand out from others. They often lack business acumen and are prepared to leave the development and exploitation of their ideas to others. They can be more interested in producing ideas rather than exploiting them commercially, and consequently many who didn't bother to take out patents to protect their inventions finished up bankrupt. Dick Fosbury won the gold medal for the high jump for the USA at the 1968 Olympics in Mexico City. He is the creator of the novel and famous "Fosbury Flop," which is now the most popular high jumping technique.

- Curiosity. Curiosity is an internal motivator of exploratory behaviour, which leads to learning, or increased knowledge. Creative people have broad interests and specific interests, and are innately curious. Their broad interest motivates them to seek out various sources of novelty, challenge and information. Their specific interest motivates them to increase the depth of their specialist knowledge and experience. Creative people whether they are artists, inventors, or scientists, share some common traits such as openness to experience. In addition, they like to question the purpose of everything and see things from a new perspective. Their need to question things may irritate others with a more practical bent of mind. James Watt invented the steam engine, after noticing the power of steam to lift the lid off a kettle. Newton is said to have formulated the law of gravity, after being hit on the head by an apple falling from a tree.

- Energy. They have high energy levels with great staying power, and are driven by an innate need to produce creative work. They believe they must put in the effort if they are to be successful in whatever they undertake. Creative people create more ideas, come up with more possibilities, and generate more schemes. They make more attempts, make more mistakes than others, and endure more setbacks. They treat mistakes as experiments to learn from. They know that if they don't make mistakes they fail to learn, let alone do anything unusual or innovative.

Nurturing creativity at home

Creative adults tend to grow up in families which provided stable homes with clear rules and boundaries, but where the parents encouraged uniqueness. These families were highly sensitive to children's needs, yet challenged them to develop skills, be different, and be adaptable. On the other hand, highly creative adults frequently grew up with hardship. Hardship by itself doesn't lead to creativity, but expediency forces children to become more flexible in dealing with problems in straitened circumstances, and flexibility helps with creativity.

Apparently the games children play in early childhood help them to grow into creative adults. Pre-schoolers who spend more time in role play tend to be more creative. It seems that acting out someone else's point of view, help develop their ability to analyse situations, and see things from different perspectives. Even when playing alone they can act out strong negative emotions such as anger, sadness and hostility, in a safe environment.

Optimistic and confident people think more positively, flexibly and creatively. With an optimistic attitude you have a belief that things will work out well, despite adverse circumstances, and that all you have to do is to figure out how. This attitude helps you to come up with innovative solutions, while pessimism may have the opposite effect. Inventors tend to be more confident and optimistic than the general population. They spend more time on their projects, even after receiving negative feedback that it is time to quit.

There is the widespread idea that fear and sadness is a spur to creativity. On the contrary, creativity is positively associated with joy and love and negatively associated with anger, fear and anxiety. People are happiest when they come up with a creative idea, but they are more likely to do so if they experience happiness beforehand.

Empowered people, or people with control over their lives, are more likely to be creative than people who believe they cannot influence the circumstances under which they live. Such people believe their lives are controlled by others, and therefore have little incentive to be creative or learn new things.

Even though some people think that they are far more creative when working under time constraints, the opposite in fact is true. Creativity requires an incubation period as previously discussed; people need time to soak in a problem, and let the ideas emerge. Time pressures stifle creativity, because people haven't the time to deeply engage with and think about the problem.

However, people may become more innovative with the challenge of recessionary times, more competition, tighter budgets, and deadlines. When your back is to the wall you are often forced to come up with more effective, smarter and less costly ways of living. The pressures and demands of wartime often give rise to an increase in useful inventions and ideas for everyday living.

Nurturing creativity at work
In general people will be most creative when they are intrinsically motivated, by the interest, enjoyment, involvement, satisfaction, and challenge of the work itself. On the other hand, this intrinsic motivation can be undermined by extrinsic motivators, that lead people to feel externally manipulated and controlled in their work. Sometimes financial rewards can have a negative effect on creativity, if they are perceived as being a means of being bribed or controlled. Financial rewards do not in themselves make employees passionate about their work, and thus may hinder creativity in the long-term.

People are most creative when they're passionate about their work, and they're stretching their skills. If the challenge is far beyond their skill level, they tend to get frustrated, while if it's below their skill level, they tend to get bored, and so a right balance needs to be struck for best results. In fact, a challenging job offering satisfaction is more important than monetary compensation.

Creativity may be easier to achieve within the smaller firm where flexibility is a key factor when addressing business opportunities. Creativity flourishes in a culture, where it is supported, valued, celebrated and recognised. People like the opportunity to engage deeply in their work and make real progress. Organisations conducive to creativity are more informal than formal, and allow people to participate, network and experiment.

Entrepreneurs are creative in that they exploit business opportunities for competitive advantage when they establish a new business. They would never undertake risky business projects, if they did not believe that their one is the one that is going to defy the odds, and be successful. They provide the basis for innovation and business growth, as well as meeting the needs of customers and creating employment opportunities for others. Optimism motivates them to work hard, while protecting them against the ever present risk of failure.

Nurturing creativity in groups

Creative individuals within organisations contribute to overall competitive advantage and organisational innovation, while teams or groups of creative individuals increase this advantage further. It is essential that the right leaders are appointed so that creativity is nurtured and encouraged. A culture within the company of openness to innovation, and acceptance of new ideas should be encouraged. Transformation leadership, in particular, stimulates creativity and innovation. They lead by example, are honest, convey a strong vision, show consideration for others, and inspire others to follow them.

People are more creative in work groups that have different experiences, expertise, perspectives and world views. The more diverse the group, the more likely they are to come up with breakthrough ideas. For example, the best ideas for Disney theme park adventures have come from older people in their 60s, 70s and 80s. So don't neglect the older generation while giving the younger generation opportunities to develop and grow! In addition, work groups that collaborate rather than compete are more creative.

The most creative teams are those that have the confidence to share and debate ideas. But when people compete for recognition, they stop sharing information. Such destructive behaviour means that nobody in an organisation has all the information required to put all the pieces of the puzzle together, and so sub-standard decisions and solutions to problems are made.

Famous Creative People

People have been creative from the beginning of human history. We have built on the shoulders of giants to get to our present state of sophisticated civilisation and comfortable lifestyles. I have taken a few inspirational figures from history and from more modern times. These demonstrate the significant effect people can have on our lives, either working alone, or in teams. We can model our behaviour on these people and learn from their achievements. Be inspired by their enthusiasm, great powers of observation, concentration, curiosity and hard work.

Historical creative figures

Many discoveries were made by people, obsessed by and totally immersed in their subjects, after much patient work and research over a long period of time. Isaac Newton, when asked about how he discovered the law of gravity, said he thought of it all the time. It seems if you are not actively looking for new discoveries, and clued in for relevancy, you will overlook them when they happen. Many people saw the apple fall but none except Newton understood its significance.

The development of the theory of evolution offers a good lesson in creative

Inspiration

"Curiosity about life in all of its aspects, I think, is still the secret of great people."
Leo Burnett

problem solving in science. The idea that all animal species were related had been around for many years. However, the mechanism of evolution, through natural selection of the survival of the fittest, went unnoticed. Both Charles Darwin and naturalist Alfred Wallace coincidentally arrived at the solution to the evolution puzzle by the same route and around the same time. Each had stepped back from the immediate problem, and noticed how relevant the ideas of Thomas Malthus were to the evolution puzzle. He had described the struggle for existence of increasing populations and reducing food supplies. This was the eureka moment and the analogy that Darwin and Wallace needed to solve the conundrum of evolution.

Creative geniuses such as Benjamin Franklin, Nikola Tesla, and Leonardo da Vinci did not simple create great things, they created things of value, highly desired and useful to people. Franklin invented bifocal glasses, Tesla invented the alternating-current electric motor which revolutionised the generation, transmission and distribution of electricity, and da Vinci painted the Mona Lisa. All of these things have enriched and have had a great impact on our lives.

Alexander Fleming is purported to have discovered penicillin by chance, and revolutionised the healthcare industry. Similarly, W.C. Roentgen accidentally discovered the X-ray while conducting a series of experiments using cathode ray tubes. His discovery led to great developments in science and medicine, and he was awarded the Nobel Prize in Physics in 1901.

Modern inventors

Dean Kamen is best known as the inventor of the Segway – the two wheeled human transporter which has been taken up by police services throughout the world – but he's far from a one hit wonder. The US entrepreneur has created many inventions, from an all-terrain wheelchair, to a water purification system for Third World villages. His obsession with innovation came gradually. He wasn't inventive as a child, but he did have one standard trait: an insatiable curiosity about the natural world. He derived great pleasure in finding unexpected uses for existing technology such as making tiny portable pumps for diabetics.

He thinks that the public have the mistaken perception that inventors have great ideas, get the parts, and make the product. However, he points out the process of inventing is not like that – it's not a linear, straightforward process. You have to be willing to adapt your ideas quickly, no matter how passionate you are about them, and just keep working patiently away until you have a worthwhile product.

Esther Takeuchi is an engineer at the State University of New York, who has turned her talent for figuring out how things work into a very successful career. She holds over 120 patents – more than any other women alive – and has received many awards for her work. While working at the technology company Greatbatch, she developed the Lilliputian battery that powers implantable cardiac defibrillators, a device that has improved the lives of thousands of heart patients. Perfecting her most famous invention took many years of hard work. She doesn't discount the importance of split-second inspiration, but emphasises that innovators need to have an extensive background of knowledge before they arrive at the eureka moment. She highlights the importance of spending sufficient time exploring and thinking about the problem, and reading extensively around it. Sometimes she sets the problem aside, and finds that she arrives at the solution in the most unexpected manner, often when doing something else.

Summary of Chapter Eight

Apart from creating something new, creativity can also involve improving, refining, changing, or combining things in new or novel ways. Creativity should not be confused with innovation which is the implementation of ideas into practical use.

Creativity is needed in all areas of business life from the top to the bottom of an organisation. In a changing world, new products, services, and technologies are appearing all the time. To keep a competitive edge, you must keep up with the best, and more often than not do better.

Creativity can happen at the most unlikely times when showering, walking, conversing, engaged in recreation or just before you fall asleep, or on waking up. Many companies now run courses and workshops to enhance the creativity of their employees. The five stages of creativity have been identified as preparation, effort, incubation, insight and evaluation. New ideas can be triggered off by the acronym CAMPERS, which stands for combine ideas, adapt a product, modify a product, put to other uses, eliminate unnecessary parts, rearrange, and simplify.

You can classify creativity techniques under three headings; paradigm preserving, paradigm stretching, and paradigm breaking. Paradigm preserving techniques are used to solve more structured problems. Paradigm stretching and breaking techniques are used to solve unstructured problems. Brainstorming is one of the better known techniques for generating ideas, and is a paradigm preserving technique. The acronym FARMS will help you remember some paradigm stretching and breaking techniques. This stands for fantasy, attribute listing, reverse brainstorming, metaphors and SWOT analysis. A systematic approach to creative problem solving was highlighted.

The barriers to creativity include conformity, evaluating too quickly and afraid to challenge the obvious. Creativity is killed off by negativity, criticism and destructive phrases. Creativity happens in all areas of our lives

Inspiration

"Creativity involves breaking out of established patterns in order to look at things in a different way."
Edward de Bono

including personal and work. People are naturally innately creative. It just has to be encouraged and drawn out. Famous creative people are remembered for the way they have enhanced and improved the lives of people.

Five Activities to Improve Your Creativity Skills

1. Memorise and understand the acronym CAMPERS, so that you will be will be able to recall easy and useful ways to enhance your ability to be creative. Study nature and be inspired by the marvellous evolutionary ways it has invented to cope with survival.

2. Memorise the five stages of the creative process; preparation, effort, incubation, insight and evaluation and make sure that you know and understand what each stage means. The acronym **P**aul **e**ffortlessly **i**ncubates **i**nsights will help you remember the stages.

3. Role play the six thinking hats, so that you can empathise with and adopts the perspectives of each role.

4. Memorise and understand the acronym FARMS; which stands for fantasy, attribute listing, reverse brainstorming, metaphor and SWOT analysis, so that you know at least five techniques for generating creative ideas. Learn the brainstorming approach. Use the acronym **S**am **f**ancies **g**ood **c**hocolate to remember the stages, or better still invent your own. Google 'creativity techniques' for more ideas.

5. Memorise the systematic creative problem solving technique SREDIM and be able to meaningfully describe each stage. In the future use this approach to solve problems.

References & Bibliography

Abraham, Curtis. (2010). One minute with ….Matthieu Ricard. New Scientist. 30/1/2010. Vol. 205. Issue 2745. P23.

Abrecht, Karl. (2002). Brain Power. T&D. Nov. Vol.56. Issue 11. P38.

Addie, Ian. (2011). Is neuroscience facilitating a new era of the hidden persuader? International Journal of Market Research. Vol. 53. Issue 3. Pp303-305.

Ahlstrom, Dick. (2011). Children likely to have greater brainpower if mother ate fish during pregnancy. Irish Times. Wednesday 11 Jan 2011.

Alex & David Bennet. (2008). The human knowledge system: music and brain coherence. The journal of information and knowledge management systems. Vol. 38. Number 3. Pp:277-295.

Beel, Joran, Gipp, Bela and Stiller, Jan Olaf. (2009). Could Mind Maps Be Used To Improve Academic Search Engines? Proceedings of the World Congress on Engineering and Computer Science. Vol 11.

Benley, Ross. (2002). Learn from the worst IT mistakes. Computer Weekly. 23/5/2002. P68.

Bennett, David. (2008). Medical mistakes new caveat in contracting terms. Managed Healthcare Executive, November 2008.

Blakeslee, Sandra. (2002). Exercising Toward Repair of the Spinal Cord. The New York Times. 22 September 2002.

Boe, John. (2011). Do It Now! American Salesman. July 2011. Vol.56. Issue 7. p15-16.

Breen, Bill. (2004). The 6 Myths of Creativity. Fast Company. Issue 89. 1/12/2004.

Brooks, Rachel, & Everett, Glyn. (2008). The predominance of work-based training in young graduates' learning. Journal of Education and Work. Vol. 21. No. 1. February.

Brozo, William G, and Johns, Jerry L. (1986). A content and critical analysis of 40 speed reading books. Journal of Reading. December 1986.

Buch, Ken. (2010). Brain Break. Understanding the Influence of Brain Functions on Organisational Effectiveness. T&D. May 2010.

Budd, John W. (2004). Mind Maps as Classroom Exercises. Journal of Economic Education. Winter 2004.

Buzan, T. (1993). The Mind Map Book: Radiant Thinking – The Major Evolution in Human Thought, London, BBC Pubications.

Calvin, William H. (2008). Review: Big Brain by Gary Lynch and Richard Granger. New Scientist. 6/3/2008. Vol. 197. Issue 2646. P48.

Camerer, Colin, Loewenstein, George & Prelec, Drwzen. (2005). Neuroeconomics: How Neuroscience Can Inform Economics. Journal of Economic Literature. Vol. XL111, March 2005. Pp9-64.

Campbell, Andrew; Whitehead, Jo & Finkelstein, Sydney. (2009). Why Good Leaders Make Bad Decisions. Harvard Business Review. Vol. 87. Issue 2.

Canas, Alberto J. (2003). A Summary of Literature Pertaining to the Use of Concept Mapping Techniques and Technologies for Education and Performance Support. The Institute for Human and Machine Cognition, Pensacola FL 32502.

Christian, Hart L; Randell, Joe A & Griffith, James D. (2007). Ironic Effects of Attempting to Remember. North American Journal of Psychology. Vol. 9. Issue 2. p201-210.

Crampton, Michael F. (2011). Gender effects in advertising. International Journal of Market Research. Vol. 53. Issue 2.

Croasdell, David T and Freeman, Lee A. (2003). Concept Maps for Teaching and Assessment. Communications of the Association for Information Systems. Vol.12. pp: 396-405.

Csikszentmihalyi, Mihaly. (1997). Finding Flow. Psychology Today. July/Aug 97. Vol.30. Issue 4. p46.

Davies, Martin. (2010). Concept mapping, mind mapping and argument mapping: what are the differences and do they matter. Springer Science + Business Media B.V. Published online: 27 November 2010.

Dixit, Jay. (2008). The Art of Now: Six Steps to Living in the Moment. Psychology Today. Nov/Dec 2008. Vol.41. Issue 6. Pp62-69.

Dolan, Kerry A. (2006). Sharp As A Tack. Forbes. Vol. 177. Issue 6. 27/3/2006.

Donovan, Elena. (2002). When is distraction desirable? Psychology Today. May/June 2002. Vol.35. Issue 3. p18.

Dourma, Michael and Ligierko, Greg. (2009). Creating Online Mind Maps and Concept Maps. 25th Annual Conference on Distance Teaching & Learning.

Eddy, Erik R; Tannenbaum, Scott I; Lorenzet, Steven J and Smith-Jentsch, Kimberly A. (2005). The Influence of a Continuous Learning Environment on Peer Mentoring Behaviors. Journal of Managerial Issues. Vol.17. No. 3. Fall 2005.

Edmondson, Amy C. (2011). Strategies for Learning from Failure. Harvard Business Review. Vol. 89. Issue 4.

Ellison, Katherine. (2006). Mastering Your Own Mind Back. Psychology Today. Sept/Oct 2006. Vol.39. Issue 5. Pp 70-77.

Fass, Alison. (2003). Duking it out. Forbes. Vol. 171. Issue 12.

Fisher, Kathleen M, Wandersee, James H and Wideman, Graham. (2000). Enhancing cognitive skills for meaningful understanding of domain specific knowledge. Center for Research in Mathematics and Science Education.

Galbraith, Diana D and Fouch, Sandra E. (2007). Principles of Adult Learning. Professional Safety. September 2007.

Gannerud, Eva and Ronnerman, Karin. (2005). Studying Teachers' Work Through Mind Maps. New Zealand Journal of Teachers' Work. Vol. 2. Issue 2. pp: 76-82.

Gelb, Michael J. (2009). Think Like Da Vinci. Harper Element, London.

Gilbert, Katie. (2006). Your Personal Time Zone. Psychology Today. July/Aug 2006. Vol.39. Issue 4. p56.

Gilkey, Roderick & Kilts, Clint. (2007). Cognitive Fitness. Harvard Business Review. November 2007.

Goldsmith, Marshall. (1996). The One Skill That Separates. Psychology Today. July 2005. Issue 96. p86.

Gopnik, Allison. (2010). How Babies Think. Scientific American. July 2010. Vol. 303. Issue 1.

Graham-Rowe, Duncan. (2011). Mind readers. New Scientist. 28/5/2011. Vol. 210. Issue 2814. P40-43.

Greenfield, Susan. (2008). Perspectives: Who are we becoming? New Scientist. 17/5/2008 Vol.198. Issue 2658. Pp48-49

Griffey, Harriet. (2010). The Art of Concentration. London. Rodale.

Gryskiewicz, Stanley S and Epstein, Robert. (2000). Cashing in on Creativity at Work. Psychology Today. Vol. 33. Issue 5.

Jackson, Thomas. (2003). This is Your Brain on Golf. Forbes. 31/3/2003. FYI Supplement. Vol.171. Issue 7.

Hallowell, Edward M. (1997). What I've learned from A.D.D. Psychology Today. May/June 1997. Vol.30. Issue 3. p40.

Hallowell, Edward M. (2005). Overloaded Circuits: Why Smart People Underperform. Harvard Business Review. January 2005. Vol. 83. Issue 1. Pp54-62.

Hamman, W.R. (2004). The complexity of team training: what we have learned from aviation and its application to medicine. Qual Safe Health Care. Vol. 13 (supplement 1).

Harris, Craig. (2006). Driven to Distraction. Canadian Underwriter. October 2006.

Heller, Victor, L & Darling, John, R. (2011). Toyota in crises: denial and mismanagement. Journal of Business Strategy, Vol. 32. Issue 5.

Herrmann, Ned. (1982). The Creative Brain 11: A Revisit with Ned Herrnann. Training and Development. December 1982.

Hlavacek, Jim; Maxwell, Craig & Williams, Jimmy, Jr. (2009). Learn From New Product Failures. Industrial Research Institute.

Holt, Jim. (2005). Of Two Minds. The New York Times. 8 May 2005.

Horn, Sam. (1991). Improve Your Concentration. London. Kogan Page.

Hubbard, Edward, M. (2006). Hearing Colours, Tasting Shapes. Scientific American Special Edition. Vol. 16. Issue 3. 1/9/2006.

Jackson, C.R. & Gibbon, K.P. (2006). Per ardua….Training tomorrow's surgeons using inter alia lessons from aviation. Journal of the Royal Society of Medicine. Vol. 99. Nov 2006.

Kamuth, John-Paul. (2008). Mind mapping software helps ice warrior meet challenges of the pole. Computer Weekly, 4/1/2008.

Kapp. Karl M. (2011). Matching the right design strategy to the right content. T&D July 2011.

Karli, Pierre. (2008). The human brain as a mediating, integrating and unifying central agency. Society and Business Review. Vol. 3. No. 2. Pp107-118.

Kayt, Sukei. (2012). The amazing memory marvels. New Scientist. Vol. 215. Issue 2878. 18/8/2012.

Kertesz, Louise. (2011). Doctors owning up to mistakes. Business Insurance. Vol. 45. Issue 48.

Kingston, Anne. (2010). Learning from Past Mistakes. Maclean's, Vol. 123, Issue 46.

Knutson, Renee Grana. (1997). The sure thing. Supervision. Vol.58. Issue 2. P9

Koznov, Dmitrij and Pliskin, Michel. (2008). Computer-Supported Collaborative Learning with Mind Maps. Saint-Petersburg State University.

Ladika, Susan. (2008). When Learning Lasts a Lifetime. HR Magazine. Vol. 53. Issue 5.

Laing, Gregory Kenneth. (2010). An Empirical Test of Mnemonic Devices to Improve Learning in Elementary Accounting. Journal of Education for Business. Vol. 85. pp 349-358.

Larson, Christine. (2007). Calisthenics for the Older Mind, on the Home Computer. The New York Times. 26 August 2007.

Larsen, Kurt and Istance, David. (2001). Lifelong learning for all. Observer, No.225. March.

Lipschutz, Robert P. (2004). Food for the Mind. PC Magazine. Vol.23. Issue 13. 8/3/2004. P37.

MacCourt, Duncan & Bernstein, Josephy. (2009). Medical Error Reduction And Tort Reform Through Private, Contractually Based Quality Societies. American Journal of Law & Medicine. Vol. 35. Pp505-561.

Malone, Samuel A. (1995). A Critical Evaluation of Mind Maps in an Adult Learning Environment, unpublished thesis, University of Sheffield.

Malone, Samuel A. (1997). Mind Skills for Managers. Gower, Aldershot.

Malone, Samuel A. (2000). Learning Skills for Managers. Oak Tree Press, Dublin.

Malone, Samuel A. (2003). Learning about Learning. CIPD, London.

Malone, Samuel A. (2005). A Practical Guide To Learning In The Workplace. The Liffey Press, Dublin.

McFadzean, Elspeth. (1999). Creativity in MS/OR: Choosing the Appropriate Technique. Interfaces. No. 29 Sept/Oct 1999.

McMahon, Walter W. (1998). Conceptual framework for the analysis of the social benefits of lifelong learning. Education Economics. Vol. 6. Issue 3.

Mendelson, Edward. (2001). MindManager Creates Tree-Diagrams of Ideas. PC Magazine. Vol.20. Issue 5. 3/6/2001.

Mento, Anthony J; Martinelli, Patrick and Jones, Raymond M. (1998). Mind Mapping in Executive Education: Applications and Outcomes. The Journal of Management Development, Vol.18. Issue 4.

Mindrum, Craig. (2011). The Twitching Organisation. Chief Learning Officer. March 2011.

McKie, Robin. (2010). Male and female ability differences down to sociali-sation, not genetics. The Observer. Sunday 15 August, 2010.

Moran, Aidan P. (2004). Sport and Exercise Psychology, A Critical Intro-duction. London, Routledge. pp: 101-130.

Moser, Philip R. (2011). Managing Unsafe Drivers & Their Unsafe Habits. Professional Safety. May 2011.

Moyers, Bill. (1993). Meditate! For stress reduction, inner peace or what-ever. Psychology Today. July/Aug 93. Vol.26. Issue 4. p36.

Murley, Diane. (2007). Mind Mapping Complex Information. Law Library Journal. Vol. 99:1

Odegard, Synnove. (2000). Safety Management in Civil Aviation – A Use-ful Method For Improved Safety In Medical Care. Safety Science Monitor. Issue 1. Article 4.

O'Reilly, Daragh. (2011). Mapping the arts marketing literature. Arts Mar-keting: An International Journal. Vol.1. No. 1. pp: 26-38.

O'Reilly, Jennifer and Samarawickrema, Gayani. (2003). Using Multime-dia concept maps to enhance the learning experience in business law. Monash University, Australia.

Orlick. Terry. (2000). In Pursuit of Excellence. Champaign, USA. Human Kinetics.

Pollitt, David. (2009). Thomas Reuters maps new relationships in learning and collaboration. Human Resource Management International Digest. Vol. 17. No. 4.

Pronovost, Peter J et all (2009). Reducing Health Care Hazards: Lessons From The Commerical Aviation Safety Team. Health Affairs. Vol. 28. No.3.

Pychyl, Timothy. (2009). Ending Procrastination – Right Now!. Psycholo-gy Today. Sept/Oct 2009. Vol.42, Issue 5. P79.

Reason, James. (2000). Human error: models and management. BMJ. Vol.320, 18 March 2000.

Robson, David. (2010). Total recall. New Scientist. 17/4/2010. Vol. 206. Is-sue 2756. P36.

Rosenbaum, Andrew. (2003). Chart the course of your negotiation. Har-vard Business School Publishing Corporation.

Roth, Gerhard. (2004). The quest to find consciousness. January 2004. Sci-entific American. Special Edition. Vol. 14. Issue 1.

Sacks, Oliver. (2010). This Year, Change Your Mind. The New York Times. 31 December 2010.

Salvador, Rommel, & Folger, Robert, G. (2009). Business Ethics and the Brain. Business Ethics Quarterly. January 2009.

Scarfino, Deborah & Roever, Carol. (2009). Team-Building Success: It's In The Cards. Business Communication Quarterly. March 2009.

Schoemaker, Paul J.H. & Gunther, Robert E. (2006). The Wisdom of Delib-erate Mistakes. Harvard Business Review. Vol. 84. Issue 6.

Shamma Al Naqbi and Ras Al Khaimah. (2011). The use of mind mapping to develop writing skills in UAE schools. Education , Business and Socie-ty: Contemporary Middle Eastern Issues. Vol. 2, No. 2. pp: 120-133.

Simon, Jon. (2010). Curriculum Changes Using Concept Maps. Accounting Education: an international journal. Vol. 19. No.3. pp:301-307, June 2010.

Simon, Jon. (2007). Concept Mapping in a Financial Accounting Theory Course. Accounting Education: an internatioinal journal. Vol. 16. No.3. pp:273-308.

Svoboda, Elizabeth. (2009). Profiles in Creativity. Saturday Evening Post. Vol. 281. Issue 5. p40-43.

Trivedi. Bijai. (2006). Healthy and happy. New Scientist. 23/9/2006. Vol. 191. Issue 2570. Pp48-49.

Tyler, Kathryn. (1999). Reading at the Speed of Life. HR Magazine, Vol. 44. Issue 5. Page 75.

Veillette, Patrick R. (2006). Whawazat!? The Importance of Managing Distractions.

Business & Commercial Aviation. March 2006. Vol.98. Issue 3. p46-50.

Veillette, Patrick R. (2007). Time Pressures. Business & Commercial Aviation. Oct 2007. Vol. 101. Issue 4.

Waldman, David A; Balthazard, Pierre A & Peterson, Suzanne J. (2011). Leadership and Neuroscience: Can we revolutionise the way that inspirational leaders are identified and developed? Academy of Management Perspectives. February 2011.

Weber, Bruce. (2009). Kim Peek, Inspiration for 'Rain Man,' Dies at 58. The New York Times, December 27, 2009.

Weiss, Ruth Palombo. (2001) The Mind-Body Connection in Learning. T&D. Sept 2001. Vol. 55. Issue 9. P60.

Wheeldon, Johannes. (2011). Is a Picture Worth a Thousand Words? Using Mind Maps to Facilitate Participant Recall in Qualitative Research. The Qualitative Report. Vol.16. No 2. March 2011. pp:509-522.

Wheeldon, Johannes & Faubert, Jacquelinge. (2009). Framing Experience: Concept Maps, Mind Maps, and Data Collection in Qualitative Research. International Journal of Qualitative Methods. Vol.8. No. 3.

Wilcox, Andrew. (2003). MindManaging Your Projects. IEE Engineering Management. June/July 2003.

Also available from Glasnevin Publishing:

In this inspiring and remarkable book you will discover the principles of success that have directed and motivated many people to make a significant contribution and difference to the world. You will also uncover the pitfalls to avoid in your quest to become the best you can be. Success in any endeavour does not happen by chance. It happens through the application of sound principles and purposeful actions such as:

- Setting realistic goals
- Making worthwhile plans
- Practising good interpersonal relationships
- Having confidence and self-belief
- Being optimistic
- Developing self-esteem
- Being persistent and resilient
- Being highly motivated
- Developing the habit of lifelong learning and continuous improvement
- Practising good personal values.

This book has an entertaining blend of inspirational real life stories, quotations, practical tips, acronyms and activities to help you acquire the right habits and practise the skills of success. The book is underscored by the best scientific research currently available which is made accessible tothe reader through clear simple language. By following the principles set out in this book you will become the happy and successful person you are destined to be.

ISBN-13: 978-0-9555781-8-2 PB 229x152mm 282pp 2011 Glasnevin Publishing

Available from Amazon.com and all good bookshops.